Save Lives or
Save the Rhetoric?

Save Lives or Save the Rhetoric?

Comparing the Logic of Evidence with the Power of Rhetoric

David H. Goldenberg

HAMILTON BOOKS
an imprint of
ROWMAN & LITTLEFIELD
Lanham • Boulder • New York • London

Published by Hamilton Books
4501 Forbes Boulevard, Suite 200, Lanham, Maryland 20706
www.rowman.com

6 Tinworth Street, London SE11 5AL, United Kingdom

Copyright © 2021 by The Rowman & Littlefield Publishing Group, Inc.

All rights reserved. No part of this book may be reproduced in any form or by any electronic or mechanical means, including information storage and retrieval systems, without written permission from the publisher, except by a reviewer who may quote passages in a review.

British Library Cataloguing in Publication Information Available

Library of Congress Control Number: 2020918261
ISBN 978-0-7618-7205-4 (paper)
ISBN 978-0-7618-7206-1 (electronic)

To all those who think for themselves
and follow the logic and the evidence wherever it leads.

Contents

List of Illustrations ix

List of Tables xi

Acknowledgments xiii

Introduction 1

PART I: LOGIC AND EVIDENCE VERSUS FALLACIES AND RHETORIC

1. What Is an Evidence-Based Approach?: Can Non-Existence be Proven? 9
2. What Is an Evidence-Based Approach?: Is Non-Proportionality Discrimination? 17
3. Basic Logic And Fallacies: Necessary versus Sufficient Conditions 29
4. Evidence, Economic Data, and How to Find It 41
5. More Fallacies 65
6. Evidence: What it Is, What it Is Not 91
7. Fallacies Based on Personal Attack 131

PART II: BASIC KNOWLEDGE FOR DECISION-MAKING AND EVALUATING POLICY

8	Making Good Decisions and Good Policy: Relative versus Absolute, Opportunity Costs, and Marginalism	151
9	Certainty versus Uncertainty: Multiple Factors, Multiple Uncertain Outcomes, Polls and Their Interpretation	183
10	Individual Preferences and Opportunities, and the State's Role: Capitalism, Communism, (Democratic) Socialism, and the Welfare State	193

Bibliography	211
Index	233
About the Author	247

List of Illustrations

4.1.	U.S. Labor Force Participation: Blacks, Whites, Ages 16+ years	46
4.2.	U.S. Employment-Population Ratio since 2008: Blacks, Whites, Ages 16+ years	48
4.3.	U.S. Unemployment Rate U3: Blacks, Whites, Ages 16+ years	51
4.4.	U.S. Civilian Unemployment Rates: U6 versus U3	53
4.5.	U.S. Blacks Have Twice the Unemployment Rate (U3) of Whites is a Static Half-Truth	54
4.6.	The Last Ten Years of Twice the Rate Rhetoric	55
4.7.	The Last Five Years of Twice the Rate Rhetoric	56
6.1.	U.S. Civilian Labor Force Participation Rate, Ages 25–54 years	100
6.2.	U.S. Employment-Population Ratio, Ages 25–54 years	101
6.3.	U.S. Unemployment Rate U3, Ages 25–54 years	102

List of Tables

4.1.	U.S. Civilian Non-Institutional Population 2018, All, and Whites and Blacks, Ages 16+ years	42
4.2.	U.S. Labor Participation Rates 2016-2018, Blacks and Whites, Ages 25–54 years	47
4.3.	U.S. Employment-Population Ratio 2016-2018, Blacks and Whites, Ages 25–54 years	49
4.4.	U.S. Unemployment Rates, 2016-2019, Blacks and Whites, Ages 25–54 years	50
4.5.	Educational Attainment of the U.S. Labor Force, 2017, by Race and Ethnicity, Ages 25+ years	58

Acknowledgments

I thank the Rowman & Littlefield Publishing Group, Inc. for signing me to write this book and for publishing it in a timely manner. At Hamilton Books (Rowman & Littlefield), I wish to thank Brooke Bures, associate editor, and Mikayla Mislak, assistant editor, for invaluable assistance throughout the review and publication process. I also wish to thank Sam Brawand for her copyediting services.

Introduction

An Evidence-Based versus a Rhetoric-Based Approach to Understanding Public Policy

This book, *Save Lives or Save the Rhetoric? Comparing the Logic of Evidence with the Power of Rhetoric*, is about rhetoric and the realities that it distorts in the name of agenda. It is also about our choices. Do we want to look at the world as others would have us, because it suits our preconceptions and biases, or do we want to try to see the realities that we face with more objectivity? Rhetoric appeals to our emotions and definitely has allure. Yet as free, independently thinking individuals, we can resist uncritically accepting it and its emotional appeal. This is a difficult choice to be sure but an important one, and it is *our* choice.

How do we see the basic logic, and illogic, of positions taken by partisans of different stripes? For what motivates those positions is often not logic or evidence, but rather the self-interest of special interest groups, and their conflicting ideologies and rhetoric. How do we learn how to cut through the fog and barriers created by (political) rhetoric?

What is the alternative to rhetoric? Simply put: a data-based approach based on theory and evidence. In this approach we look at the *data*. This is not easy in a world where the purveyors of news and information often leave out relevant data. Human beings are plagued by numerous *biases* and news providers are human beings. It is relatively easy to promote a narrative that some factions want to hear, particularly on the Internet and through social media. By presenting a one-sided view of the evidence, one-sided conclusions tend to follow.

There is a lesson here. Perhaps we should have some degree of skepticism before we allow others, on both sides of the aisle, to base policies and billions/trillions of dollars on false ideas and their rhetoric, no matter how much we want them to be true? And we should not succumb to the pressure to *do something* under the fallacy that doing something is always better than doing nothing.

Doing something usually means government action, at the expense of the taxpayer of course. This suits the government because it grows their monopoly. On the one hand, whether any given government mandate actually benefits the people it intends to help is not always clear, or even testable. On the other hand, some government mandates (minimum wage laws and other price controls) have demonstrably hurt particular groups of people, including those they intended to help.

The first part of this book, "Logic and Evidence versus Fallacies and Rhetoric," discusses basic logic and logical fallacies with numerous real-world applications. It also posits an alternative: an evidence-based approach based on correct logic, and it gives examples of how to apply that approach.

The second part of the book, "Basic Knowledge for Decision-Making and Evaluating Policy," has a different focus and objective than the first part. Its goal is to present a whirlwind course in concepts and methods that any intelligent citizen may apply in order to make informed decisions about policy proposals. There are at least two ways to make judgments on policy proposals. One is on the basis of rhetoric—what other people want you to believe. The second way is an informed approach and it is based on the evidence. Many can benefit from this part of the book, given the material in part I.

There are really three components discussed herein: rhetoric and its logical fallacies, falsifiable hypotheses (not facts) well formulated on the basis of theory which in many of our cases comes from logic and economics, and the testing of those hypotheses using appropriate non-cherry-picked evidence (data) and proper applications of data analysis.

It is a tall order and I have had to make many choices along the way. This includes the choice of examples and links, which was based on relevance, timeliness and data availability.[1] Examples and cases exhibiting both the rhetorical approach and the evidence-based approach are particularly useful in contrasting these two approaches.

My goal is pedagogical, not political. I do not engage in the Herculean task of presenting an exhaustive treatment of any of the topics considered. Nor do I attempt to resolve, once and for all, any of the major issues of the day. The initial goal for the reader is simply to gain and practice the skill of recognizing the many faces of rhetoric and the fewer faces of evidence. Ultimately, the reader will make their own judgments in the bright light of that distinction. The goal of the examples, theory, case studies, economics, statistics, historical documents, and data analysis offered in *Save Lives or Save the Rhetoric?* is to provide citizens with an *informed* approach to examining and evaluating the issues, the rhetoric, and the evidence in order to ultimately make their *own* informed decisions

Since the rhetoric is operative around the clock I need not repeat it, except to use it as illustration. The purveyors can feel free to justify their own rhetoric—with valid fallacy-free reasoning and evidence—and not simply repeat it nor demand that their opponents prove them wrong. The same requirement applies of course to those who reject the rhetoric. In this way, the minimum necessary condition for a productive discussion, which is rarely happening now, will be put in place.

There are many different points of view (usually opinions) as the rhetoric goes, implying that they are all equally valid (fallacies of relativism/subjectivism and of political correctness).[2] But not all are equally valid nor are they all based on evidence. Instead, many positions are rhetoric-based. And the goal of rhetoric is not the same as that of the evidence-based approach. It is to stay alive, hence the term "save the rhetoric"—and to persuade and thereby control the populace.

Rhetoric does not adapt well to evidence but is better suited to confirmation bias. Repeat the lie is its mantra. Unfortunately, lives are often held in the balance since bad policy can and has damaged and has even cost many lives. The evidence-based approach insists that we reject the fallacious and the counter-evidential hypotheses and move on. Its motto is science in the interest of the truth and the policy goal of improving and saving lives.

However, there is a scientific way of incorporating alternative viewpoints which this book employs. For example, if one believes that gun controls do not save lives, we could take that as the null hypothesis to be examined, since it is falsifiable. Then alternative views are all those contained in the alternative hypothesis by definition, that gun control laws do save lives (the negation of the null hypothesis).

This is standard scientific method and it will be used to benchmark the discussions relative to the null hypothesis. The alternative views are then supported in so far as the null hypothesis is rejected. The procedure is quite reasonable because it gives equal a priori weight to both the null hypothesis (the hypothesized view) and the alternative hypothesis (the alternative views).

Practically, it is not possible to scientifically consider the large array of the specifics of alternative views and their underlying theories, data sources, data analysis methods, and implied policy proposals in one fell swoop. This is why researchers write papers and explicate their methodologies in detail. An active competition is thereby fostered without the partisan interference of government officials trying to pick and choose the research results that suit their political agendas. From the latter it is a small step to the Propaganda

Ministry. The alternative marketplace for rhetoric is well supported by media outlets through their echo chambers.

The discussion questions are an integral part of the book and I encourage the reader to examine, think about, and discuss them. They are meant simply to stimulate discussion and to apply the methods discussed in the book. For it is discussion we need in today's polarized environment, not the restriction of discussion in the name of ideology.

The current fashion is to politicize *everything* via the fallacies of false dichotomy and ad hominem. Rhetoric aims to polarize à la Marxist class warfare. To do so, it labels then targets and marginalizes its enemies.[3] This is not done with logic or evidence but with more rhetoric.[4] The rhetoric is all about *taking sides*, the central proposition of Marxist class warfare, and it is a very limited view of the world. Taking sides is premised on a serious fallacy which is false dichotomy. There are usually not just two sides, and no one in a non-totalitarian country has to take sides, fixed unto eternity. Suspend judgment if you do not know and look for the evidence, if there is any.

This book is not about taking positions but about learning how to *analyze* and *assess* them using logic, evidence, data analysis, and economics—not confirmation bias. Hopefully the reader will resist the rhetoric, with its reductionism and polarization, by depoliticizing their approach to this book's intent and content.

Keep an open mind (by taking fixed positions rhetoric does anything but that) while we learn to analyze the rhetoric, logic, evidence, and economics of some of the hot button issues of the day. These are the same issues for which unaccountable political partisans routinely and glibly pretend to have all the answers in their oracular pronouncements (usually rhetoric) to millions. The only problem is that they never give the details, including any evidence, until it is far too late. Be independent, use this book as a guide, and do your own non-partisan research.

The reference website links will be accessible in the ebook format and they may also appear on a personal website strictly devoted to the book (savelivesorsavetherhetoric.com). I sincerely hope that you enjoy the book, learn from it, and apply the material in your everyday lives, and not go the route of confirmation bias (or at least recognize the tendency to do so). Now we are ready for the first steps of our journey in part I.

NOTES

1. Public policy is an *applied* field and this is an applied book. Therefore, as needed, we must go to the public domain: online economics libraries such as *Econlib* with articles by the best economists in the country/world most of whom are academi-

cally trained, articles from online journals on current events, (government and other) source reports where we can read the real (not second-hand) words of actors on the world stage, data sources and explanations, books on background material such as (basic) economics, economic fallacies, history and historical documents, and yes, examples of rhetoric—as befits a book on that topic.

All of this material has been carefully selected to illustrate the specific, contextualized content presented and indicated in the section and sub-section titles. The entire book, including its sources and methods, is meticulously researched and yet designed to be accessible (non-technical) to the general reader.

Feel free to investigate other sources (that is the whole point) keeping in mind the goals, which are to recognize fallacies and to see if you can apply the material. This is done by looking for the evidence, if there is any, and for the rhetoric and then distinguishing between the two. Being able to do so is a major takeaway from this book. Keep in mind the difference between hypotheses and facts. Hypotheses without evidence are just that, and depending upon the standard for proof, negative hypotheses can be very difficult or impossible to empirically and conclusively prove.

2. Logically Fallacious, "Subjectivist Fallacy," *Logically Fallacious*, n.d., https://www.logicallyfallacious.com/tools/lp/Bo/LogicalFallacies/171/Subjectivist-Fallacy (accessed November 23, 2019); and Logically Fallacious, "Political Correctness Fallacy," *Logically Fallacious*, n.d., https://www.logicallyfallacious.com/logicalfallacies/Political-Correctness-Fallacy (accessed November 23, 2019).

3. The thirteenth rule: "Pick the target, freeze it, personalize it, and polarize it" (Saul D. Alinsky, *Rules for Radicals: A Practical Primer for Realistic Radicals* [New York: Vintage, 1989], 134).

4. Such as the well-worn and by now ineffective ad hominem "racist" and "Nazi" shaming tactics applied to all who challenge or debunk the rhetoric. Alinsky's fifth rule: "The fourth rule carries within it the fifth rule: Ridicule is man's most potent weapon. It is almost impossible to counterattack ridicule. Also it infuriates the opposition, who then react to your advantage." (*Rules for Radicals*, 132). Learn Liberty below argues that Alinsky's fifth rule is ineffective at changing hearts and minds. If it cannot do that then the populace may revolt when the partisans try to execute the power grab and then force their system on them (the real Fascism). To grab power you need a willing populace. The purveyors have failed to learn from economics that the more people use a tactic, the less effective it becomes. Perhaps it is time to extirpate it? It has been almost fifty years since the Alinsky book was published. This is our first example of the reluctance of rhetoric to change. See Learn Liberty, "Shaming Someone Doesn't Change Their Mind," February 1, 2017, YouTube video, 1:57 min., https://www.youtube.com/watch?v=4qU7KVTAMIU (accessed November 23, 2019).

Part I

LOGIC AND EVIDENCE VERSUS FALLACIES AND RHETORIC

Chapter One

What Is an Evidence-Based Approach?
Can Non-Existence be Proven?

What is an *evidence*-based approach to understanding public policy proposals and solving social problems, as opposed to a *rhetoric*-based approach?

The rhetoric-based approach starts from rhetoric, emotion, and wishful thinking. These are then filtered through confirmation bias which selects the juicy bits. Finally, its expression is accomplished in the form of opinion-based speculation which is elevated to the status of "fact." Verification is performed by group think: assembling a like-minded special interest group and an echo chamber for confirmation.[1]

The evidence-based approach starts with reasoning, solid theory based on fallacy-free logic, and then empirical observations (evidence).[2] The theory suggests provisional, testable hypotheses (not facts). Then data is collected in *random* samples, which thereby control for confirmation bias and cherry picking, and the results are used to test the provisional hypotheses. Acceptance (non-rejection) of the hypotheses is based on the weight of the empirical evidence.[3]

Well-formulated (falsifiable) hypotheses that are not disproven are allowed to stand, until better theories are produced and/or better data is obtained, and then tested in like manner. This, in a nutshell, is a scientific method. We will illustrate the process in examples and case studies throughout the book.

Contrast the evidence-based approach with the rhetoric-based approach, which has little use for valid theory or for evidence that is not cherry picked. In the latter approach, one goes with what one and one's special interest group wants to believe. Only if anyone who matters asks for evidence, and the media apparently never asks, is it then carefully selected (cherry-picked), and then leaked to the media in the hopes that it will create enough selective moral outrage for the group to capture hearts, minds, votes, and most importantly, funding. The trouble with rhetoric is that it can be used to manipulate the facts. This can be done in a number of ways including cherry-picking specific statistics and choosing time-periods that support the rhetoric.[4]

Rhetoric gives people a voice to what they want to hear, based on their confirmation biases, which will be discussed in chapter 6. The evidence-based individual suspends judgment until all or enough of the facts are in. That individual admits that they do not really know because they do not have the actual information to make a judgment. Information is needed to make an evaluation of, rather than a rush to judgment on, almost anything.

What we presume the facts to be are not necessarily the actual facts until the evidence is brought to light. Numerous things that people have thought to be true have turned out to be flat wrong. That the earth is the center of the universe was standard wisdom for millennia.

Nor can we necessarily go by what people say. Talk is cheap and getting cheapened by some pundits, some in the media, and some partisans. Peoples' actions often tell us much more about their true intent and what drives them. It is a truism that people can and do lie, depending on the stakes involved. They may not even know what they truly think.

Economists James E. Roper and David M. Zin discuss the Paul Samuelson term for getting at their true intent: "revealed preference."[5] For example, a person says they like ice cream better than watermelon and can afford both. But, given the choice, they keep choosing watermelon. This says a lot about their real preferences. They may indeed prefer healthy eating to unhealthy eating. When presented this way, they may change their preferences and consumption choices.

HYPOTHESIS TESTING

We will start with a sharp formulation that includes the hypothesis to be tested. This is called the *null* hypothesis. Then we examine what would constitute disproof or proof of the null hypothesis. The book is intended to help you with reasoning skills. To do so, it is a good idea to dispose of ambiguity at the outset. Unfortunately, we are constantly exposed to rhetoric and it thrives on ambiguity.

Example No. 1

This example first states the null hypothesis, and then the elements needed to determine disproof and proof.

> *Null Hypothesis A*: There was no voter fraud in the 2016 U.S. Presidential election.

We can easily disprove (falsify) *Null Hypothesis A* with evidence.

Disproof: A single example of fraud.

Proving *Null Hypothesis A* is another matter.

Proof (?): Reviewing every single ballot and confirming that all of them are not fraudulent.

Of course, this may not be possible and there are cases that could escape this effort—because there are types of voter fraud that could not be detected. So the exercise does not conclusively confirm the hypothesis. In other words, this negative (non-existence) hypothesis is not empirically verifiable. But this is far less important in the world of science than its falsifiability, which is where we should concentrate our efforts, and is a characteristic of a well formulated empirical hypothesis. *Null Hypothesis A* is well-formulated (falsifiable) because, as noted, it is possible to *disprove* it.

One of the lessons of this example, which occurs in numerous contexts, is that you generally cannot empirically prove a negative. It is very difficult or impossible to empirically and conclusively prove non-existence.[6] However, there are some special cases in which it is possible. Keep in mind that the ability to prove or not prove a negative hypothesis depends on the standard of proof. We will sometimes drop the word "conclusively" henceforth but understand that it represents a high standard of proof, as high as the standard for disproof— when disproof is possible.

Now to apply this further, an example of rhetoric is when partisans attempt to empirically prove that there was no voter fraud. Consider the title of the Brennan Center for Justice article, "Debunking the Voter Fraud Myth."[7] This title is equivalent to claiming to empirically prove that there was no voter fraud. As such, it can never be empirically proven simply by debunking any number of instances of alleged evidence of fraud. Why? because there could always exist some non-debunkable evidence of fraud. Attempting to prove this negative is the knowing more than you could ever know fallacy.

The inability to prove the negative hypothesis of no fraud does not establish that there was fraud, only the *possibility* that there could have been fraud. The latter is a far different assertion. Playing this game of trying to empirically prove negatives is an illogical sleight of hand because generally you cannot empirically prove non-existence. Unfortunately, political discourse is riddled with this error, and it often goes undetected or unacknowledged.

The negative hypothesis can only be disproven through real evidence of real fraud. In the absence of real evidence of fraud, logic dictates that we provisionally do not reject the hypothesis that there was none. In other words, innocent (no fraud) until proven (by providing evidence, not simply accusations) guilty (fraud).[8]

Let us try another example with a positive formulation.

Null Hypothesis B: There was fraud in the 2016 election.

Proof: In this case proof, provided there is evidence, is a single case of fraud.

Disproof (?): Note that denying *Null Hypothesis B* just returns us to *Null Hypothesis A*. We have seen that it is a negative and in this case it cannot be empirically proven. Once again the potential disproof is that of non-existence.

Conclusion: While *Null Hypothesis B* is provable—until evidence that does so is produced—it is far more important that it is falsifiable and it is not. Therefore, from a scientific point of validity, it is not a well-formulated hypothesis. We can prove a positive hypothesis (in our example fraud) by evidence through one case of fraud. We can try to disprove it (prove no fraud), but we cannot really prove that there was no fraud. We cannot conclusively disprove *Null Hypothesis B* because its negation is a negative hypothesis.

Policy debates are filled with positive hypotheses that are not falsifiable. While not scientifically valid, positive hypotheses do permit evidence that supports them. (Negative hypotheses do too, but the issue is whether such evidence is conclusive.) What is inadmissible is not to provide such evidence, and then to shift the burden of proof to the naysayers by demanding that they prove the hypotheses wrong. This is a rhetorical tactic because doing so is an impossible task. It is incumbent upon the purveyors to "prove" their hypotheses by standards of proof that are just as high as the standards for disproof, when disproof is possible. And the naysayers are then welcome to assess their evidence. The inability of naysayers to not "prove them wrong" (an impossible task) does not thereby prove them right. Only the evidence has any chance of doing that.

Next, we apply what we have learned to proving guilt or innocence of a crime.

Example No. 2

Consider *Null Hypothesis C*.

Null Hypothesis C: X is not guilty (innocent) of a crime.

Proof: The potential proof is that of a negative, not guilty.

As discussed, this is impossible to conclusively prove because there could be some currently unknown data that establishes guilt. DNA testing opened up the door to such evidence in some cases. This is the logical, not simply legal, reason that we presume innocence until guilt is proven. In general, we cannot conclusively prove innocence. But we can disprove it (prove guilt), the legal standard, if we have hard evidence. Therefore *Null Hypothesis C* is a well-formulated (falsifiable) hypothesis.

> *Disproof*: Providing data that supports the hypothesis of guilt. Note that here the disproof is of the negation of a negative, which is a positive. Not "not guilty" is guilty.

Rhetoric cannot substitute for evidence because it is antithetical to it. Rhetoric usually *begs the question* (assumes the conclusion), but proves nothing because it does not provide evidence. Finally, consider the positive version of *Null Hypothesis C* which is *Null Hypothesis D*.

> *Null Hypothesis D*: X is guilty of a crime.
>
> *Proof*: Hard evidence.
>
> *Disproof*: Here not guilty (innocent) takes us back to proving a negative. You cannot conclusively prove innocence nor should you be required to do so, despite the demands of the rhetoric and its partisans. It is not provable because there will always be some potential data that suggests otherwise.[9] *Null Hypothesis D* is not well-formulated because it is not falsifiable.

Conclusion: While the standards of evidence vary by type of proceedings, presumed innocent until proven guilty is the way to go and it is the law in the United States of America and in many other countries.[10] Guilty until proven innocent is an inescapable logical trap because it requires the allegedly guilty party to empirically and conclusively prove that they are not guilty. This puts the burden on the accused to conclusively prove that which is generally impossible to conclusively prove. Whereas innocent until proven guilty requires the *accuser* to simply provide hard evidence to establish guilt. This puts the burden on the accuser to prove something that is possible to prove with hard data—not with opinion or rhetoric.

CASE STUDY NO. 1: ABSENCE OF *ACTUAL* EVIDENCE OR ABSENCE OF ALL *POSSIBLE* EVIDENCE?

Partisans can and do make the fallacious argument that we have been discussing in their rhetorical question concerning an opponent's actions: how do we know a crime was not committed? This is a negative and in general it cannot be answered. The framing of the investigation biases it toward taking a person and finding (or manufacturing) their alleged crime(s). In the words of Stalin's police chief Lavrentiy Beria quoted by Bob Barr: "Show me the man and I'll find the crime."[11]

Discussion Questions

(1) What constitutes real evidence of real crimes that justifies investigations of one's political opponents and imposing special prosecutors? Who decides?

(2) Is it the job of special prosecutors to *exonerate* people and thereby protect the world from crime?

(3) Are our laws about attaching crimes to opponents and criminalizing political differences?

(4) What budget of other peoples' money are special prosecutors entitled to spend (millions, unlimited?); and how must they account for their spending? Should they be audited?

(5) Evaluate the claim by Alan M. Dershowitz: "An investigation by a special counsel is not a search for objective truth. It is a search for incriminating evidence sufficient to charge."[12]

The logical fact is that empirically and conclusively "proving" a negative can be extraordinarily difficult or impossible. Unfortunately, the illogic of doing so is deficient because we live in a world of uncertainty where we can never know with absolute certainty that a crime was not committed. The rational thing to do is to adjust our expectations to this fact, something the rhetoric and its partisans avoid. After all, their goal is to save their *agendas*. In order to accomplish that, saving the rhetoric is a necessary condition.

Going after a person, as opposed to evidence of a crime, that is based on an agenda which assumes they must have committed a crime is called begging the question (assuming the conclusion in the premise). The effort is tainted by conflicts of interest and Beria's dictum: guilty until proven not guilty. The agenda is then expressed through rhetoric and sometimes raw incitement and intimidation. Confirmation bias, further examined in chapter 6, kicks in to cherry pick for evidence (real or manufactured), and then speculation is elevated to the status of fact.

Case study no. 1 opens up a set of issues under the topic of speaking truth to prosecutorial power.[13] In their essay, Philip Keefer and Stephen Knack present a model of public investment under unaccountable governments.[14] It is a confirmed fact that millions of dollars of taxpayer money can be wasted on (government) boondoggles without their consent. A government boondoggle may be defined as government or government subsidized unproductive production of public goods. The investigation and study of the company, Solyndra, a solar panel manufacturer outlined by David Boaz, is one of many examples (half a billion dollars) and it makes a good example of government decision-making.[15]

Boaz makes the case illustrating the role of "green energy rhetoric" and partisanship in affecting the government's subsidization of the unproductive production of public goods. It also illustrates the lack of research and transparency that plagues these Presidential pet projects. Not least is the knowing more than they know or can know fallacy, to which even Presidents are not immune. In concluding Boaz lists the hallmarks of government decision making. These are well worth understanding and discussing.

- "officials spending other people's money with little incentive to spend it prudently,
- political pressure to make decisions without proper vetting,
- the substitution of political judgment for the judgments of millions of investors,
- the enthusiastic embrace of fads like "green energy,"
- political officials ignoring warnings from civil servants,
- crony capitalism,
- close connections between politicians and the companies that benefit from government allocation of capital,
- the appearance—at least—of favors for political supporters,
- and the kind of promiscuous spending that has delivered us $18 trillion in national debt."

NOTES

1. Goodwill Community Foundation, "What is an Echo Chamber?" *Digital Media Literacy*, 1998–2019, https://edu.gcfglobal.org/en/digital-media-literacy/what-is-an-echo-chamber/1 (accessed November 19, 2019).

2. The evidence has to be sourced and shared, and failure to do so calls both the data and the results based on it into question.

3. Different unbiased parties can use different samples, different theories, and different statistical methods to test the hypotheses. Thus different explanations will compete with each other, improving and self-regulating the process.

4. Eugene Kiely, "Obama's Economic Sleight of Hand," *FactCheck.org*, June 15, 2012, https://www.factcheck.org/2012/06/obamas-economic-sleight-of-hand (accessed November 23, 2019).

5. James E. Roper and David M. Zin, eds., "Revealed Preference Theory," *Encyclopedia Britannica, Economics*, December 30, 2013, https://www.britannica.com/topic/revealed-preference-theory (last updated May 24, 2016; accessed November 19, 2019).

6. Logically Fallacious, "Proving Non-Existence," *Logically Fallacious*, n.d., https://www.logicallyfallacious.com/logicalfallacies/Proving-Non-Existence (accessed

November 25, 2019). Note that I am not considering mathematical or mathematical economics theorems that are negatively expressed. They can indeed be proven and there are several in this book, Arrow's impossibility theorem and the Chamley-Judd redistribution impossibility theorem.

7. Brennan Center for Justice, New York University School of Law, "Debunking the Voter Fraud Myth," March 12, 2017, https://www.brennancenter.org/sites/default/files/analysis/Briefing_Memo_Debunking_Voter_Fraud_Myth.pdf (accessed November 29, 2019).

8. John Gibbs, "Voter Fraud Is Real. Here's The Proof," *Federalist*, October 13, 2016, https://thefederalist.com/2016/10/13/voter-fraud-real-heres-proof (accessed November 29, 2019).

9. Ryan Saavedra, "Pelosi Scraps Presumption of Innocence: Trump Needs to Prove He Is Innocent," *Daily Wire*, November 17, 2019, https://www.dailywire.com/news/pelosi-scraps-presumption-of-innocence-trump-needs-to-prove-he-is-innocent (accessed November 30, 2019).

10. Andrew C. McCarthy, "Is 'Guilty Until Proven Innocent' the New Standard?" *National Review*, April 26, 2018, https://www.nationalreview.com/2018/04/trump-russia-investigation-guilty-until-proven-innocent-new-standard (accessed November 30, 2019).

11. Bob Barr, "Show Me the Man and I'll show You the Crime," *Townhall*, June 28, 2017, https://townhall.com/columnists/bobbarr/2017/06/28/draft-n2347508 (accessed November 19, 2019).

12. Alan M. Dershowitz, "The Mueller Waiting Game," *Gatestone Institute, International Policy Council*, April 4, 2019, https://www.gatestoneinstitute.org/14005/mueller-report-waiting (accessed November 19, 2019).

13. John C. Eastman, "The General Warrant and the Politics of Personal Destruction," *American Greatness*, June 20, 2017, https://amgreatness.com/2017/06/20/general-warrant-politics-personal-destruction (accessed November 30, 2019).

14. Philip Keefer and Stephen Knack, "Boondoggles, Rent-Seeking, and Political Checks and Balances: Public Investment under Unaccountable Governments," *Review of Economics and Statistics* 89, no. 3 (2007): 566–72, available online at http://pscourses.ucsd.edu/ps200b/Keefer%20Knack%20Boondoggles,%20Rent-Seeking,%20and%20Political%20Checks%20and%20Balances.pdf (accessed November 19, 2019).

15. David Boaz, "Solyndra: A Case Study in Green Energy, Cronyism, and the Failure of Central Planning," *CATO Institute*, August 27, 2015, https://www.cato.org/blog/solyndra-case-study-green-energy-cronyism-failure-central-planning (accessed November 19, 2019).

Chapter Two

What Is an Evidence-Based Approach?
Is Non-Proportionality Discrimination?

Following the evidence-based approach, as opposed to going down the well-worn rhetoric road, requires a great deal of mental discipline. We will start this section with an example that illustrates several fallacies.

Person X did action Y. Therefore, they must be guilty of possessing mental characteristic Z. In other words, having characteristic Z is the only possible explanation for why anyone, X in this case, would do Y.

One can already sense that something is awry here. How can we attribute uniqueness of causation to something as complex as human behavior? Indeed, the *unique cause* fallacy (causal reductionism) assumes precisely that.[1] In fact, there are multiple equally plausible reasons for many, if not all, behaviors. Let us apply this idea.

CASE STUDY NO. 2: ARE POLICE DISCRIMINATORY?

A police officer shoots and kills an African American (hereafter black) person in the course of their police duties. We will assume the police officer is a white person in accordance with the rhetoric's claim. Otherwise the argument falls apart.

Conclusion: The police officer must be discriminatory.

Note that we follow the US Census race categories used to define the data.[2] These may or may not correspond to any ideologies.[3] Further, the definition of American for statistical, not ideological, purposes is North American unless stated otherwise. Cross-sectional studies of non-comparable data sets across countries are notoriously flawed, as we shall discuss later.

Note the vagueness of the question in the title of case study no. 2, which is typical of rhetoric. There are whites, blacks, Asians, as well as many other self-identifying ethnic and racial groups in America. The police force includes at least all three, so discrimination is possible between all of the groups. For example, there can be black discrimination against whites and Asians.

When it comes to police activity, the rhetoric has focused exclusively on blacks as automatic victims. The rhetoric appears to be that every encounter of white police with a black person is discriminatory. In particular, the policy innuendo appears to be that the ordinary laws do not or should not apply to blacks.[4] Rhetoric is not usually as explicit as this because it loses power when its lack of evidence and confirmation bias appeal are brought to light.

Discussion Questions

(1) Why are blacks as allegedly and always "victims" of whites the exclusive focus of the rhetoric? Is this cherry picking or not?

(2) Is the focus agenda driven? What agendas are possible?

(3) Are there any circumstances when deadly force is justified against any particular individual minority member?

(4) Do the murders of inactive police sitting in their squad cars count as discrimination also? Or, are they just hate crimes?

(5) One would think that if discrimination were the real issue of the rhetoric then why do not all forms of it matter? Sticking to one category represents agenda-based bias and a partisan narrative.

Let us look at the issue for the categories of whites and blacks only. In order for the "are police discriminatory?" implied claim to work in each and every case, it must be assumed that all white police are discriminatory. What exactly are their incentives to kill African Americans? There are many disincentives including losing one's livelihood and going to jail for the rest of one's life. These work to hold some of them accountable, assuming their actions are unjustified.

We clearly cannot mind-read every single (or even one) white police officer's mind. Nor are we, after the fact, in the exact situation that a police officer was in at the time of a killing. Even if we could, mind-reading is not evidence. As in many discrimination claims, the conclusion cannot be verified without data. The rhetorical approach has led to a dead-end. You either believe the assertion or you do not. Confirmation bias kicks in immediately (see chapter 6).

What other reasons could there possibly be for the killing? The officer might have been threatened by the individual, for example. Fearing for their life, they responded. What other responses could there have been, short of deadly force? The answer is that, in general, we do not know. Needless to say, a ten second video does not allow us to presume what some other person should have done in the exact same situation. And, videos suffer from a lack of all the relevant information. The usual format shows the police officer exercising force and ignores what preceded it. That is enough for the rhetoric, and more might damage it, so cherry-picking is used to selectively present data (lie by omission) and create selective moral outrage.

How can we use an evidence-based approach, rather that the usual rhetorical one, to address this issue? We can start by looking at the crime statistics in our search for non-speculative evidence. Statistics are just numbers and depend on how much reality you want your analysis to reflect. Seemingly simple questions have to be asked and answered in order for the numbers to mean anything. That subject is applied statistics—how to collect data and properly use statistics to draw conditional inferences.

Statistics do not prove anything. They merely confirm or deny that the available evidence is consistent with the asserted hypotheses. They recognize that there is a chance (typically one percent to five percent) of being wrong in rejecting true hypotheses. It is the opposite of dichotomous, cut and dry thinking, since it acknowledges:

1. The world is a world of uncertainty wherein we are constantly dealing with probabilities, not certainties,
2. No one has all the relevant data to make or confirm any given hypothesis. Statistical inferences are usually made with random samples of the overall population which constitute partial—not full—information.

Think about this before falling into the trash statistics camp, where blanket claiming that the polls are always "wrong" is a classic example. We will examine the latter claim under the topic "Polls" in chapter 9. For now, simply recognize that statistics makes probability assertions, not statements about what must (with 100% certainty) be true. Most people who deal with actual data, as opposed to rhetoric and theoretical models of the perfect world, are skeptical of the latter type of assertions because they claim to have more knowledge than is available. That is another fallacy.

AN EVIDENCE-BASED ANALYSIS

How many fatal shootings were there of blacks by white police in 2018? This question is in absolute terms. We will later discuss the relevance of absolute, as opposed to *relative* numbers. A relative point of view asks: how many fatal shootings of blacks were there by white police in 2018, compared to the share of blacks in the US population?

At the time of this writing, the databases describe fatal shootings by all police. They did not split it up by race of the police officer. However, Joseph Cesario and David Johnson, provide a new database that tracks 917 fatal shootings by on-duty police officers in the U.S. in 2015. White police officers were involved in 79 percent of those shootings.[5]

Their methodology examines their empirical null hypothesis: "If fatal shootings of minority civilians are due to bias by white officers, we would expect that when white officers are involved in a fatal shooting, the person fatally shot would be more likely to be black or Hispanic." They find that their data does not support the hypothesis.

Some would conclude that if that percentage is greater than their population share then discrimination is obvious. To put some real world numbers on this discussion, according to Statista, a market and consumer data provider, in 2018 there were 996 people shot and killed by police.[6] The number of black "victims" (note the rhetoric) of those 996, was 209. This gives a percentage of 209 / 996 = 20.98%. According to U.S. Census Bureau data for 2018, "Black or African American alone" constituted 13.4 percent of the U.S. population of roughly 327 million.[7]

Conclusion: Indisputable proof that blacks are targeted by police at a ratio of 1.56 = 20.98/ 13.4. This is interpreted as obvious proof of discrimination and the case is closed according to the rhetoric which thereby achieves its goal. Note that the implicit assumption here, rarely explicitly stated, is that *fairness demands strict proportionality.*

Discussion Questions

(1) The Statista (http://statista.com) data uses the *Washington Post* as a source and Statista provides useful graphics, but the latter requires payment for some of its data.[8] After reading this article and website methodology, "Fatal Force: 994," 2015, discuss economic reasons for paying or not paying for their data.

(2) David R. Henderson's essay "Rent Seeking," explores monetizing activities for political gains.[9] After reading his essay, answer the following: Is the *Washington Post*'s data source site in item (1) for the years 2016 to 2019 an example of this by monetizing death statistics? or not?

(3) After reviewing the data provided in the *Washington Post* website from item (1), answer the following: Is this data offered neutrally or it is employed to support a narrative and spark moral outrage? Address the extra large number 994 in orange (the color of incarceration, another hot-button issue), the black stick

figures for shootings by police per month in 2015 (do they suggest excessive force?), the lack of any statistical analysis, discussion of the validity of the multiple news sources, or of their comparability, and the subtle suggestion that we are supposed to believe that the numbers imply that the fatalities are all victims.

(4) How do you emotionally respond to this post ? Does it suggest that there is an outrageous number of killings by police and that we must immediately do something about it? Click the Read More link to 'This database is based on news reports, public records, Internet databases and original reporting.' Examine the titles of some of the articles for shock value, the misuse of raw numbers at which we are supposed to be morally outraged even though no benchmark is presented, and for bias or innuendo.

(5) Compare the Washington Post's "Fatal Force: 994, 2015" approach to presenting the data to that of Joseph Cesario and David Johnson. Which, if either, is relatively more dispassionate?

In looking at media (including social media) sites, which often provide no data, learn to distinguish between evidence and rhetoric; remember to recognize the difference between an evidence-based approach, which is based on data and its analysis, and a rhetoric-based approach which is based on persuasion and emotional appeal.

Now let us take a step back and look at the assumptions behind this data analysis. It is probably a good idea to define discriminatory before accusing any person or group of persons of it. Unfortunately, the word is often used as rhetoric and it is like ketchup because you can put it on anything. Its use also brings the potential for libel. Discrimination usually is by one group against another, in this case presumably white (police) against blacks (victims).[10]

It follows that fatal shootings of blacks by other blacks cannot be attributed to discrimination. There are currently at least sixteen times more such fatalities than those from police shootings. However, that is an inconvenient fact and it is not consistent with the discrimination rhetoric. Hence the rhetoric ignores it.

Discussion Questions

(1) Should we rank the relative importance of social issues by criteria such as discrimination, or by the number of lives forfeited, saved, or improved?

(2) Should we save lives or should we save the rhetoric?

The Washington Post data just documents shootings of blacks by all police and it does not disaggregate it by the race of the police. That produces an over estimate and suits the rhetoric. At a minimum, we would have to try to determine the race of the police officer who shot. Why is this important?

Because, otherwise we cannot say that *all* police shootings of blacks are discriminatory.

From the same census data, 76.5 percent of the U.S. population was white in 2018. Therefore, assuming as an approximation that white police officers represent the population, the maximum number of shootings of blacks by white police officers would be 76.5 percent of 209, or 160. Other estimates of the percentage of white police include 77.7 percent (close to 76.5%), so white police do represent the population.[11]

160 represents a percentage of 16.06 percent of all fatal shootings (using 77.7% we obtain 16.30%). Now we are a lot closer to the 13.4 percent black share of the population. And there was no magic or sleight of hand here. These are just adjustments that anyone familiar with basic statistics would make.

Statistics are based on *randomization*. But, despite the rhetoric, police do not randomly go about shooting other people. They go to where the crime is.[12] Given that fact, the proportional to their share of the population weak standard of fairness falls apart because it is based on the assumption of random selection in the process being considered. Since police shootings are not random (nor should they be), arguing that their outcomes for different ethnic groups should be that of a random process in order to be unbiased is an error.[13]

In other words, when dealing with data you have to know what you are doing and what your criteria are for acceptance of a hypothesis such as "police are discriminatory." If police randomly shot people, then all minorities would tend to appear proportionally. This is a definition of "random" and it makes good statistics, but inefficient policing. Good policing aims at *minimizing deaths*, not at being random. The proportionality criterion, if adopted, would fail to protect the populace. This is an example of how saving the rhetoric (proportionality = fairness) costs lives.

The analysis so far suggests that relative crime rates are a better metric for assessing discrimination claims than relative shares of the population.[14] Of course, you would have to know something about how police operate in order to go beyond the canned proportional-to-the-population metric. That is another feature of rhetoric. It takes a shallow approach or the one most likely to startle its audience, reality notwithstanding. Rhetoric is nothing if it fails to get attention.

How do we define relative crime rates? First an example. Suppose a population at large consists of one hundred people. A minority accounts for 10 percent of that population. If every person and group commits crimes at the same rate then we would expect strict proportionality of crime rates to population share.

For example, if the crime rate is two crimes per person then using the population of one hundred persons as in the example above, overall two hundred crimes will be committed by the entire population and twenty by the minority for a percentage of 20 / 200 or 10 percent which is its population share. So far so good. But crime rates are not constant across subgroups of the population. What then?

Suppose now that a subgroup commits crimes at a rate twice that of the rest of the population (assumed to be two per person).[15] Then 90 percent of the population will commit 90 x 2 = 180 crimes, while the subgroup commits 4 x 10 = 40 crimes. The total number of crimes goes up to 180 + 40 = 220. The subgroup now commits 40 / 220 = 18% while the remainder of the population commits 180 / 220 = 82%.

Is this evidence of discrimination? No, it is just arithmetic. Even though the result can be interpreted to look biased in that 90 percent of the population commits 82 percent of the crime while 10 percent commits 18 percent, it is not biased given the different crime rates. Otherwise we get theater of the absurd: that the 90 percent majority better hurry up and commit relatively more crimes to get its proportion up. Or should legislation be created that provides incentives for the majority to commit more crimes and thereby make society more fair?

Let us apply some numbers to this example. Look at the FBI homicide statistics by race and by offender for 2018.[16] We find that blacks committed 6,318 of the 16335, or 38.68 percent of the total number of homicides recorded, while whites committed 4884 of the 16335, or 29.90 percent. With blacks roughly 13.4 percent of the population this shows that they commit homicides at a rate of 2.89 =38.68% / 13.4% times their share of the population. They are therefore going to show up in fatal police officer shootings much more often than their population share suggests.

Whites committed homicides at a rate of 29.90 percent but constituted 76.5 percent of the population in 2018 so their crime rate was 0.39 = 29.9% / 76.5%.[17] Going back to our example of one hundred persons, it will have on average 13.4 blacks and 76.5 whites if that sample is randomly sampled. We calculate how much more often blacks commit homicides, adjusting for relative population size.

Say that "y" represents the total number of homicides committed. Blacks committed 0.3868y in 2018 while whites committed 0.2990y in 2018. For example, in a random sample of of one hundred crimes from the total crimes and in a random sample of one hundred persons from the overall population, there will on average be 38.68 crimes committed by 13.4 African Americans. That is 38.68 / 13.4 = 2.89 crimes per each African American.

Similarly, in that same random sample of one hundred crimes, whites committed 29.90 crimes on average in 2018. But there are 76.5 whites on average in a random sample of one hundred. This means that there were 29.9 / 76.5 = 0.39 crimes committed on average by each white. This also says that each African American committed 2.89 crimes on average for each 0.39 crimes committed by each white. Therefore, the relative crime rate of African Americans compared to whites was 2.89 / 0.39 = 7.41. That constitutes a rate 7.41 greater.[18]

The inescapable conclusion based on this data is that blacks committed 7.41 times as many homicides as whites on average in 2018, each relative to their population shares (per capita). That is why blacks appear disproportionately in crime statistics. Disproportionality is not automatic evidence of discrimination—because the data tells us that any group will appear disproportionately in excess (deficit) of their share of the population as long as they commit relatively more (fewer) crimes. For example, Chinese crime rates also are out of proportion to their share of the population. In this case their crime rate is too low.

This is an alternative explanation of the data at least as plausible as the discrimination claim, whose hypothesis is essentially untestable because it requires a testable definition of discrimination and it employs mind-reading.

Why the black minority has a relatively higher per capita crime rate is a different question. Partisans might attribute that to discrimination too, amplifying the rhetoric. And even more by demanding that the State immediately fix it. This is a whole other issue since the State could itself have affected the higher crime rate in the first place by mandating minimum wage laws that price black youth out of the labor market—thereby producing more unemployment and crime. Or by soak the rich schemes that drive the tax base out. And because it assumes that the State is omnipotent and can fix anything. But that is another topic. We will discuss it under "utopianism" in chapters 8, 9, and 10.

This example illustrates that multiple explanations of a phenomenon are possible and plausible (evidence is available), and that lack of proportionality does not automatically imply blanket discrimination. Other factors can and do cause non-proportionality.[19]

In his essay, Thomas Sowell notes that:

Discrimination is just one factor among many and cannot be automatically presupposed to be the most powerful factor, however politically convenient that assumption might be. In practical terms, there is neither unlimited time nor unlimited resources available for dealing with racial issues. In order to maximize the impact of those resources, we must first decide whether our top priority is to smite the wicked or to help the less fortunate.[20]

Discussion Questions

(1) Consider the hypothesis noted above that "police are discriminatory." Is it rhetoric that is logically lacking, while imbued with rhetorical emotion?

(2) Does it mean all police, including black, Hispanic, and Asian-American police?

(3) Is each and every use of force on any minority discriminatory, or are some justified and non-discriminatory?

(4) Are some police possibly discriminatory and do they act on it? How does one know which ones?

Sample Discussion: That is possible and, if it could be decided, must be examined on a case-by-case basis in the context of the event and applying the laws of the country—not by the mob in the court of public opinion. Blanket labeling is a common rhetorical device and mind-reading is not evidence. The real evidence is the determining factor and the laws, not the partisan agenda.

(5) Are all police discriminatory because some might be?

Sample Discussion: That is the meaning of the concept known as the fallacy of composition, what is true of the part is true of the whole.

Before ending this chapter let us look at another much bigger social problem alluded to earlier in the chapter. If we look at killings of blacks by blacks in gang warfare we see that other factors come into play. Discrimination has nothing to do with such killings, hence such internecine killings (a major problem in Chicago) are ignored by the partisans.

What is the relative size of this problem compared to the alleged discriminatory police problem? In 2018, there were 2,925 murders of black victims according to FBI statistics.[21] Of these 2,600 were committed by black offenders. The percentage is 88.89 percent.

As previously noted, in 2018 the total number of killings of blacks by all police was 209, with 160 estimated in the calculation above to be by white police, based on their 76.5 percent (or 77.70%) contribution to the police force. The percentage of killings by estimated white officers to the total number of black victims (160 / 2,925) was 5.47 percent in 2018. Therefore, homicides committed by blacks against other blacks is a far greater problem: more than sixteen times greater 16.25 = 88.89% / 5.47%. Why has so little attention been devoted to them? Conspiracy theories are the stuff of rhetoric. In this book we will learn how to stick to the evidence, no matter how tempting it is to speculate.[22]

However, with limited resources (usually tax payers'), it is a good principle to rank problems by their magnitude, and attack them in the order of their bang for the buck. In this case, that means by how many lives they are likely to save. Citizens, not the punditry nor the government, need to decide what is more important: saving lives or saving the rhetoric.[23]

NOTES

1. Logically Fallacious, "Causal Reductionism," *Logically Fallacious*, n.d., https://www.logicallyfallacious.com/tools/lp/Bo/LogicalFallacies/64/Causal-Reductionism (accessed January 6, 2020).

2. U.S. Census Bureau. "About Race." January 23, 2018. https://www.census.gov/topics/population/race/about.html (accessed November 19, 2019).

3. Note that the self-identified, data-based U.S. Census Bureau race categories are used to facilitate consistent data definition acquisition and comparability. If you keep changing them as does the rhetoric to accommodate its narrative, you lose compatibility. This is of no concern to the partisans of the rhetoric because consistency and comparability are not on their agendas. Persuasion is the goal and emotion is the mechanism. It is not important what the facts are, but rather what people think they are.

4. For example, see Rich Morin, Kim Parker, Renee Stepler, and Andrew Mercer, "Behind the Badge," *Pew Research Center, Social & Demographic Trends*, January 11, 2017, https://www.pewsocialtrends.org/2017/01/11/behind-the-badge (accessed November 19, 2019). It is interesting to examine how police perceive themselves compared to what the pundits and partisans say to promote the politically motivated counter narrative. That being said, one would expect black crime to increase—because the penalties to black crime have decreased, though the data to test this hypothesis is hard to find.

5. Joseph Cesario and David Johnson, "Our Database of Police Officers in Fatal Shootings Reveals Who Shot Citizens," *Foundation for Economic Education* (*FEE*), July 23, 2019, https://fee.org/articles/our-research-of-police-shootings-reveals-who-is-the-likeliest-to-be-shot-by-police (accessed November 19, 2019).

6. Statista Research Department, "People Shot to Death by U.S. Police, by Race 2017–2019," last edited October 30, 2019, https://www.statista.com/statistics/585152/people-shot-to-death-by-us-police-by-race (accessed November 19, 2019).

7. U.S. Census Bureau, "Quick Facts," July 1, 2018, https://www.census.gov/quickfacts/fact/table/US/PST045217 (accessed November 19, 2019).

8. Washington Post, "Fatal Force: 994," 2015, *Washington Post*, https://www.washingtonpost.com/graphics/national/police-shootings (last accessed November 19, 2019). Available on this page are links to the methodology and data for 2015–2019.

9. David R. Henderson, "Rent Seeking," *Library of Economics and Liberty*, n.d., https://www.econlib.org/library/Enc/RentSeeking.html (accessed November 19, 2019).

10. This terminology echoes Marxist class warfare rhetoric. Karl Marx and Friedrich Engels, "Manifesto of the Communist Party: I. Bourgeois and Proletarians," n.d., *Avalon Project*, Yale Law School, Lillian Goldman Law Library, 5, https://avalon.law.yale.edu/19th_century/manone.asp (accessed December 3, 2019).

11. Data USA, "Police Officers: Race and Ethnicity," n.d., https://datausa.io/profile/soc/333050 (accessed January 7, 2020).

12. When a bank robber was asked why they rob banks, they responded: because that is where the money is.

13. The rhetoric might respond by asking why police do not randomly police, begging the question. The answer is that crime is not randomly distributed across ethnic groups.

14. David J. Johnson, Trevor Tress, Nicole Burkel, Carley Taylor, and Joseph Cesario, "Officer Characteristics and Racial Disparities in Fatal Officer-Involved Shootings," ed. Kenneth W. Wachter, *PNAS* 116, no. 32 (2019): 15877-82, https://www.pnas.org/content/116/32/15877 (accessed November 19, 2019).

15. Note that we could adjust for the relative crime rates of each subpopulation for which we have data.

16. U.S. Department of Justice, Federal Bureau of Investigation, "2018 Crime in the United States, Murder Offenders by Age, Sex, Race, and Ethnicity," 2018, https://ucr.fbi.gov/crime-in-the-u.s/2018/crime-in-the-u.s.-2018/tables/expanded-homicide-data-table-3.xls (accessed November 19, 2019).

17. U.S. Census Bureau, "Quick Facts," July 1, 2018.

18. Note that this does not say that each black committed 2.89 homicides in 2018. One has to understand the notion of "on average" to properly understand the correct interpretation. It is that if we repeatedly take random samples of one hundred homicides and random samples of one hundred people from the overall population and average the number of blacks and homicides committed by them in those samples, then the averages will be 13.4 blacks and 38.68 homicides committed by them. That amounts to 2.89 crimes per black person if we spread out the 38.68 homicides equally across the 13.4 persons, which is the standard method for determining per capita numbers. What would the rhetoric say? We do not know. But, based on its usual response or non-response, it would ignore the data and the calculations and say that it is 'racist' to point out any facts that negate its narrative.

19. Furthermore, proportionality is in general an invalid way to measure inequities (in our example, discrimination) in society for the simple reason that it assumes that the only "fair" allocation of the resources (including human capital) of society is the uniform distribution. That does *sound* reasonable though and is all that matters to the rhetoric, because it means that many people can be easily manipulated into believing it. Thereby its authors, the partisans who want to use public approval to justify their agendas, gain unearned credibility from their dichotomous thinking.

20. Thomas Sowell, "Discrimination, Economics, and Culture," in *Beyond the Color Line: New Perspectives on Race and Ethnicity in America*, ed. Abigail Thernstrom and Stephan Thernstrom (Stanford, CA: Hoover Institution Press, 2002), 176–77, https://www.hoover.org/sites/default/files/uploads/documents/0817998721_167.pdf (accessed November 19, 2019).

21. U.S. Department of Justice, Federal Bureau of Investigation, "2018 Crime in the United States, Race, Sex, and Ethnicity of Victim by Race, Sex, and Ethnicity of Offender," 2018, https://ucr.fbi.gov/crime-in-the-u.s/2018/crime-in-the-u.s.-2018/tables/expanded-homicide-data-table-6.xls (accessed November 19, 2019).

22. Some conspiracy theories (the term itself can be used as rhetoric) could be true, others not. If they could be properly formulated as testable and falsifiable hypotheses then the evidence or counterevidence would decide, not the rhetorical label.

23. And then try to force their representatives to implement their choices. In a democracy this is done by imposing term limits and/or voting them in and out.

Chapter Three

Basic Logic And Fallacies
Necessary versus Sufficient Conditions

Fallacies are powerful errors that cloud thinking. They muddy one's judgment and make rational decision-making impossible. They establish false conclusions, and thereby policies based on them are flawed.[1] They occur frequently, especially in (political) discussions where rhetoric and partisanship are intimately connected, and they include issues all the way from gun control to climate change. The antidote? Knowing what they are, how they operate, and applying basic logic. And most importantly, getting and looking at the evidence.

There are hundreds of fallacies. We will stick to some of the most commonly occurring ones:

1. Failure to understand and distinguish between *necessary* and *sufficient* conditions.
2. *False Dichotomies* (dichotomous thinking): the only alternative to a given policy choice is the worst case scenario (Armageddon). Failure to consider all the feasible *alternatives* is characteristic of this fallacy.
3. Fallacy of *Composition*: what is true of the *part* is true of the *whole*.
4. Fallacy of treating *aggregates* as if they are *individuals*.
5. Fallacy of claiming to *know more than one knows or can know*.
6. Fallacy of confusing *rates* with *stocks* of underlying quantities.
7. *Post Hoc Ergo Propter Hoc*: if one event follows another in time then the first one *must* have caused the second. This is also called the failure to distinguish *correlation* from *causation*.
8. *Tu Quoque*: answering the claim by an opponent that one has a certain characteristic or has done a certain action by the counterclaim that the opponent has exactly the same characteristic or has done the same action (two wrongs make a right).

9. *Ad Hominem*: attacking the person's *character*, not their *argument*.
10. *Straw Man* Argument: *changing* the person's argument by replacing it by an argument easier to refute (straw man), refuting the straw man, then concluding that the opponent's original argument has been refuted.
11. *False Comparisons and False Analogies*: comparing the incomparable. For example, saying those who disagree with you *must* be Nazis simply by virtue of disagreeing with you.[2]
12. *Non Sequitirs:* the conclusion(s) *do not follow* from the premise(s).
13. *Begging the Question: assuming* the conclusion(s) in the *premise(s)*.
14. *Psychobabble*: pseudo-scientific, fraudulent accusations of your opponent's mental health by those without the qualifications to make them, and who have never met their targets (very common online and by some pundits). A form of item (9) above, ad hominem, is one popular alternative to having a valid argument supportable by credible evidence.
15. *Claiming Moral Authority* for spurious reasons, without earning it, and *Morally Suspect Equivalencies*.
16. *Victimology*: getting a blanket pass to make unsupported claims and disarming your opponents by falsely claiming that all of their arguments are victimizing you.[3]
17. *Pot Shot fallacy*: merely critiquing the policies, actions, words, and morality of an opponent implies that you automatically have better policies, actions, words, and morality. No evidence is needed or given. This is a form of non-sequitir and of claiming (stealing) moral authority for spurious reasons.

NECESSARY AND SUFFICIENT CONDITIONS

Basic logical reasoning is necessary in order to understand rhetoric and its alternatives. It is interesting how little the important distinction in the title of this section is understood, Further, confusing necessary with sufficient conditions is also involved in another related fallacy, affirming the consequent.[4]

In the following statement, P and Q stand for assertions.

Truth Statements:
(1) P
(2) ~ P (not P)
(3) P and Q
(4) P or Q
(5) If P then Q (P is sufficient for Q)
(6) If ~Q then ~ P (Q is necessary for P)

(7) If Q then P (Q is sufficient for P)
(8) If ~ P then ~ Q (P is necessary for Q)

Examples:
   (1) 1 + 1 = 2
   (2) 1 + 1 ≠ 2
   (3) 1 + 1 = 2 and 2 + 2 ≠ 4
   (4) Either 1 + 1 = 2 or 2 + 2 ≠ 4
   (5) If I am a nationalist then I must be a Nazi.
   (6) If I am not a Nazi then I am not a nationalist.
   (7) If I am a Nazi then I must be a nationalist.
   (8) If I am not a nationalist then I am not a Nazi.

Items (1), (2), (3), and (4) are easy and self-evident. We will use the more interesting (and easily dismissed as rhetoric) hypercharged example item (5) to illustrate necessary and sufficient conditions—and their differences.

Look at the example in item (5). Does it follow from logic or history? Or is it rhetoric, an attempt to shame anyone who embraces nationalism? Is it a rhetorical challenge to prove you are not a Nazi (a negative, hence cannot be conclusively proven) by rejecting nationalism? See item (6) which is equivalent to item (5). Since no one can ever empirically and conclusively prove that they are not a Nazi, the rhetorical accusation can be and perpetually is used by some partisans against their opponents. It shares this feature with the discrimination rhetoric.

Item (5) does not pass the test of either logic or history. From the logical perspective it asserts that embracing nationalism is a sufficient condition for being a Nazi. That is quite a bold claim, which is false. But it clearly is not a sufficient condition even if one agrees that all Nazis were nationalists. We are back to the unique versus multiple explanations of human behavior argument and the single cause fallacy in chapter 2.

In order to be a Nazi, one has to have not just one defining characteristic of Nazis but all of them. The single biggest one missing here is their anti-Semitism. I can well be a nationalist without being an anti-Semite and therefore not a Nazi. In other words, nationalism is not a uniquely defining characteristic of Nazism. Item (5) mistakenly makes the claim that having a single alleged characteristic of Nazis makes one a Nazi.

From the historical perspective, there were many nationalists who fought the Nazis, so presumably they were not all Nazis. These include the British, the French, the Poles, eventually the Russians, the Americans, the Canadians, Winston Churchill, and many more. Why? Because Nazis usually do not oppose Nazis, and because the above list were not all anti-Semites; and anti-Semitism is one of the defining characteristics of Nazis.

Going back to logic, the purveyors probably mean item (7), being a Nazi is sufficient for being a nationalist (all Nazis were nationalists). Then they mistakenly jump to the conclusion that all nationalists must be Nazis. That move is a sleight of hand. Whether one agrees with item (7) or not, it is not the same as item (5).

In order to verify item (7), one would have to claim that all Nazis were nationalists (being a Nazi is a sufficient condition for being a nationalist)—which under pain of death at the time "nationalist" meant supporters of Hitler. But even the statement in item (7) is highly questionable. Were those Nazis who attempted to assassinate Hitler nationalists? One could say they were true nationalists, but that was not Hitler's definition, who killed both them and their families. As noted, item (5) is not equivalent to item (7).

It would make sense that the purveyors might try to equate nationalism to Nazism if they are against nationalism. But nationalism is neither a necessary nor a sufficient condition for Nazism. The purveyors of this rhetoric confuse necessary with sufficient conditions, in addition to being ill informed about the actual history. A common partisan tactic is to re-write history to suit the rhetoric.

Let us further try to understand necessary versus sufficient conditions. Consider the example: "If I say $1 + 1 \neq 2$ then I am lying." The assertion assumes that I know that $1 + 1 = 2$. The statement is true and is equivalent to its contra-positive which states: "If I am not lying then I would not say $1 + 1 \neq 2$."

Saying $1 + 1 \neq 2$ is sufficient for someone lying. It is not necessary though because there are numerous other ways a person can be lying. Necessary means that if someone is lying then they must say that $1 + 1 \neq 2$ —a statement that is not true. There are numerous other ways someone can lie; saying $1 + 1 \neq 2$ is just one of them.

We conclude that the if-then statement "If P then Q" says both that P is sufficient for Q and that Q is necessary for P (without Q there can be no P). "If Q then P" says both that Q is sufficient for P and that P is necessary for Q (without P there can be no Q). Thus "If P then Q" and "If Q then P" are very different statements. Here is our example:

Statement A: (If P then Q) "If I say $1 + 1 \neq 2$, then I must be lying."
Statement B: (If Q then P) "If I am lying, then I must say $1 + 1 \neq 2$."

Statement A is true; statement B is false.

P and Q are not equivalent. "Equivalent" means that P is a necessary and sufficient condition for Q. It follows that Q is a necessary and sufficient condition for P if P and Q are equivalent. Be on the lookout. This is a very common confusion and it enables much rhetoric.

CASE STUDY NO. 3: CONFUSION OF NECESSARY WITH SUFFICIENT CONDITIONS

On a Twitter post, Jeffrey Toobin writes, "Happy people do not obstruct justice."[5] In other words, the null hypothesis (not a fact) is that being happy is a sufficient condition for not obstructing justice. The other way to phrase this is the contra-positive assertion: if a person obstructs justice then that person must not be happy.

This could be a null hypothesis because it is falsifiable, but it is rhetoric because it is untestable. It was offered as a test of whether someone does not obstruct justice. All that one needs is an assessment of whether the person is happy, which some will be willing to assert through mind-reading and psychobabble, neither of which constitute real evidence.

Unfortunately, even the rhetoric is garbled and confuses necessary and sufficient conditions. The quoted assertion, even if true, fails to establish what the author is apparently attempting to establish, because it states only that happiness is a sufficient condition for not obstructing justice. It is not a necessary condition.

> (1) Is being happy a necessary condition for not obstructing justice? That is: if a person does not obstruct justice then that person must be happy.

Or the contra-positive:

> (2) If a person is not happy, then that person must obstruct justice.

Note carefully the difference between item (2) and the original assertion that states "Happy people do not obstruct justice." Even if the original assertion is true, item (2) "If a person is not happy, then that person must obstruct justice" does not follow. That fact, in essence, is the difference between sufficient and necessary conditions.

Looking at item (1), this statement is clearly false. Not obstructing justice is not enough (sufficient) to make every person happy. Or item (2), the single feature called unhappiness is not itself a sufficient condition for obstructing justice. Perhaps some unhappy people obstruct justice, others do not, even when faced with the opportunity to do so.

Item (2) is an inference. One could equally well say that the penalties may inhibit some unhappy (and happy) people from obstructing justice. The latter statement is supported by economic reasoning: the greater (lower) the penalty for an activity, the less (more) the activity will occur. Aaron Chalfin and Justin McCrary examine this hypothesis in detail in Criminal Deterrence: A Review of the Literature.[6]

34   *Chapter Three*

Further, even the single sufficient condition unhappiness in item (2) is dubious as the sole explanatory variable for obstructing justice. Many other allegedly sufficient conditions required for someone to obstruct justice could be posited, other than just unhappiness alone. For example, thinking one could get away with it is one such condition.

The analysis here is the same as it is for the statement: "If you are a nationalist then you must be a Nazi." Nationalism per se does not establish Nazism. Just like happiness does not make you not an obstructer of justice. Therefore, a single condition, let alone "happiness" as one of them, does not establish the desired result.

As discussed, sufficient conditions must be proven to be necessary. The two conditions are different. The moral of this, and the Nazism example, is that to prove obstruction of justice you have to provide hard evidence, not political rhetoric such as an implied syllogism based on flawed logic.

We can use case study no. 3 to learn about decision-making, and contrast the public sector approach with the private sector approach. So we are back to the special prosecutor. The rhetoric-based approach ignores some salient facts:

1. The special prosecutor, with unlimited resources, found that: "the investigation did not establish that members of the Trump Campaign conspired or coordinated with the Russian government in its election interference activities." (U.S. Department of Justice, Special Counsel Robert S. Mueller III, "Report On The Investigation Into Russian Interference In The 2016 Presidential Election," [redacted], 2 vols., March 2019 (volume 1, p. 2).[7]
2. Volume 2 of the Report does not establish—by presenting evidence, not rhetoric or speculation—that obstruction of justice by the Trump campaign occurred either: "Fourth, if we had confidence after a thorough investigation of the facts that the President clearly did not commit obstruction of justice, we would so state. Based on the facts and the applicable legal standards, however, we are unable to reach that judgment. The evidence we obtained about the President's actions and intent presents difficult issues that prevent us from conclusively determining that no criminal conduct occurred. Accordingly, while this report does not conclude that the President committed a crime, it also does not exonerate him."[8]

Item (2) is a convoluted, equivocal statement and it purports to being able to empirically and conclusively prove a negative. Hence it lends itself nicely to becoming rhetoric, which is precisely what happened. Either there is evidence that the President committed a crime or there is not. Exoneration has nothing to do with it and is a red herring. Both volumes 1 and 2 confirm that he did not commit a crime of either collusion or obstruction—because no evidence was provided to the contrary.

1. Attorney General Barr's summarizes the entire sequence of events and its conclusions.[9]
2. The notion of 'exoneration' is discussed, with references, in case no. 10 in chapter 9. Briefly, one can never empirically and conclusively prove that no crime was committed (a negative). The fact that one cannot conclusively prove non-existence of a crime does not prove a crime was committed, only that it is possible.

   Possible is a probability statement that does not mean some crime was actually committed. Evidence is required to prove that a crime was committed. Hence it is impossible to exonerate anyone with 100 percent certainty. Nor is this the premise under which the U.S. Justice system works. Therefore, Special Prosecutor Mueller's exoneration statement in volume 2 represents an invalid legal opinion bordering on rhetoric. For him to state it as if it had any operational meaning is a classic example of government overreach—and why we need to hold government officials accountable. It is no wonder that it generated so much rhetoric in the aftermath.
3. We are led back to the *unaccountability* of government officials who execute massive government boondoggles at the tax-payers' expense. It is unlikely that the partisans, with limited resources, will do better than the special prosecutor, due to decreasing marginal returns to searching. We will discuss when a search should be ended in part II. We will also introduce the opportunity cost notion there, and show how to use it as part of a decision making criterion for the acceptance or rejection of projects, including investigations.

In the rhetoric-based approach one can endlessly search for something that confirms one's own confirmation bias using cherry picking, just as there may be the chance of finding evidence for the guilt of anyone. However, as long as credible confirmable evidence is not produced then that person is innocent—without qualification.

CASE STUDY NO. 4: DISCRIMINATION VERSUS NON-PROPORTIONALITY IN THE LABOR MARKET

We have already looked at the premise that "proportionality to population share equals fairness" in chapter 2. It is false in the context of relative crime rates. We found it lacking because it is based on randomization—which does not work when it comes to enforcing our crime laws.

Now we turn to the labor market to examine racial disparities (departures from randomized-based proportionality) in labor market outcomes. The null hypothesis (not a fact) is: "A disproportionate number of minority employees in an industry or company must be the result of discrimination." That is, (1) discrimination causes non-proportionality, and (2) discrimination is the only possible cause, according to the rhetoric. Of course, the negative of the above null hypothesis cannot be empirically and conclusively proven, so the negative should be the null hypothesis.

Let us apply reasoning to assertions (1) and (2). Assertion (1) is a possibility that cannot be dismissed. However, (2) does not follow from (1). Even if discrimination causes non-proportionality it does not follow that it is the only such cause. Nor even that it is automatically the main one.

Could discrimination be one cause of non-proportionality in the labor market? What else could cause it? We discussed this in chapter 2 in the context of relative crime rates and concluded that proportionality as a percentage of the population is a flawed metric (based on randomization) that itself causes the lack of proportion.

Discrimination may be one of many sufficient conditions, but not a necessary condition, for non-proportionality. Of course, sufficiency assumes that those making the hiring decisions are on average discriminatory. Can minority members hiring other minority members be discriminatory? The disincentives are the anti-discrimination laws that expressly forbid it and the penalties for violating those laws.[10]

Is it a necessary condition? This would be the assertion that "if there is non-proportionality then there must be discrimination." In other words, you would never have non-proportionality were it not for discrimination. Let us examine this assertion. We already did so for crime rates in chapter 2.

To do so in the context of the labor market, one has to look at the reasons that non-proportionality exists. There are numerous reasons for non-proportionality including:

1. A firm could locate where there is a non-proportional distribution of a specific minority. Minorities are not uniformly distributed across all regions of the United States.[11]
2. Hiring minorities in certain fields (academia for example) may be relatively costly compared to hiring non-minorities. Therefore fewer, more costly minorities will be hired. After all, minorities are by definition in short supply in certain industries relative to non-minorities. In order to hire a minority faculty member to meet affirmative action requirements, which

is effectively what the government is demanding, universities would get into bidding wars for minorities. This increases the price of hiring in a manner similar to bidding wars for housing.

Firms in a competitive economy demand less of a more costly input, not because they are discriminatory, but because they need to limit factor input costs in order to survive.

3. Using basic economics, for any given demand schedule for labor, the equilibrium price (wage rate) for comparable minority labor should be relatively higher.[12]

Is it reverse discrimination that a minority member will command a higher wage than an equivalent non-minority member? Or does that reality simply reflect the neutral economic fact that minorities are in relatively short supply, which drives up their relative wages?

4. There are lower cost substitutes for domestic minority labor in certain industries, for example, (illegal and legal) foreign agricultural labor. In certain fields foreign labor may be plentiful relative to domestic labor. That will bid down the relative price of foreign labor, inducing firms to substitute it for domestic labor. The degree of substitution will depend on the elasticity of demand for the type of labor.[13]

Discussion Questions

(1) Those who accuse others of discrimination against foreigners seeking to enter the country as migrant workers might consider that open entry could cause non-proportionality in hiring *domestic* labor—because foreign labor would partially displace domestic labor. Hence according to the partisan logic, would open entry increase discrimination against domestic laborers? How and why?

Sample Answer: This shows that something else can cause non-proportionality. And, that the something else has nothing to do with the discrimination rhetoric. Just as consumers switch to substitutes when the relative price of a consumer good increases, so too do firms switch to lower cost labor inputs, or even to capital versus labor. The overall demand for all labor (not just minority labor) decreases as firms become relatively more capital intensive.

(2) Should the government create laws that prevent consumers from switching to margarine when the relative price of butter increases? Would the rhetoric then say that not creating such a law discriminates against butter producers and the entire supply chain? So must we do something immediately?

We now continue with the causes of non-proportionality.

5. The theory of *Comparative Advantage* implies non-proportionality. Individual people, like nations, can and should choose to specialize in what

they are relatively good at (do that which has the lowest relative opportunity cost to them).[14]

We take job choice as a basic human right in a free society. However, talent is not proportionally distributed among individuals. Therefore, given individuals could be disproportionally under-represented in fields of endeavor in which they have little comparative advantage. It is not likely that proportionality will reign supreme in any field of endeavor. Why? Because people choose to work as they wish in accordance with their individual talents and opportunities.

Discussion Questions

(1) Does freedom supersede equality? Define the terms. Using them, answer the following: Is equal but not free a deal with the devil?

(2) How is the government able to either determine or to enforce proportionality? And at what cost? What particular expertise and information does it have?

(3) How is the government to be held responsible for not abusing these extraordinary powers?

(4) If we allow the government to determine and enforce labor market proportionality by gender, race, sexual preference, age, religion, minority status, and other criteria would not a sub-optimal distribution of labor result in and across industries? Why? or why not?

(5) Would special interest groups, based on the factors listed in item (4), lobby the government for special treatment? How do we know the government would not give such special treatment?

(6) Will all this be determined at birth, based on what will have to be introduced as our analogue of the industry planning models of the central planners, as was instituted in the former Soviet Union?

(7) How can our freedom to choose how we wish to work not be sacrificed to a potentially infeasible concept of equality?

(8) As long as people have equal opportunity to enter the field of their choice, is not proportionality of the outcomes up to their merit (subject to demand and supply in the labor market) and not up to the government officials?

NOTES

1. Sometimes advocates will support good policies despite their fallacious/or incomplete logic. More often than not, however, their rhetoric leads them down the path to bad policies.

2. Outrageously false comparisons get attention, so partisans use them often to create selective moral outrage in their base.

3. Victimology is a common tactic designed to insulate partisans from any criticism of their ideas.

4. Logically Fallacious, "Affirming the Consequent," *Logically Fallacious*, n.d., https://www.logicallyfallacious.com/tools/lp/Bo/LogicalFallacies/14/Affirming-the-Consequent (accessed November 23, 2019).

5. Post to *Twitter*, by Jeffrey Toobin, April 18, 2019, 7:34 a.m., https://twitter.com/JeffreyToobin/status/1118885464914714624 (accessed November 20, 2019).

6. Aaron Chalfin and Justin McCrary, "Criminal Deterrence: A Review of the Literature," *Journal of Economic Literature* 55, no. 1 (2017): 5–48, https://doi.org/10.1257/jel.20141147; https://eml.berkeley.edu/~jmccrary/chalfin_mccrary2017.pdf (accessed January 27, 2020).

7. U.S. Department of Justice, Special Counsel Robert S. Mueller III, "Report on the Investigation Into Russian Interference in the 2016 Presidential Election," [redacted], vol. 1, 2, March 2019, https://www.justice.gov/storage/report_volume1.pdf (accessed November 20, 2019).

8. U.S. Department of Justice, Special Counsel Robert S. Mueller III, "Report on the Investigation Into Russian Interference in the 2016 Presidential Election," [redacted], vol. 2, 2, March 2019, https://www.justice.gov/storage/report_volume2.pdf (accessed November 20, 2019).

9. William Barr, "Mueller Report: AG William Barr's Full Press Conference," *USA TODAY*, YouTube video, 21.23 min., Streamed live on April 18, 2019, https://www.youtube.com/watch?v=FeFGk6JbkJo (accessed November 20, 2019).

10. L & E Global, "Anti-Discrimination Laws in USA," March 24, 2017, *L & E Global*, https://knowledge.leglobal.org/anti-discrimination-laws-in-usa (accessed November 20, 2019).

11. U.S. Bureau of Labor Statistics, "Career Outlook: Blacks in the Labor Force," February 2018, https://www.bls.gov/careeroutlook/2018/article/blacks-in-the-labor-force.htm (accessed November 20, 2019).

12. Craig A. Depken II, *Microeconomics Demystified*. (Emeryville, CA: McGraw-Hill, 2006).

13. Minority labor in certain industries could, instead of substituting, be complementary to domestic labor.

14. Arnold Kling. "Ricardo's Difficult Idea Eludes Wonks" *Econlog at Econlib*, January 13, 2004, https://www.econlib.org/archives/2004/01/ricardos_diffic.html (accessed November 25, 2019).

Chapter Four

Evidence, Economic Data, and How to Find It

Still using the labor market of case study no. 4 from chapter 3 for illustration, this chapter is a mini-course on data acquisition, data presentation, and data analysis, using *source* data and not relying on interpretations by third parties. If this material is new to you please stick with it. I have only used relatively few charts and tables.

Many people have to form their opinions based on what other people tell them and confirmation bias, particularly when it comes to data. And those others may simply be repeating what other people told them (cf. echo chambers). If the original source—assuming there is one—is in error, then the error propagates itself all through the chain. There is a way to get out of this syndrome. Look at the source data. This approach creates much more independence.

Are employed blacks (henceforth short form for African Americans) in aggregate (ages 16+ years) under-represented in the United States compared to their relative share of the population (the civilian non-institutionalized population)? What does the source data in aggregate say?

The U.S. Bureau of Labor Statistics (BLS) states,

> In 2018, there were 257.8 million people [ages] 16 years or older in the U.S. civilian non-institutionalized population (CNIP). Of those, about 32.8 million (12.71%) were Black or African American. The Civilian Labor Force was 162.1 million people (62.9% of the CNIP).[1]

Note, once again, that share of the entire population is not relevant since it includes those who are inmates of institutions or are employed in the US Military. So we can narrow it down at first to the CNIP. This measure also includes people not employable, or who choose not to be employed (voluntarily

Table 4.1. U.S. Civilian Non-Institutionalized Population (CNIP) 2018, ages 16+ years, All, and White and Black Population (in thousands)

Letter	Category	Total	White	Black
A	CNIP	257,791	200,221	32,761
B	% of CNIP	100%	77.67%	12.71%
C	Number Employed	155,761	121,461	19,091
D	Number Employed / CNIP	60.4%	60.7%	58.3%
E	Number Employed / Total Employed	100%	77.98%	12.26%
E-B	Discrepancy	0.0%	+0.31%	-0.45%

Sources: U.S. Bureau of Labor Statistics, "HOUSEHOLD DATA ANNUAL AVERAGES, 3. Employment Status of the Civilian Noninstitutional Population by Age, Sex, and Race," 2018, https://www.bls.gov/cps/aa2018/cpsaat03.htm (last modified date: January 18, 2019).

unemployed), hence are not in the potential labor force. It does not include people working illegally because where would any government agency get such data? People generally do not admit to illegal behavior.

The data we first need here are approximated by the number of all individuals (all genders, races, ages 16 years and over) in the CNIP. Table 4.1 presents the 2018 data first.

First note the fact that only 60.4 percent of the entire CNIP is employed. One reason is voluntary unemployment (for example students and retirees) and that occurs both among blacks and whites. Surely this is not due to discrimination?

As a percentage of their component of the CNIP, the discrepancy between black and white workers, ages 16+ years, employment is 60.7% - 58.3% = 2.4% minus statistical error (Table 4.1, row D). But the CNIP includes people who are not employable or who are voluntarily unemployed, so a more relevant number is percentage of the employed, not percentage of the CNIP.

Now if we use the employed to measure contributions to the total employed we find that: blacks account for 19,091 / 155,761 = 12.26% of the number employed. Compared to their share of the CNIP, they are under-represented by 12.26% - 12.71% = -0.45 %. That is less than half a percent. In absolute terms 0.45 percent of the black CNIP is 147,425 persons. Whites are 121,461 / 155,761 = 77.98% of the employed population, which means that whites are over-represented by 0.31 percent. Again, less that half a percent. In absolute terms 0.31 percent of the white CNIP is 620,685 persons.

For reference, 2.454 million non-farm jobs were added in 2018 so the absorption of 147,425 (0.45%) persons could happen in one month at this rate.[2] The discrimination rhetoric claims that any non-proportionality in outcomes must represent discrimination (see chapter 3). The present analysis of the data in Table 4.1 indicates that the current degree of non-proportionality is minimal and could easily be eliminated. Further, Table 4.2 indicates that discrepancies in the *labor participation rate* are decreasing and faster for blacks. Therefore, by the logic of the discrimination rhetoric itself, "discrimination" is decreasing.

The question is not whether real, empirically verifiable discrimination—not simply non-proportionality—is a potential issue in specific, legitimate cases. The discrimination rhetoric begs the question by assuming that because it asserts it, without valid evidence, it is a major issue. Our question here is whether the discrimination rhetoric is empirically verifiable.

Rhetoric does not like good news that contradicts it, because such good news causes it and its purveyors to be irrelevant. It also does not like having to follow its own logic, although it hypocritically insists that everyone else must. But it must be held accountable to do so and follow its own illogic and rules.

Therefore partisans might still claim discrimination, since rhetoric cannot afford to change its narrative. Once the rhetoric is solidified in the minds and hearts of the populace through constant repetition, revising it becomes counterproductive. Believers in the class warfare/"struggle" rhetoric of Karl Marx would say that the 0.45 percent deficit in employment of blacks is directly caused by the 0.31 percent surplus of employment by whites.[3] Why? Because all non-proportionality in labor market outcomes represents discrimination by and only by whites against people of color only. The mechanism is that whites are taking jobs that blacks should have. If so, then they should be taking 620,685 jobs, not the 147,425 jobs blacks are in deficit. Whites are doing a very bad job of depriving blacks.[4]

Discussion Questions

(1) Define workers and capitalists.

(2) Explain the precise difference between them. For example, are the self-employed workers? Are CEOs workers?

(3) Why is it a given that whites are the ruling class (capitalists) and that they necessarily "exploit" blacks (workers) in modern day America?[5] Are there no black capitalists? Do we have a false dichotomy here?

(4) What is the evidence, as opposed to the rhetoric, for the allegation in item (3)?

(5) In rhetoric versus evidence, is the emotional appeal all that is needed to rouse the base?

This rhetoric fails because the false dichotomy fallacy applies to both workers and capitalists. The BLS data consists of those employed, whether they work for others (workers) or for themselves (self-employed), or as CEOs (capitalists).

Furthermore, the jobs that account for the white surplus are not necessarily the same jobs as those that account for the black deficit. Even the Marxian rhetoric updated in the form of neo-Marxism tells us so: all whites are "oppressors" (therefore capitalists) and all blacks are "oppressed" (therefore workers) and the classes are dichotomous, by definition.[6] Therefore, they cannot have the same jobs—if the rhetoric is to survive.

Neo-Marxism justifies this Marxist-based reasoning and is worth considering because it is at the root of much of the current rhetoric. Its fundamental hypothesis (not fact) is stated by Georgi Boorman in "How The Theory Of White Privilege Leads To Socialism": "Briefly, neo-Marxism divides the world between oppressor and oppressed and identifies a system, or systems, by which the oppression takes place. In classical Marxism, the oppressed were the proletariat, the oppressors were the bourgeoisie, and the system of oppression was capitalism. The Marxist framework has been adapted to categorize and pit against each other various group identities, all toward the end of establishing socialism. . . . In race, whites are oppressors, people of color the oppressed, and "white supremacy" is the system of oppression."[7]

Discussion Questions

(1) Is rhetoric specific or non-specific; and does it lack evidence? or not?

(2) Does rhetoric rely on ideology or on evidence?

(3) Is rhetoric laden with emotional appeal, which sells it by making its adopters feel morally superior (a free good and does not have to be earned)? or not?

In contrast to the rhetoric-based approach, the evidence-based approach insists on testing properly formulated and testable hypotheses with data, not accepting them outright.

ALTERNATIVE APPROACHES TO LABOR MARKET DISCREPANCIES

Labor Force Participation Rate, Age 16+ Years

We now look at the U.S. Labor Force Participation (LPR) rates for blacks and whites. The *civilian labor force* consists of those employed and those *actively looking* for work (the definition of unemployed according to the BLS). The LPR is the ratio of the civilian labor force to the CNIP.

The civilian labor force consists of two categories: the employed and the unemployed. Note that to be counted as unemployed you have to be actively looking for work. Those who are not—discouraged workers and natural exits—are not considered to be unemployed. They have exited the labor market.

Unemployed Persons According to the Current Population Survey

The BLS defines "Unemployed persons (Current Population Survey)," as "Persons aged sixteen years and older who had no employment during the reference week, were available for work, except for temporary illness, and had made specific efforts to find employment sometime during the four-week period ending with the reference week. Persons who were waiting to be recalled to a job from which they had been laid off need not have been looking for work to be classified as unemployed."[8] That is, the BLS does not count everyone who is jobless as unemployed.

Now for our next challenge we have to look for the LPR for blacks, ages 16+. According to the data provided by the BLS in 2016, it was 61.6 percent. Next we find the LPR for whites, ages 16+. It was 62.8 percent at the end of 2016. So we have a discrepancy of 1.2 percent to explain. Note that the discrepancy is changing through time. Part of that discrepancy is due to sampling error which according to the BLS is small.[9]

In 2017 the discrepancy was 62.8% (whites) - 62.3% (blacks) = 0.5% with the white LPR decreasing and the black LPR increasing compared with the prior year.[10] To be consistent (rhetoric rarely is), the rhetoric would have to say that this represents decreasing discrimination—because, according to it, all discrepancies in labor market outcomes must be the result of discrimination. There was little change to these numbers in 2018: 62.8 percent for whites versus 62.3 percent for blacks.[11] By November 2019, the numbers are 63.2 percent for whites and 62.3 percent for blacks for a divergence under 1.0 percent.[12]

Generally, convergence to parity is occurring (see figure 4.1). This result says that as a percentage of the population (CNIP), those employed plus those unemployed and actively looking for work were roughly equivalent for both blacks and whites. One argument for this convergence is that as the labor force ages people exit the labor market. Blacks and whites age at the same rate on average.[13]

We can also change our focus from ages 16+ years to look at the relative LPR for blacks and whites of *prime working age* (ages 25 to 54 years). This removes the retirement age and student effects in the larger population. But it includes both the employed and those actively looking for work.

For blacks in 2016 this number was 78.9 percent. For whites it was 82.1 percent. The discrepancy was therefore 3.2 percent. Since 2016, with the increased recovery rate of the economy, that discrepancy has declined further. In 2017 the total LPRs were 79.8 percent for blacks (ages 25 to 54 years) and 82.4 percent for whites for a discrepancy of 2.6 percent. By 2018 both black and white LPRs increased, but the difference remained constant. Overall the black LPR improved more than or by an amount equal to the white LPR's improvement (Table 4.2).

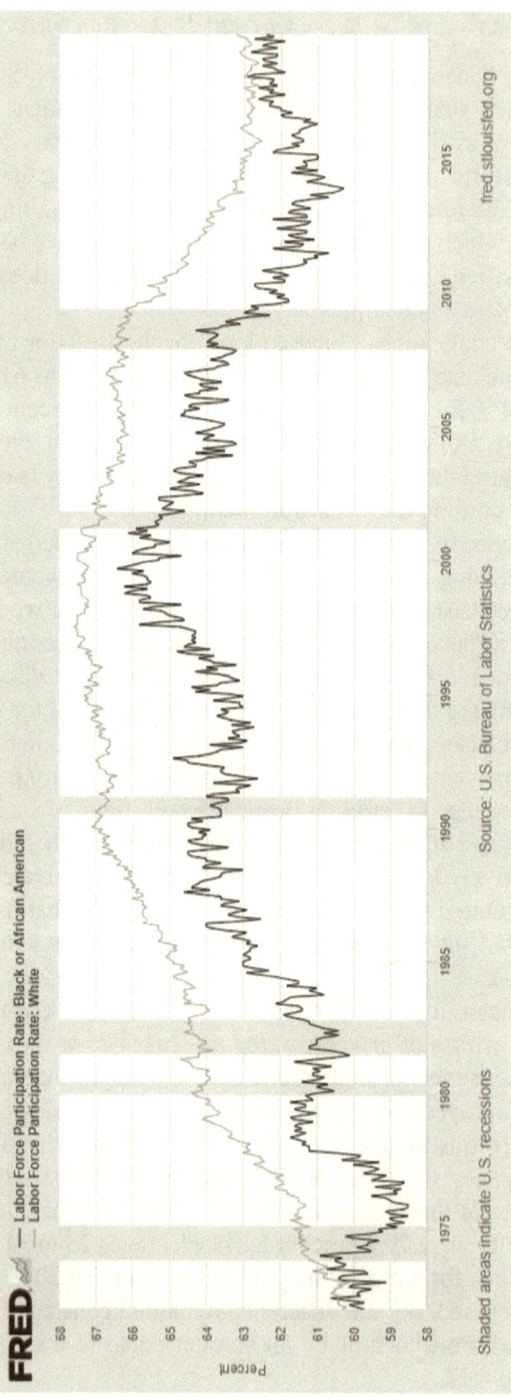

Figure 4.1. U.S. Labor Force Participation: Blacks, Whites, Ages 16+ years.
Source: U.S. Bureau of Labor Statistics, Labor Force Participation Rate: Black or African American, retrieved from, FRED, Federal Reserve Bank of St. Louis, https://fred.stlouisfed.org/series/LNS11300006 (accessed November 4, 2019); and U.S. Labor Force Participation Rate: White, retrieved from FRED, https://fred.stlouisfed.org/series/LNS11300003 (accessed November 4, 2019).

Table 4.2. U.S. Labor Participation Rates, ages 25-54 years, Blacks and Whites (by percentage)

Year	(1) Blacks	(2) Whites	Discrepancy (col. 2 minus col. 1)
2016	78.9%	82.1%	3.2%
2017	79.8%	82.4%	2.6%
2018	80.1%	82.7%	2.6%

Sources: U.S. Bureau of Labor Statistics, "HOUSEHOLD DATA ANNUAL AVERAGES, 3. Employment Status of the Civilian Noninstitutional Population by Age, Sex, and Race," column 3, 2016, https://www.bls.gov/cps/aa2016/cpsaat03.htm (last modified date: February 8, 2017); 2017, https://www.bls.gov/cps/aa2017/cpsaat03.htm (last modified date: January 16, 2019); and 2018, https://www.bls.gov/cps/aa2018/cpsaat03.htm (last modified date: January 18, 2019).

There is no single magic number that captures the complex dynamic U.S. labor market, so labor economists look at multiple measures. This harkens back to our discussion of unique versus multiple factor explanations and is part of the scientific verification process in the evidence-based approach.

Employment to Population Ratio

The different measures are related to each other. In our case,

Employment-Population Ratio
= Employed / CNIP
= (Employed / Civilian Labor Force) x (Civilian Labor Force / CNIP)
= (1-Unemployment Rate) x Labor Participation Rate

A little piece of theoretical knowledge like this allows us to understand how to increase the employment-population ratio, which is by lowering the unemployment rate and/or increasing the LPR.

Figure 4.2 summarizes the employment-population ratio for blacks and whites, ages 16+ years. We conclude that the gap has been narrowing in the last ten years with the black employment percentage improving while the white employment percentage remained stable.

Nonetheless, the rhetoric might insist that a (much) greater *proportion* of prime working age blacks relative to that of whites were not employed. We already did this exercise for ages 25 to 54 years, when looking at the LPR (see Table 4.2). Now we will do it for the employment-population ratio.

Note that if we look just at the employed component of the prime working age labor force (the employment-population ratio) in 2016, we obtain 73.3 percent for prime working age blacks and 79.1 percent for whites. The actually employed prime working age discrepancy was 5.8 percent in 2016 (Table 4.3).

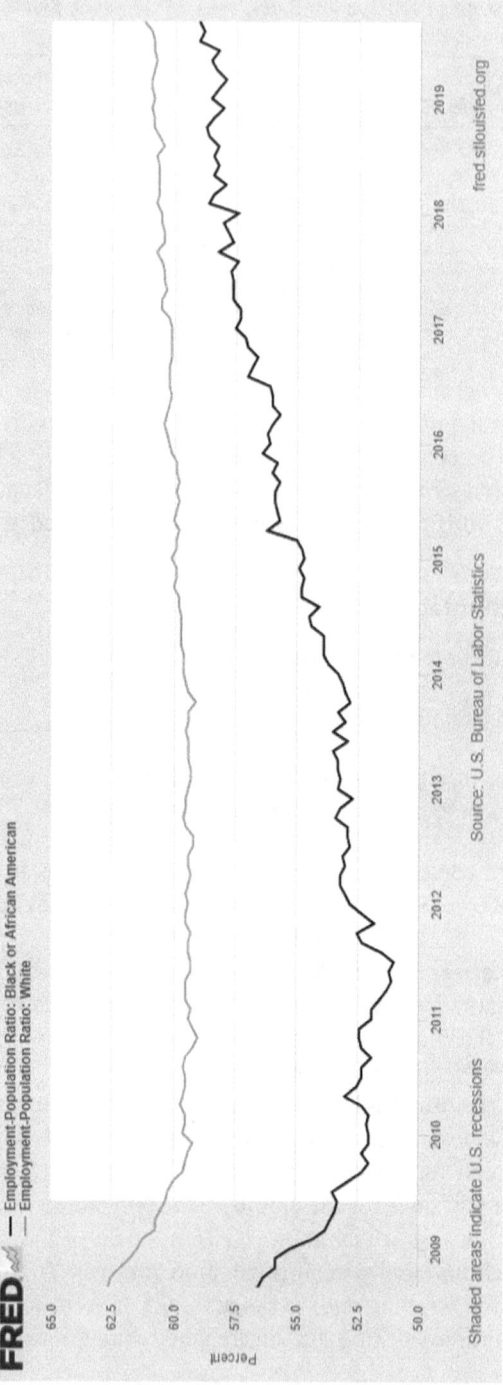

Figure 4.2. Employment-Population Ratio: since 2008: Blacks, Whites, Ages 16+ years.
Source: U.S. Bureau of Labor Statistics, Employment-Population Ratio: Black or African American, retrieved from, FRED, Federal Reserve Bank of St. Louis; https://fred.stlouisfed.org/series/LNS12300006 (accessed November 4, 2019); and Employment-Population Ratio: White, retrieved from FRED, https://fred.stlouisfed.org/series/LNS12300003 (accessed November 4, 2019).

Table 4.3. U.S. Employment-Population Ratios, ages 25-54 years, Blacks and Whites (by percentage)

Year	(1) Blacks	(2) Whites	Discrepancy (col. 2 minus col. 1)
2016	73.3%	79.1%	5.8%
2017	74.6%	79.7%	5.1%
2018	75.7%	80.3%	4.6%

Sources: U.S. Bureau of Labor Statistics, "HOUSEHOLD DATA ANNUAL AVERAGES, 3. Employment Status of the Civilian Noninstitutional Population by Age, Sex, and Race," column 5, 2016, https://www.bls.gov/cps/aa2016/cpsaat03.htm (last modified date: February 8, 2017); 2017, https://www.bls.gov/cps/aa2017/cpsaat03.htm (last modified date: January 16, 2019); and 2018, https://www.bls.gov/cps/aa2018/cpsaat03.htm (last modified date: January 18, 2019).

Table 4.3 gives the data for 2016, 2017 and 2018 from which we see again that both blacks and white employment-population ratios were improving,[14] with blacks improving relatively more and the discrepancy declining.

How can the discrepancy in the LPR (ages 25 to 54 years) in 2016 be 3.2 percent (Table 4.2, row 1) while the discrepancy in the employed component of it is 5.8 percent (Table 4.3, row 1)? The reason for the jump in the numbers as we move from employed plus actively looking (LPR) to simply employed (employment-population ratio) is that in 2016 some estimated 7.1 percent prime working age blacks were actively looking for work (unemployed) while only 3.6 percent of prime working age whites were doing so. The actively looking are not yet employed but they have not exited the labor market.

Now we summarize what happened over time, we examine the null hypothesis that "all discrepancy must be discrimination," and also whether alleged discrimination increased or decreased in the last few years. From Tables 4.2 and 4.3 we see that under both measures, the LPR and the employment-population ratio, the discrepancies have decreased over the years 2016 to 2019. The employment-population ratio for prime working age workers for blacks was 74.6 percent in 2017 while for whites it was 79.7 percent. Therefore the discrepancy decreased to 5.1 percent from 5.8 percent in 2016 (see Table 4.3).[15] Then it further decreased.

Decreasing discrimination must be the inescapable conclusion, at least according to the discrimination rhetoric—which ignores all other factors as is typical of dichotomous thinking. Note further that the discrimination rhetoric assumes that blacks and whites apply for the same jobs. If not, then we are comparing apples to oranges.

This suggests that there is a better explanation for the discrepancies than the rhetoric-based "discrimination." The data suggests that *improvements in the labor market* better account for the discrepancies. With the improvement in the labor market, the discrepancies have all decreased, while it is very

Table 4.4. U.S. Unemployment Rates, ages 25-54 years, Blacks and Whites (by percentage)

Year	(1) Blacks	(2) Whites	Discrepancy (col. 1 minus col. 2)
2016	7.1%	3.6%	3.5%
2017	6.6%	3.3%	3.3%
2018	5.5%	2.9%	2.6%
2019 Q3	4.7%	2.8%	1.9%

Sources: U.S. Bureau of Labor Statistics, "HOUSEHOLD DATA ANNUAL AVERAGES, 3. Employment Status of the Civilian Noninstitutional Population by Age, Sex, and Race," column 7, 2016, https://www.bls.gov/cps/aa2016/cpsaat03.htm (last modified date: February 8, 2017); 2017, https://www.bls.gov/cps/aa2017/cpsaat03.htm (last modified date: January 16, 2019); 2018, https://www.bls.gov/cps/aa2018/cpsaat03.htm (last modified date: January 18, 2019); and "HOUSEHOLD DATA NOT SEASONALLY ADJUSTED QUARTERLY AVERAGES, E-16. Unemployment Rates by Age, Sex, Race, and Hispanic or Latino Ethnicity," cols. 6 and 3, 2019 Q3, https://www.bls.gov/web/empsit/cpsee_e16.htm (last modified date: October 4, 2019).

unlikely that white (black) employers are any less discriminatory against blacks (whites) in their hiring practices. Why would they be? Furthermore, how many people hiring blacks are blacks themselves? They cannot be discriminatory by definition. Conversely, how do we know there is no discrimination from blacks hiring whites?

Discussion Questions

(1) Why are the questions raised in the previous paragraph never or far less investigated, just as blacks killing blacks is relatively ignored? Provide evidence if you find it.

(2) Is the data (not opinions) that is needed to investigate these issues available?

U3 Unemployment Rate

Even the most flawed and politicized measure of unemployment, U3, tells the same tale.[16] The discrepancy between black and white unemployment rates has decreased over at least the last ten years (see fig. 4.3). The discrepancy usually increases during recessions and decreases during booms, which means that the *business cycle* is another factor behind the discrepancy. Unlike amorphous discrimination, the business cycle is an observable measure.

The U3 rate is influenced by *exits*, people giving up searching for jobs. If you exit the labor market you are not considered unemployed and the U3 measure will therefore decrease due to exits alone (because exits are no longer counted as unemployed by the BLS).

Therefore, the fact that the U3 rate is declining does not always signal increased employment, specifically when the LPR is decreasing due to exits. Historically, blacks have proportionally more exits than whites.[17] When the

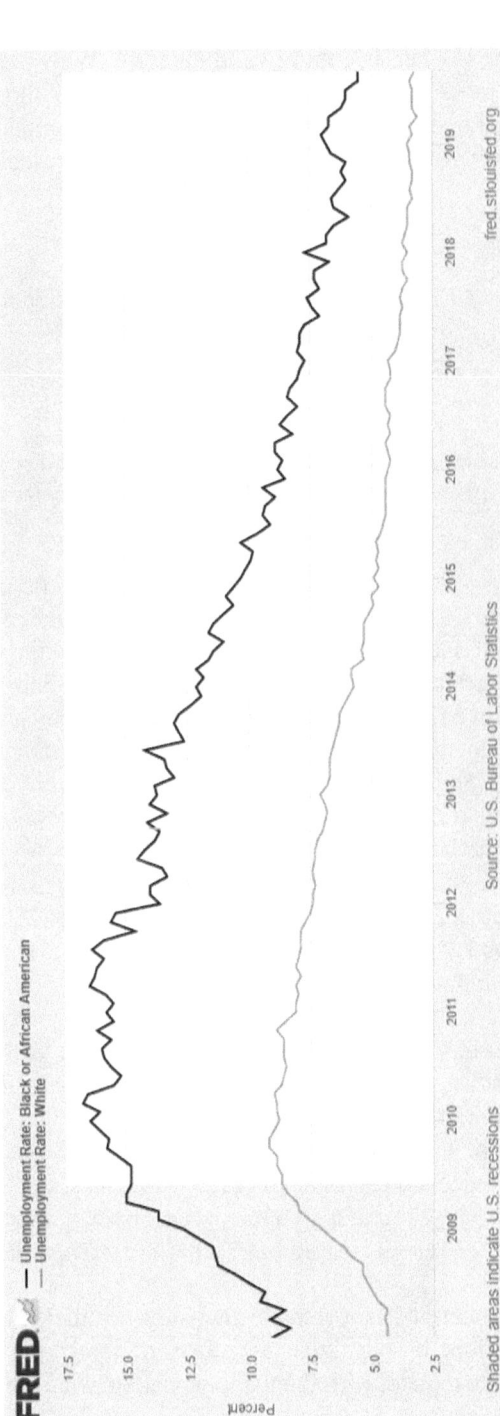

Figure 4.3. U.S. Unemployment Rate U3: Blacks, Whites, Ages 16+ years.
Source: U.S. Bureau of Labor Statistics, Unemployment Rate: White, retrieved from FRED, Federal Reserve Bank of St. Louis; https://fred.stlouisfed.org/series/LNS14000003 (accessed November 4, 2019); Unemployment Rate: Black or African American, retrieved from FRED, https://fred.stlouisfed.org/series/LNS14000006 (accessed November 4, 2019).

LPR is increasing, the U3 rate is a more valid measure. We will expand on this in chapter 6. A measure that accounts for exits and for those marginally attached to the labor force (part-time workers and marginally attached workers) is U6, but it is hardly ever discussed in the popular media (see n16 below).

Discussion Questions

(1) Are the U6 rate and its analysis missing from the news because it is much harder to politicize?

(2) Is there evidence to support the hypothesis in item (1)?

(3) Is item (1) a conspiracy theory?

(4) Should all hypotheses currently lacking data to test them be dismissed out of hand as conspiracy theories; or are some of them untested hypotheses? Why or why not?

The discrepancy between whites and blacks (prime-aged workers) for the U3 unemployment rate decreased to 2.6 percent in 2018 from 3.5 percent in 2016 (see Table 4.4). It decreased even more to 1.9 percent in the third quarter of 2019. The number of unemployed workers decreased both for blacks and whites as they moved from the category of looking to being employed. Not only that, black unemployment went down relatively more than white unemployment.

For the third quarter (Q3) of 2019, the U3 discrepancy between all (ages 16+ years) blacks in the labor market versus all whites (ages 16+ years) was 5.6 % - 3.4 % = 2.2 %.[18] The rate of 5.6 percent is not double 3.4 percent. It is less than double, by 1.2 percent. The discrepancy for ages 25 to 54 year olds, as just noted, was 1.9 percent for 2019 Q3 (see Table 4.4). There is some sampling error in these numbers.

The Fallacy of Composition is built into the rhetoric to the contrary, in that it implies as innuendo that it must always be twice, or above, and that all of it is discrimination. Must the government be called in to instantly "fix the crisis" by creating more unenforceable legislation?

As indicated in figure 4.5, typically the U3 rate for blacks, ages 16+ years, has averaged around twice the corresponding rate for whites, ages 16+ years (except around 2012). The 2012 unemployment rate anomaly drop occurred, not because the black U3 rate decreased but because of exits, a defect of the U3 measure.

But, this does not mean it has to remain that way nor that it is a consequence of discrimination. In July 2016 and forward something new happened: the black U3 rate dipped, with fluctuations, below twice the white rate (see figs. 4.6 and 4.7).

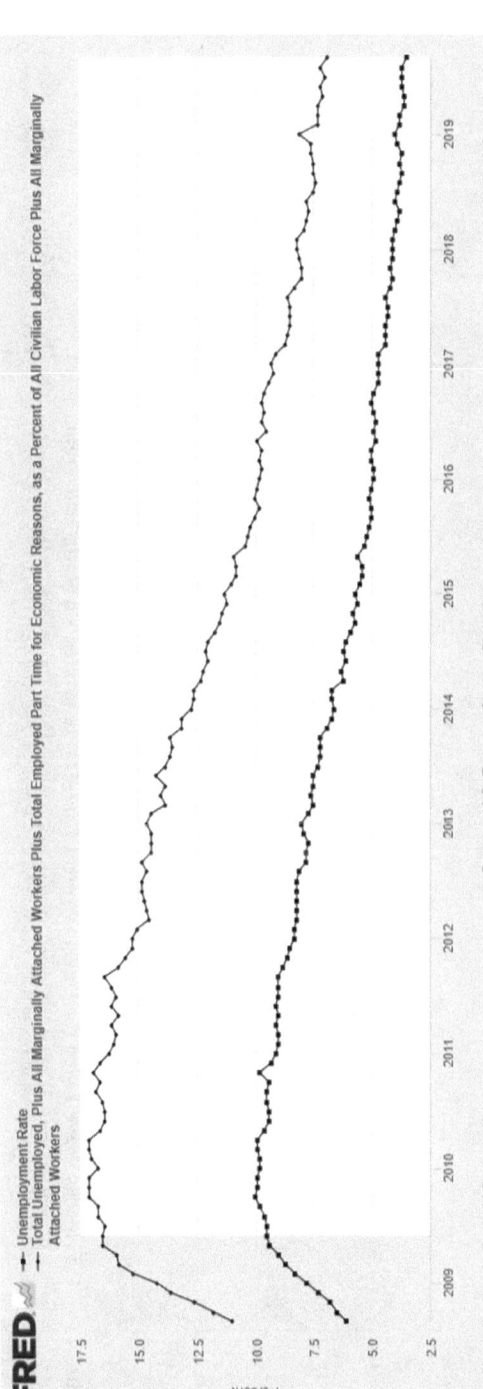

Figure 4.4. U.S. Civilian Unemployment Rates: U6 versus U3.

Source: U.S. Bureau of Labor Statistics, Unemployment Rate, retrieved from FRED, Federal Reserve Bank of St. Louis; https://fred.stlouisfed.org/series/UNRATE (accessed November 2, 2019); and Total Unemployed, Plus All Marginally Attached Workers Plus Total Employed Part Time for Economic Reasons, as a Percent of All Civilian Labor Force Plus All Marginally Attached Workers, retrieved from FRED, https://fred.stlouisfed.org/series/U6RATE (accessed November 4, 2019).

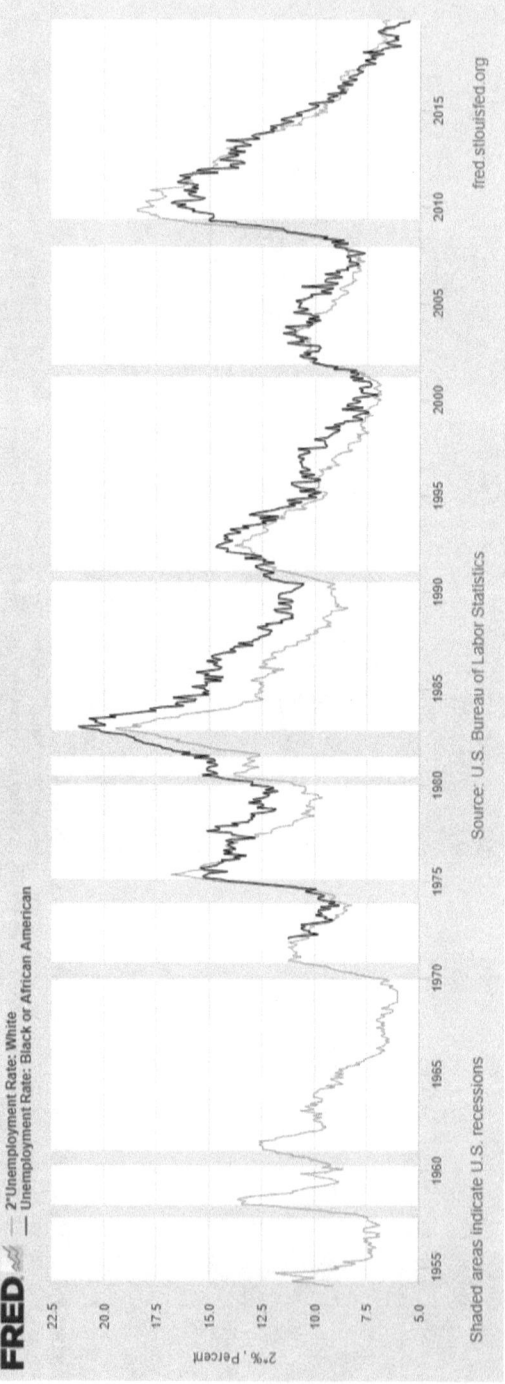

Figure 4.5. U.S. Blacks Have Twice the Unemployment Rate (U3) of Whites is a Static Half-Truth.
Source: U.S. Bureau of Labor Statistics, Unemployment Rate: White, retrieved from FRED, Federal Reserve Bank of St. Louis; https://fred.stlouisfed.org/series/LNS14000003 (accessed November 4, 2019); and Unemployment Rate: Black or African American, retrieved from FRED, https://fred.stlouisfed.org/series/LNS14000006 (accessed November 4, 2019).

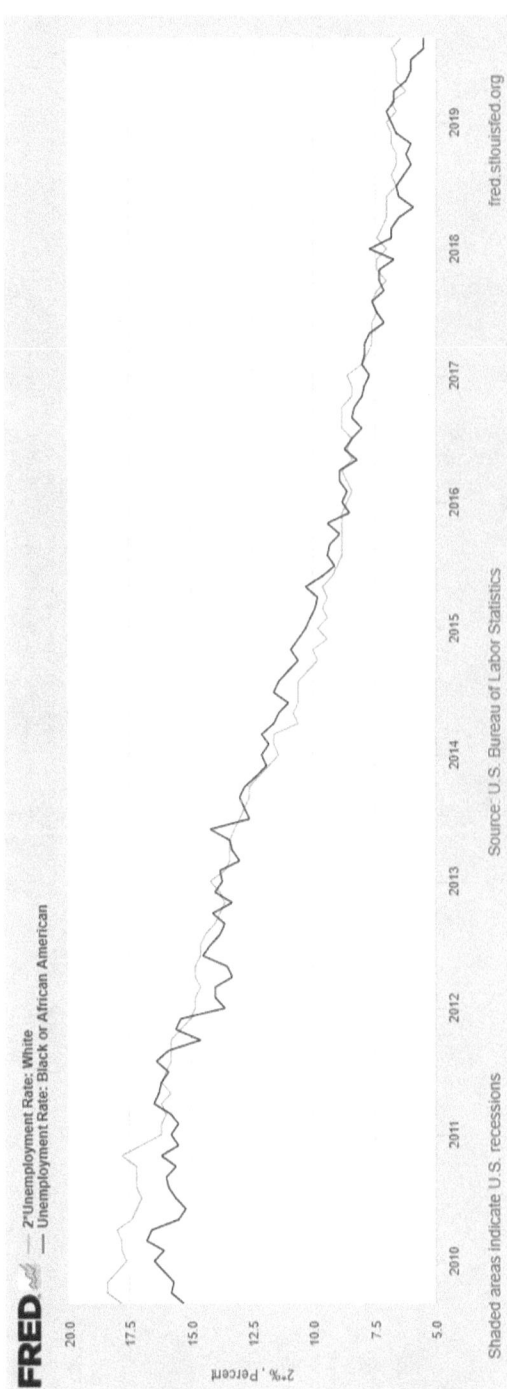

Figure 4.6. The Last Ten Years of the Twice the Rate Rhetoric.

Source: U.S. Bureau of Labor Statistics, Unemployment Rate: White, retrieved from FRED, Federal Reserve Bank of St. Louis; https://fred.stlouisfed.org/series/LNS14000003 (accessed November 4, 2019); and Unemployment Rate: Black or African American, retrieved from FRED, https://fred.stlouisfed.org/series/LNS14000006 (accessed November 4, 2019).

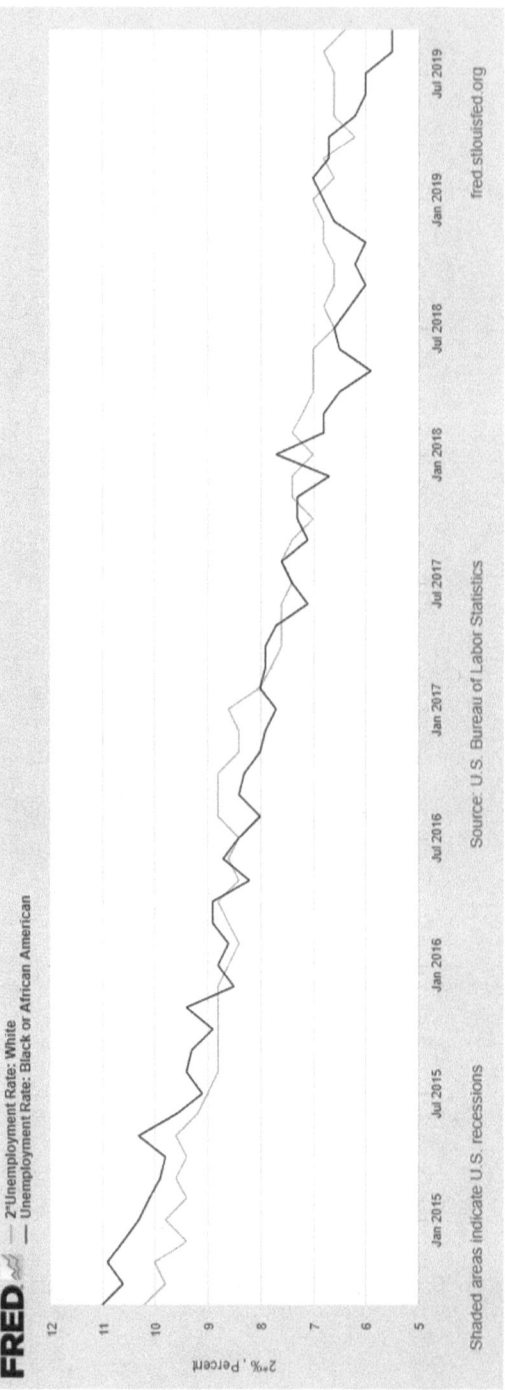

Figure 4.7. The Last Five Years of the Twice the Rate Rhetoric.
Source: U.S. Bureau of Labor Statistics, Unemployment Rate: White, retrieved from FRED, Federal Reserve Bank of St. Louis, https://fred.stlouisfed.org/series/LNS14000003 (accessed November 4, 2019); and Unemployment Rate: Black or African American, retrieved from FRED, https://fred.stlouisfed.org/series/LNS14000006 (accessed November 4, 2019).

Of course, statistical games can be played with the data by averaging, or even by using moving averages. Since the rates for both whites and blacks have both been going down (it is not a zero-sum game as assumed by the Marxist class warfare rhetoric)[19], averaging from previous periods when both the rates and the discrepancy were higher will make the current discrepancy look higher. Try it. Edit the graph and use quarterly averages for example. For Q3 2018, the discrepancy is now 2.9 percent. Now use semi-annual averaging, same data. For the first half of 2018, the discrepancy is now 3.2 percent. It is good to know how the data is collected.[20]

There is an argument to be made for not averaging and just taking the month-by-month data. The labor market's past is gone. The counterargument is that averages are less noisy estimates. In any case, the discrepancy is decreasing and with it doubt is cast on the double unemployment rate discrepancy therefore discrimination syllogism.

Also note the rate versus absolute fallacy. Unemployment rates for both blacks and whites are down; therefore, many actual people benefit, even if the rate discrepancy were to remain constant which it has not. Saving the rhetoric becomes irrelevant compared with saving actual people by taking them out of unemployment, even if we do not have statistical rate equality.

This takes us back to a basic point, necessary versus sufficient conditions discussed in chapter 3. Equating non-proportionality with discrimination says that non-proportionality is a necessary and sufficient condition for discrimination, when it may only be sufficient. One can have non-proportionality without discrimination, just as one can have nationalism without Nazism. In other words conflating (equating) non-proportionality with discrimination is a logical error. And, it is not supported by the data.

The Theory and Its Literature

There are many theoretical and empirical studies of discrimination:

1. Gary S. Becker, *The Economics of Discrimination.*
2. Kenneth J. Arrow, "What Has Economics to Say about Racial Discrimination?"
3. Walter E. Williams, *Race and Economics: How Much Can Be Blamed on Discrimination?*
4. Kevin Lang and Jee-Yeon K. Lehmann, "Racial Discrimination in the Labor Market: Theory and Empirics."[21]

Lang and Lehmann (see 4 above) conclude: "Since we have concluded that none of the existing models of race discrimination in the labor market

Table 4.5. Educational Attainment of the U.S. Labor Force, 2017 Annual Averages, age 25+ years, by Race and Ethnicity (by percentage)

Educational Attainment	Hispanic or Latino/a	Asian	Black or African American	White
Less than a high school diploma	25%	6%	7%	7%
High school graduates, no college	31%	17%	31%	26%
Some college, no degree	15%	9%	21%	16%
Associate's degree	9%	7%	12%	11%
Bachelor's degree and higher	20%	61%	30%	40%

Sources: U.S. Bureau of Labor Statistics, "Labor Force Characteristics by Race and Ethnicity, 2017," https://www.bls.gov/opub/reports/race-and-ethnicity/2017/home.htm (last modified date: August 2018).

explains the major empirical regularities, it should not be surprising that we are reluctant to draw strong policy conclusions from the existing literature."[22]

Of course, it is easier to invoke the discrimination-for-everything explanation rhetoric, but reality is much more complicated. There are usually several—not one—variables involved in explaining many things, including black-white disparities. For example? Lang and Lehmann further state: "First, much of the difference in labor market outcomes between blacks and whites undoubtedly reflects the skills workers bring to the labor market. The models we have discussed, especially those with dynamic elements, show how premarket investment decisions may be affected by expectations about how workers will be treated in the labor market. Therefore, labor-market oriented policies can affect these investments."[23]

Here is some evidence on educational achievement by race which is related to relative skill levels and job qualifications. Asian and Hispanic/Latino/a minorities are also included for comparison.

Note that in Table 4.5 provided is the 2017 annual average of educational attainment for those ages 25 and older, and that there is a discrepancy between the numbers for those with bachelor's degrees and higher; for whites (40%) versus blacks (30%). Their relative lack of higher education compared with whites (but not with Hispanics or Latinos/a at 20%) hurts blacks in the labor market for bachelor's degree jobs. This provides another source of evidence that blacks are not competing with whites for the same jobs. If they wish to do so, then they will have to get their bachelor's degree rate up and be competitive with whites. Conversely, the Asian population examined shows 61 percent of the population with a bachelor's degree or higher. By the same argument, whites will be viewed as non-competitive with Asians for bachelor's degree jobs.

Unfortunately, people may feel they are being discriminated against when the real discrimination is in determining whether they are suited for the job, and this requires the maximum educational attainment needed for the respective jobs. There is empirical evidence that: "Therefore, the higher incidence of unemployment among blacks suggests to us that we require a model in which blacks are more likely to take jobs for which they turn out to be poorly suited."[24]

Discussion Questions

(1) So, is there discrimination in the labor market?

(2) What percentage of labor market discrepancies between racial groups is the result of discrimination?[25]

(3) What are the other factors related to labor market discrepancies, such as government imposed minimum wage laws that price unskilled labor out of the market?

(4) What is the relative importance of each of the factors, ranked from most to least important?

(5) If there is discrimination, do we recognize that an alternative explanation for some of it is government policies themselves that meddle with prices?

(6) Are some government policies and labor discrimination related?

(7) Do some government policies, ostensibly to protect the public, reduce the cost of racial discrimination, thereby increasing racial discrimination?

(8) Are minimum wage laws an example of such government policies?

(9) What about rent control? Does it incentivize landlords to discriminate against renters?

Therefore, a better option here that might actually help minorities, is to eliminate such laws rather than shaming people into proving the impossible, which is that they are not discriminatory.[26]

Rhetoric rarely goes beyond the most superficial, declaring as obvious what is not known at all. What is the goal of the discrimination rhetoric? If the goal is to produce a state of no discrimination (a utopian fantasy) then that goal can never be achieved, nor proven to exist. You cannot empirically and conclusively prove a negative, namely that there is zero discrimination.

Or is the goal to have the government take over and execute another government boondoggle orchestrated by the partisans? This happened for the war on poverty that by 2012 had cost twenty-two trillion dollars (inflation-adjusted) and had had zero impact.[27]

But the zero discrimination goal becomes an endless source of the discrimination rhetoric (similar to the rhetoric "prove you are innocent"), because there could always be some discrimination somewhere. Perhaps this is why the discriminatory charge continues to be exploited by political partisans against their political opponents, particularly during election seasons.

According to the bad logic, it is up to the opponents to prove they are not discriminatory, which is of course impossible. Not being able to empirically prove the impossible is then a guilty verdict, according to the flawed logic. Note that this rhetorical tool permits discrimination against innocent parties and takes us back to the days of kangaroo courts and their show trials. Is it morally acceptable to cause the loss of lives in order to save the rhetoric, a practice that continues to this day?

Discussion Questions

(1) Is the government the only or best mechanism for controlling alleged discrimination? Why or why not?

(2) How can the government control labor market discrepancies having little to do with discrimination but something to do with its own (partisan) wage-fixing legislation? Why would the government do so?

(3) Has such legislation materially hurt the very people it was intended to help?

These are just some of the questions that can be asked and answered, based upon logic and the evidence, not the rhetoric.

Discussion Questions

(1) Can we expect any self-reflection, economic logic, or historical knowledge from unaccountable government legislators that will result in the reversal of their ill-founded legislation? (That is, of their own legislation that creates some of the labor market discrepancies.)

(2) Or, is it just the nature of bureaucracies to never admit their errors while calling out those of their political opponents?

(3) Can we legitimately argue that government legislators are 100 percent unbiased angels, and if not, should we replace them by those who are (assuming they exist and we could find them)?[28]

NOTES

1. U.S. Bureau of Labor Statistics (BLS), "HOUSEHOLD DATA ANNUAL AVERAGES, 3. Employment Status of the Civilian Noninstitutional Population by Age, Sex, and Race." 2018. https://www.bls.gov/cps/aa2018/cpsaat03.htm (last modified date: January 18, 2019).

2. U.S. Bureau of Labor Statistics, FRED, Federal Reserve Bank of St. Louis, "All Employees, Total Nonfarm," November 1, 2019, https://fred.stlouisfed.org/series/PAYEMS (accessed November 21, 2019).

3. Karl Marx and Friedrich Engels, "Manifesto of the Communist Party : I. Bourgeois and Proletarians," n.d., *Avalon Project*, Yale Law School, Lillian Goldman Law Library, 5, https://avalon.law.yale.edu/19th_century/manone.asp (accessed December 3, 2019). By using the word "struggle" vs. "warfare" partisans attempt to steal moral authority and legitimize all of their actions. *Any* group can call its ideology a "struggle" to justify its behavior. The word demonizes the alleged "oppressors" and lionizes the alleged "victims." Hitler and other dictators were masters of this rhetoric. Controlling the language is controlling the people, and rhetoric insists on doing so.

4. To see if whites are taking jobs away from other minorities, we could analyze the appropriate numbers.

5. Matt Zwolinski and Alan Wertheimer, "Exploitation," in *The Stanford Encyclopedia of Philosophy* (Summer 2017 edition), ed. Edward N. Zalta, https://plato.stanford.edu/archives/sum2017/entries/exploitation (accessed November 23, 2019).

6. Marx and Engels, "Manifesto," 5.

7. Georgi Boorman, "How The Theory Of White Privilege Leads To Socialism," *Federalist*, June 26, 2018, https://thefederalist.com/2018/06/26/theory-white-privilege-leads-socialism (accessed December 2, 2019).

8. U.S. Bureau of Labor Statistics, Glossary, "Unemployed persons (Current Population Survey)," 2019, https://www.bls.gov/bls/glossary.htm#U (accessed November 22, 2019).

9. U.S. Bureau of Labor Statistics, Handbook of Methods, "Error Measurement," 2019, https://www.bls.gov/opub/hom/topic/error-measurements.htm (accessed November 21, 2019).

10. For 2016 and 2017, see U.S. Bureau of Labor Statistics, "HOUSEHOLD DATA ANNUAL AVERAGES, 5. Employment Status of the Civilian Noninstitutional Population by Age, Sex, and Race," line 3, 2016–2017, https://www.bls.gov/cps/aa2017/cpsaat05.htm (last modified date: January 16, 2019).

11. For 2018, see BLS, "HOUSEHOLD DATA ANNUAL AVERAGES, 3," https://www.bls.gov/cps/aa2018/cpsaat03.htm.

12. U.S. Bureau of Labor Statistics, "Graphics for Economic News Release, Civilian Labor Force Participation Rate," 1999–2019, https://www.bls.gov/charts/employment-situation/civilian-labor-force-participation-rate.htm (last updated October 2019).

13. U.S. Bureau of Labor Statistics, FRED, https://fred.stlouisfed.org provides useful visualizations of the BLS data. An interactive version is provided by the U.S. Bureau of Labor Statistics, "Graphics for Economic News Release, Civilian Unemployment Rate," 1999–2019, https://www.bls.gov/charts/employment-situation/civilian-unemployment-rate.htm (last updated October 2019).

14. They have to, by our theoretical equation, if the LPRs and/or the unemployment rates are improving.

15. The data tells us this must be decreasing discrimination if all discrepancies must be due to discrimination, as the one variable rhetoric assumes.

16. The U3 unemployment rate, often noted as U3, is the most commonly reported unemployment rate for the United States. There is also another rate, U-6, or

U6, which includes the unemployed workers (U3), as well as the discouraged and underemployed workers. More information on U-rates may be found at: U.S. Bureau of Labor Statistics, "Graphics for Economic News Release, HOUSEHOLD DATA, Table A-15. Alternative Measure of Labor Underutilization," 2018-2019, https://www.bls.gov/news.release/empsit.t15.htm (last updated October 2019).

17. This can be gleaned from the CPS data (last column titled "Not in labor force") referenced for Table 4.3:

Sources: U.S. Bureau of Labor Statistics, "HOUSEHOLD DATA ANNUAL AVERAGES, 3. Employment Status of the Civilian Noninstitutional Population by Age, Sex, and Race," col. 5, 2016, https://www.bls.gov/cps/aa2016/cpsaat03.htm (last modified date: January 18, 2019); 2017, https://www.bls.gov/cps/aa2017/cpsaat03.htm (last modified date: January 16, 2019); and 2018, https://www.bls.gov/cps/aa2018/cpsaat03.htm (last modified date: January 18, 2019).

18. U.S. Bureau of Labor Statistics, "HOUSEHOLD DATA NOT SEASONALLY ADJUSTED QUARTERLY AVERAGES, E-16. Unemployment rates by age, sex, race, and Hispanic or Latino ethnicity," 2018-2019 Q3, https://www.bls.gov/web/empsit/cpsee_e16.htm (last modified date: October 4, 2019).

19. See n3 and n5. The zero sum game description is a modern way to indicate that the winners always win their always allegedly unearned spoils at the alleged expense of the losers (alleged victims), and it underlies Marx's exploitation of the worker hypothesis. This is powerful rhetoric, a throwback to the 1800s, and is exploited by modern day pundits, the media, candidates for the Presidency, and others. Under the thin veil of unearned moral authority and hypocrisy, the latter never tire of pushing for the resurrection of demonstrably failed Marxist based policies including: soaking the rich, demonizing corporations, nationalization of industries, price and wage controls, apocalyptic "environmentalism," and government control of how the populace thinks, feels, and behaves through the restriction of constitutional freedoms. Being about blaming others, it retains its evergreen popularity and victimology. Hitler exploited it in his "race struggle" which he stole from Marx's "class struggle," and modern day purveyors exploit the rhetoric as often as possible to demonize "the enemy." Unfortunately, it is rarely recognized that this blaming ideology lies at the heart of real, not rhetorical discrimination. Lest the reader conclude that this only applies to the Democrats, it does not. Republicans are not always that different ideologically, and some have also been influenced by Marxist hypotheses. See Tom Mullen, "You Deserve a Tax Break and Your Boss Does Too," *Foundation for Economic Education*, November 16, 2017 https://fee.org/articles/you-deserve-a-tax-break-and-your-boss-does-too (accessed November 21, 2019).

20. See U.S. Bureau of Labor Statistics, "Labor Force Statistics from the Current Population Survey, How the Government Measures Unemployment," 2015, https://www.bls.gov/cps/cps_htgm.htm (last updated October 8, 2015). The employment numbers collected by the BLS are based on sample surveys of about 60,000 eligible households in the sample for this survey. A sample is not the whole population and is therefore subject to sampling error (see the polling section in chapter 9). Therefore, some of the discrepancy is a statistical artifact and reflects the various errors involved in sampling procedures.

21. See Gary S. Becker, *The Economics of Discrimination*, 2nd ed. (London and Chicago: University of Chicago Press, 1971); Kenneth J. Arrow, "What Has Economics to Say about Racial Discrimination?" *Journal of Economic Perspectives* 12, no. 2 (1998): 91–100; Walter E. Williams, *Race and Economics: How Much Can Be Blamed on Discrimination?* (Stanford, CA: Hoover Institution Press, 2011); and Kevin Lang and Jee-Yeon K. Lehmann, "Racial Discrimination in the Labor Market: Theory and Empirics," *Journal of Economic Literature* 50, no. 4 (2012): 959-1006.

22. Lang and Lehmann, "Racial Discrimination in the Labor Market," 1001.

23. Lang and Lehmann, "Racial Discrimination in the Labor Market," 1001.

24. Lang and Lehmann, "Racial Discrimination in the Labor Market," 1000.

25. See Williams, *Race and Economics*.

26. As opposed to making them a permanent victim/welfare dependency class beholding to their partisan rescuers.

27. See chart one in Rachel Sheffield and Robert Rector, "The War on Poverty After 50 Years," *Heritage Foundation*, September 15, 2014, https://www.heritage.org/poverty-and-inequality/report/the-war-poverty-after-50-years (accessed January 8, 2020).

28. William F. Shughart II, "Public Choice," *Library of Economics and Liberty*, n.d., https://www.econlib.org/library/Enc/PublicChoice.html (accessed November 21, 2019).

Chapter Five

More Fallacies

It should be noted that some of the issues considered so far are highly emotionally charged and polarizing with confirmation bias the deciding factor. Neither the emotion nor the consequent confirmation bias is helpful in proposing viable solutions. Therefore, the first step is to recognize that the associated rhetoric (and the incitement that goes along with it) simply adds fuel to the fire, poisons and deters any rational discussion, and ultimately costs lives.

DICHOTOMOUS THINKING: FALSE DILEMMA

How can partisans make a valid case for discrimination and determine its relative importance as potentially one of many explanatory factors, but not necessarily the main one, for black and white labor market discrepancies?

The first step is to avoid *dichotomous thinking*. It is unlikely that discrimination explains everything. That assertion is not supported by the evidence and is lazy thinking (rhetoric). The alternatives constitute a false dichotomy: either 100 percent of differences in black and white labor market outcomes are caused by discrimination or 0 percent are thus caused. Therefore, if one fails to rail at black versus white disparities, one cannot be accused of discrimination, simply because there are other factors causing the disparities. Only the equation of all such disparities with discrimination could possibly justify the discrimination accusation.

Second, in order for any scientific hypothesis to be valid, it has to be falsifiable. This means that it must be possible to find evidence that does not support it. If this minimal criterion cannot be met then the assertion is a matter of faith, not fact. From a rational perspective, "a theory that explains everything, explains nothing" (attributed to scientific philosopher Karl Popper).[1] For an example, it was an article of faith that the earth is the center of the universe. The assertion has been falsified by the empirical evidence.[2]

Karl Popper also shows how confirmation bias occurs in science by asserting: "The discovery of instances which confirm a theory means very little if we have not tried, and failed, to discover refutations. For if we are uncritical we shall always find what we want: we shall look for, and find, confirmation, and we shall look away from, and not see, whatever might be dangerous to our pet theories. In this way it is only too easy to obtain what appears to be overwhelming evidence in favor of a theory which, if approached critically, would have been refuted."[3]

How is an assertion fabricated to be not falsifiable when it in fact is falsifiable? This is done by saying or acting as if no amount of evidence could ever disprove the assertion. Nothing could ever convince the purveyors. There are many such assertions, including the rhetoric that some theory or phenomenon is settled science because it is endorsed by an alleged majority of scientists. Such material is in the domain of religion.[4]

A majority of physicists also endorsed Newton's theory of gravitation until Einstein presented a theory wherein it was not strictly correct. Einstein's theory explains phenomena that Newton's cannot. Einstein was in the minority, so a majority voting system would have voted his theory out—until evidence was determined that strongly supported it.

Real science evolves and is not decided in the way elections are, politically. What the rhetorical term "settled science" means is that it is settled for political purposes. One characteristic of rhetoric is cherry picking and lying by omission by leaving out important details. Further, the politicization of science and its co-option by the government will, in the long run, distort the goals of real science and damage individuals—particularly the poor—via misguided governmental policies. The evidence is in history.

Glaring examples of such governmental boondoggles are price and wage controls which can be found in policies going back four thousand years, outlined in Robert L. Schuettinger and Eamonn F. Butler's 1979 book, *Forty Centuries of Wage and Price Controls*.[5] Price and wage controls have never worked, but they are still go-to measures for policy makers. In other words, they are empty promises in the form of empty rhetoric.

Not only do they not work, they have unintended but fully predictable consequences including the potential deaths of millions.[6] Price controls rarely *control* inflation. They just hide it. But they are very effective in restricting production. When producing food becomes economically infeasible due to the government's price controls, food will not be produced in sufficient quantities to meet demand, and starvation (famine) may very well result.

An example, discussed in a recent essay by Peter Wilson, is in modern day Venezuela.[7]

Partisans use false dichotomies frequently. Here is an example illustrating the topic and its rhetoric.

Example No. 1

1. If you do not believe that minimum wage laws work;
2. Therefore, you must be in favor of people starving,
3. Item (2) means you are also immoral.

The rhetorical implication is that only people who believe in a minimum wage are the moral ones. This is called the moral superiority fallacy. The responses are yes to item (1), no to the non-sequitir item (2), and no to item (3) (also a non-sequitir). Choose either minimum wages or starvation is a false dichotomy. Why? The alternative to a minimum wage rate is not starvation, since there are numerous transfer mechanisms such as welfare and unemployment insurance run by the government. Further, the government can mandate minimum wages but corporations do not have to hire people. Thus the actual wage might be zero which is true starvation, as opposed to rhetorical "starvation."

Furthermore, being for a minimum wage rate does not make the proponent morally superior since such wage laws price teenage black youth out of the labor market. Minimum wage laws reduce (unskilled) youth employment and the reduction is greater for black youth employment.[8] Some may able to overcome the minimum wage barrier to entry through education that will price them above the minimum wage. Some workers who are not able to enter the job market will turn to crime.[9] In either case, the government is putting an unnecessary barrier in their road. Also, minimum wage laws reduce the cost to employers of discriminating, thereby increasing it.[10] This is in direct contradiction to the government's anti-discrimination laws.

We will talk about non-sequitirs below. For now, a non-sequitir is an argument wherein the conclusion(s) do not follow from the premise(s) as in item (3) not following from items (1) and (2). In fact, item (2) does not follow from item (1) either, so there are two non-sequitirs in Example No. 1.

Example No. 2

The only alternative to being in support of neo-Marxist ideologies is being alt-right (a fascist, a Nazi, a racist, and a white supremacist). The false dichotomy is rhetoric designed to shame and marginalize opponents and, by innuendo, infer that the opposing ideologues are morally superior. There are many alternatives to supporting neo-Marxist ideology other than the alt-right position. This false dichotomy is another example of trying to save Marxist class warfare rhetoric, and its basis is a fallacy.

Discussion Questions

(1) Read the endnote survey data article and then comment on: "Alt-right" is hard to define, identify, and quantify.[11] What three characteristics define it, according to the author?

(2) Is the alt-right label used as a rhetorical smear to refer to alleged Trump supporters and thereby blanket delegitimize them?

(3) If the rhetoric is to be believed, the alleged alt-right movement consists of the 62,984,824 registered voters who voted for Trump. Is this claim a true conspiracy theory in that it lacks evidence and exaggerates the magnitude?

(4) Is item (3) innuendo in the form of guilt by association and hence rhetoric?

(5) Compare the alt-right label with the "all nationalists are Nazis" rhetoric.

(6) The alt-right movement is allegedly an instance of white identity politics and the consequent alleged white nationalism. Is it discriminatory?

(7) Comment on the hypothesis: identity politics is a modern product of cultural Marxism—and the notion of white privilege ends up demonizing all white men.

Is that discriminatory?

(8) Is the hypothesis that the alt-right category is partially a reaction to the hypothesis in item (7) plausible?[12]

FALLACY OF COMPOSITION

The fallacy of composition is *very* common and makes the logical error that what is true of the part must also always be true of the whole.

Example No. 1

"If one illegal alien is a criminal, then all must be."

Expressed in this manner, the conclusion does not follow from the premise (a non-sequitir) and is patently absurd. Here is another fallacy that is very common among pundits who benefit from it. It is called the Expert Fallacy.

Example No. 2

"I am an expert at X therefore I am an expert at everything."

An expert journalist is not thereby an expert forecaster, an expert economist, an expert cook, or an expert at anything else. What is true of the part (journalist) is not true of the whole (everything else).

Adam Smith in his 1776 *An Inquiry into the Nature and Causes of the Wealth of Nations*, had much to say about specialization of labor.[13] A specialist in a particular form of labor has no automatic specialty in all or in any other forms. Therefore, the founders of social media companies, for example, have zero automatic credibility in economics or politics, and therefore should be given little automatic attention or respect in those fields

CASE STUDY NO. 5: HIGH GOVERNMENT OFFICIALS TURNED PAID MEDIA PERSONALITY PUNDITS

Discussion Questions

(1) Discuss the following article by *New York Post* editors, "Mueller's Conclusions Expose Disgrace of Obama's Spy Chiefs," March 26, 2019?[14] (make sure the role of the expert/authority fallacy is explained).

(2) Assess the following statement by John O. Brennan: "I do not know if I received bad information, but I think I suspected there was more than there actually was."[15] Is the Brennan statement verifiable, or is it rhetoric?

(3) What is the red herring fallacy? Is "bad information" a red herring in this context?

(4) Is it acceptable that ex-head of the CIA, Mr. Brennan, does not know whether the information he "receives" is good or bad, and yet relies on it without qualification in his public pronouncements—while being employed by the media?

(5) Is the following hypothesis a conspiracy theory or not? Point out errors of logic and fallacies (if any):

An equally plausible explanation of Mr. Brennan's rhetoric, partisanship, and attempt to influence millions (while being employed by the media) is that he was lying, had no information nor credible evidence (as established by the special prosecutor), and manufactured a narrative to support the anti President Trump smear campaign. After all, no evidence, just hate speech rhetoric, was ever produced by him. He knew that his expertise and automatic authority would be used by the media and the public as substitutes for evidence. In other words, he leveraged the authority/expert fallacy.

(6) What evidence would support or deny the following hypothesis that Mr. Brennan was one of those hired to smear and to delegitimize the President based on false claims?

(7) Mr. Brennan is currently under investigation by John Durham.[16] Should he be required to prove his innocence, given that the President is required to do so, according to the President's political enemies? What fallacies are operative here?

The *Expert Fallacy* here is that political partisanship, an agenda, confirmation bias, corruption, and hypocrisy led experts to make massive forecasting errors. Mr. Brennan is not an expert in predicting collusion, nor is he qualified to be a journalistic pundit, which is why a special prosecutor was invoked.

Mr. Brennan admits that he was fooled by his own information yet considers himself a historian as well. Brennan posts to *Twitter*, "When the full extent of your venality, moral turpitude and political corruption becomes known, you will take your rightful place as a disgraced demagogue in the dustbin of history," he tweeted at the president. Russia "may have something" on Donald J. Trump, he told the world. Now he thinks he suspected he did not know as much as he had thought?[17]

Discussion Questions

(1) Where is any data, not opinion, for Mr. Brennan's statements?

(2) Did any journalist ask Mr. Brennan for any evidence? Cite your sources.

(3) How does confirmation bias enter into political rhetoric?

(4) Should we accept everything political entities say based on the expert fallacy?

(5) Should we give political entities unearned credibility and a pass?

This is precisely why we have to *demand* the evidence, not assurances that it exists, from partisans. For partisans can and do lie and may think they will never be held accountable. By partisans demanding that sensitive information (unredacted) be made public, national security is compromised. The political tactic, which apparently overrides national security, is that once information is public they can try to twist it to attach guilt, or attempt to discredit it entirely. A useful technique is to change the ordinary meaning of the English language to promote the rhetoric. These options are much better politically than dropping the confirmation bias and admitting their errors.

Example No. 3 (Polls)

Another example is when someone says: "the polls say." Few ever ask which polls. If they did, the logical error would be manifest. One poll does not extrapolate to all polls. Furthermore, individual polls are loaded with statistical error and small sample bias. This is where *averages* of polls become important, since averages reduce the noise in individual polls.

There is also another common fallacy in interpreting polls, and that is in assuming that being descriptive implies being predictive, and being predictive implies being perfectly (with 100% accuracy) predictive. A predictive poll is still an educated guess. We will take up these issues in chapter 9.

CASE STUDY NO. 6: SOCIAL DEMOCRATIC NORDIC WELFARE STATES VALIDATE SOCIALISM IN OTHER COUNTRIES

When partisans say: social democracy "works" in Norway, they wish to imply that it must also work in the United States. This is the fallacy of composition. Just because one political system allegedly works in one country it does not follow (a non-sequitir) that it will work in any other country.

Why? Because first, we do not know that it actually works (see below on correlation versus causation). Second, even if it does, different countries have different histories, different cultures, different institutions, different people, different expectations, different constitutions or none at all, and different levels of freedom—all of which have to be taken into account.

Discussion Questions

(1) Why is extrapolating one system from one country to another not only the fallacy of composition, but also the knowing more than you know and can know fallacy? A good example to examine is the USSR and its transition to capitalism.

(2) Will all countries democratize when faced with the opportunity?

Sample Answer: Thinking that all countries will democratize when faced with the opportunity is the fallacy of composition. Some countries are theocracies. Some citizens of some countries are used to a *strong man*, top-down, paternalistic leadership, and accept the notion that the government always knows better than the millions of its own citizens.

The new rhetorical twist is to equate the Nordic welfare state to (democratic) socialism, which is logically similar to equating nationalism to Nazism. Unfortunately, the welfare state to socialism equation is not based on the ordinary (as opposed to the politicized) meanings of the two terms—which are rarely defined (see chapter 10). It is rhetoric.

72   *Chapter Five*

Further, the problem here is that the Nordics, who actually live in the Nordic countries, as opposed to the writers who live in their offices in the United States, and the far-removed-from-reality politicians, reject this equation. The Nordics flirted with socialism starting in the 1960s/1970s but ended that social experiment in the mid 1990s when it failed to produce the great prosperity both relative to the rest of the world and absolutely.[18] Sweden is a test case for which there is data.

The Nobel prize winner economist Gary Becker in 1990 summarizes the results of the thirty year social experiment of the Welfare State in Sweden in "As Role Models Go, Sweden Is Suspect": "The good habits and deep respect for the work ethic slowly built up in Sweden during the previous century have been gradually eroded by the adverse effect on incentives of twenty-five years of expanded taxes and regulations. Unfortunately, the new governments in Eastern Europe don't have such a cushion, for forty-five years of Communist mismanagement have already eroded habits of work discipline in those countries."[19]

Discussion Questions

(1) What does the rhetoric say about this evidence?

(2) Do some of our Presidential candidates capitalize on the ignorance of history of their targets through rhetoric that includes falsifications, utopian fantasies, and Marxist class warfare to rouse a relatively younger audience?

(3) Does everyone love something for nothing? Do they still love "free" things when they ultimately have to pay for them?

(4) Why study the history of communism/socialism?

Further, having a welfare state does not in and of itself make a country a socialist country (see chapter 10). Does a welfare state imply that there is no private sector? There is a private sector in all of the Nordic states. The United States has a welfare state and a private sector. Most would argue that the United States is not a socialist country.[20]

Discussion Questions Part 1

(1) Do the partisans assume as fact (not hypothesis) that the adoption of welfare states in the Nordic countries *caused* the alleged net benefits for taxpayers—if there were any after-tax benefits received?[21]

(2) Does the causation assertion in (1) confuse correlation with causation?

Sample Answer: An alternative hypothesis is based on the fact that the Nordics (take Sweden for specificity) adopted capitalism *before* their welfare state and used its fruits to fund it (à la Marx's theory of capitalism quoted earlier). It was before and after the great social experiment in the high tax statist welfare state that they received the benefits of creating and expanding a private sector (that is, capitalism).[22]

Discussion Questions Part 2

(1) Can the public sector create wealth or only redistribute it? How?

(2) Is the term "redistribution of wealth" (not originally distributed but earned) rhetoric?

(3) Can the private sector create wealth?

(4) How does the private sector distribute earnings? and to whom?

(5) Is providing opportunities to earn wealth an alternative to redistributing the earned wealth of others?

(6) What is the role of government when it comes to claiming its share of private property by threat of force and incarceration?

(7) See *Debunking Utopia: Exposing the Myth of Nordic Socialism* by Nima Sanandaji.[23] What is his basic premise?[24]

(8) Distinguish between what non-Nords, including Presidential candidates, think about Nordic societies and what Nords themselves think. Who is likely to be more informed?

FALLACY OF TREATING AGGREGATES LIKE INDIVIDUALS

Another related fallacy is treating aggregates as if they are as real as the individuals they aggregate. The false extrapolation is from the individual to the collective. One constantly hears the phrase "the American people" in the news. Politicians and pundits claim to know what the American people think, feel, and want, and then claim to represent them.

Let us take a closer look. The phrase "the American people" is an aggregate of all individual American people. It is not an individual. It is an abstraction. Only individuals actually exist, in this case individual Americans.

How could one ever know exactly what the American people think without querying each and every individual American? Polls attempt to answer this question but they are limited by sampling error.[25] Such a census is likely to come up with a diversity of opinion; so the American people do not think any one thing. The claim to have knowledge that one does not have and cannot have is another logical fallacy.

Perhaps what is meant by the aggregate "the American people" is the majority of individual Americans. Here too there are serious informational problems. Does that mean the actual voting Americans who express their preferences at the ballot box? Unfortunately, while a majority, those do not extrapolate to the entire "American people" because, in the 2016 election for example, only 61.4 percent of the voting age population actually voted.[26]

Discussion Questions

(1) Do we really know that all votes cast in elections in the United States were cast by living American citizens?

(2) What is meant by *gaming the system*?

(3) Is the assumption that there is always zero gaming dichotomous thinking? After all, there are billions of dollars in known Social Security and Medicare fraud (not including the unknown successful cases); why should voter fraud be different?[27] Or, is that a false analogy?

(4) Does the zero gaming assumption suggest the knowing more than we can know fallacy?

(5) Is there a perfect voting system on the planet or would that exist only under utopianism?

(6) After reviewing some of the cases of voter fraud documented by Heritage Foundation, "Election Fraud Cases [by state]" (see endnote link), does the evidence support the existence of voter fraud?[28]

Continuing our discussion of the fallacy of treating aggregates like individuals we ask: what is meant by the "majority" in the popular vote system versus the electoral vote system? If we take the voting interpretation of "the American people" we find that, yes, under our electoral system a candidate has to win an absolute *majority* of electoral votes. But this is not so under the popular voting system. The winner under a popular vote system has to win only the *plurality* (more than other candidates) of popular votes; not a majority (over 50%).

In the 2016 Presidential election, Hillary R. Clinton got 48.2 percent of the popular vote, therefore it is impossible for the rhetoric to say that the majority of the American people wanted that candidate. In fact, the majority (51.8%) did not want Hillary R. Clinton. Donald J. Trump received 46.1 percent of the popular vote, so the majority did not want him either. The majority did not want any candidate. This is one of the many flaws of a popular vote system in a world of more than two parties and it is one of many reasons the electoral college votes decide.

President Donald J. Trump won 306 (56.9%) electoral votes while Hillary R. Clinton won 232 (43.1%) electoral votes. Despite the rhetoric, Hillary R. Clinton lost the election by the rules in place. However, Donald J. Trump did win the popular vote in thirty states, a majority, so the majority of states wanted him.[29] Hillary R. Clinton's 2.8–2.9 million vote popular vote lead was from California alone.[30] Donald J. Trump also won more than five times as many individual counties as did Hillary R. Clinton.

Rhetoric always leads back to confirmation bias. If a partisan prefers Hillary R. Clinton, then they would prefer the popular vote system and Presidential candidates would woo California and New York voters, whose votes become relatively more important in determining who gets to rule the country—than those of the relatively low population states. The electoral system is designed to mitigate this problem and prevent tyranny both of the majority and of the minority.[31]

With regard to informational problems, the information to assess the popular vote is not even standardized. In the United States, votes are compiled by individual states according to their voting rules, which differ from state to state and even from district to district. Then certificates of ascertainment are sent in to the federal government and aggregated to get the popular vote.[32]

Is the majority of the peoples' votes (tyranny of the majority) or a majority of individual mini state elections the appropriate metric? The popular versus electoral vote confusion rests on the rhetoric that America is a democracy (popular vote wins), when in fact America is a constitutional republic (electoral votes win). The founders saw this distinction and tried to prevent tyranny of the majority, which is also facilitated by voter blocs.

Discussion Questions

(1) Contrary to determinism, there are numerous potential errors, incentives, and opportunities for fraud in any vote count. Do we live in a world of uncertainty, or in one where everything is written in stone?

(2) If the popular vote is a unique number why do different media outlets report different numbers?

(3) Why are vote recounts sometimes needed if the matter is so cut and dry?

(4) Is the assertion that Hillary R. Clinton won the popular vote in the 2016 election by almost 3 million votes a deterministic (zero error) statement? or, is it a red herring?

Sample Answer to Item (4): More refined counts suggest that the U.S. Democratic candidate's lead was 2,833,224 (2.8 million votes), but that too is a deterministic statement. It is measured with error which includes voter miscounts.

And it ignores voter fraud. Statisticians have developed statistical methods to detect voter fraud.[33] We now turn to further examples of the fallacy being discussed in this section.

Example No. 1

Considering the not all party members believe the party's policy red herring defense, note that when a member of a party takes a position that is questioned, one response is that not all party members take that position. In other words, party members are all individuals with no group position. It is, of course, legitimate to differ as an individual. But this response leads to another question: who actually represents the collective (the party) then; and what is its position?

Of course, if your personal positions differ wildly from that of the party leaders you probably would not be a member that party. Therefore, if still in the party, you probably have more in common with the party's positions than you differ from them, despite the rhetorical response. That party members are individuals with no consensus position is an admission of the failure of collectivism.

Since there is rarely a consensus, this is also one of several reasons that centralized power systems that require it can and historically do degenerate into dictatorships, with the dictator making all the decisions and then pretending to represent the *collective will*. There is no collective will, therefore nothing to represent. It is a myth, an anthropomorphism, and it illustrates the fallacy of composition. Only individuals have wills and they cannot be easily extrapolated to the collective, which is an abstract composite—not an individual.

Example No. 2

Statistical brackets, the top 1 percent, are not individuals. Take the top 1 percent of the earners in the country, reviled à la Marxist class warfare rhetoric. What are we to make of it? First, it is a statistical artifact, an aggregate, not an individual. Second, it is not a stable group of the same individuals because it changes over time with individuals entering it and other individuals exiting it, just like the category eighteen to twenty year olds.

The rhetoric based on it is meaningless. Any group will always have a top 1 percent, even if we could take all of their income and distribute it to the bottom 1 percent. There will now be a new top 1 percent and a new bottom 1 percent. This is basic arithmetic. What government policy would redistribute wealth from a changing top 1 percent to a changing bottom 1 percent?

Furthermore, no policy aimed at income equality could work in general. Income equality is not about producing wealth. It is about re-distributing it, a notion that is rhetoric given that income was not distributed in the first place. There is perfect income equality between people all earning or having transferred to them $1,000 per month. If that $1,000 is all they are allowed to have then everyone will be temporarily equal but poor. Tax revenues are based on taxable income generated and they would therefore decrease making even that $1000 policy infeasible. If they are allowed to earn more, then there is not income equality.

Discussion Questions

(1) Where then are the rich that several of our Presidential candidates, both in the top 1 percent of income earners, want to soak?

(2) What is meant by "fair" in "pay their fair share" and who decides?

(3) Is item (2) Marxist class warfare rhetoric that begs the question?

(4) Are some of our Presidential candidates guilty of Tu Quoque, the same alleged "unfairness" that they accuse others of in the top 1 percent?

Nor would a poor country be able to issue debt on favorable terms. Printing money would not work either, achieving inflation or hyper-inflation. Incentives to become more educated would also be damaged. The notion that government officials are going to be able to micro-manage any of this is not supported by evidence from its management of past social experiments, noted by Robert Higgs's *Against Leviathan*.[34]

Even without any re-distribution, the statistical categories of top 1 percent and bottom 1 percent will change their composition over time. This is called *income mobility*. We do not have a caste system in the United States. Referring to it as if it were a unitary entity is fallacious. Exactly the same arguments apply to other aggregated categories, such as the capitalists, the working class, the poor, and the rich.

The class warfare rhetoric is based on the fallacy that everything in the economic system is a zero sum game. That the top 1 percent *exploits* the remaining 99 percent by preventing anyone in the 99 percent from joining its club is patently false. In fact, that is much more likely under a communist/socialist system where the oligarchs can expropriate all private property, including wealth and the returns to natural resources, and thereby monopolize it. This is precisely what the historical record shows in all cases including those where it is a state secret.

Under capitalism one has to compete (work) and serve the needs of the populace in order to earn what then becomes the return to one's investment, just as wages are the return to workers for their work. Did Karl Marx suggest that the workers wages be absconded by the State, or were wages their private property just as they should be? Interesting to note is that Marxism continually rails against workers' undervaluation and exploitation, and simultaneously rejects private property. Presumably the Marxian rhetoric is that workers will do better when they are slaves to the state or, better yet, as the proletariat dictators.

Do workers have any ownership claims to their own human capital? If not, then someone or something else owns them and they are slaves. Marx's *Deus ex machina* (god from machine) was the prognostication (not testable) that the state will eventually disappear. Even then, it is a non-sequitir that all our problems will then magically disappear, as the rhetoric promises.

Discussion Questions

(1) What is the state?

(2) What is the role of the state vis-à-vis the individual?

Example No. 3

Is America a discriminatory country? A country is an aggregate, not a person, so a country can be neither discriminatory nor non-discriminatory per se. Only individuals can have that characteristic. But perhaps people mean that the state is discriminatory? The state being the government and the mechanism of discrimination based on its laws. In that case we ought to be awfully careful not to give the state too much power, allowing it to abuse its power by imposing and enforcing laws supporting discrimination. This applies to systems like socialism, which is a form of statism.

People who make this claim of discrimination ought also to be careful not to exaggerate. Nazi Germany officially became a discriminatory state when it imposed its *Nuremberg Laws* (1935). Before that there were just anti-Semites running amok.

Discussion Questions Part 1

(1) Read classic books on the Third Reich and the Holocaust.[35] Then define "Nazi."

(2) Is the accusation of being a Nazi over-used? By calling everyone who disagrees with a partisan position a Nazi, a fallacy is committed. Which one?

(3) Has the word "Nazi" been redefined by partisans to shut down their opponents?

(4) Do you have evidence, or is it rhetoric, that the United States is comparable to Nazi Germany? If so, then point to our allegedly discriminatory laws. That is, provide evidence to support the hypothesis—which is not a foregone conclusion. In the absence of such evidence is the claim established?

(5) Are some individuals in America discriminatory?

(6) Are the majority of Americans discriminatory? Concluding that the whole is discriminatory based on a part is which fallacy?

(7) Is mind-reading needed to determine who is and who is not discriminatory?

(8) What should we do with the alleged discriminatory persons? Should we force the majority to hand over power to the reformers who will determine their penalties?

(9) In a free country, as in all countries, will there be individuals with less than desirable characteristics (who decides?) and behaviors (who decides?)?

Discussion Questions Part 2

(1) Is it the job of the state to reform us?

(2) Besides laws against discrimination in hiring, renting, and more, would we want the government to try to control what we think?

(3) Is thought control through the media the hallmark of a totalitarian state?

(4) As long as people are following laws that prohibit discrimination where it counts, and those who do not are held accountable, then is America not a discriminatory country?

(5) What are the limits to government anti-discrimination legislation?

Example No. 4

One can confuse ideology (an abstraction) with its practitioners (individuals); anti-Christianity, for example, is an ideology. Anti-Christian words and deeds are expressed and carried out by the purveyors of that ideology. Ideologies have consequences put into action by anti-Christians.

Condemning an ideology while not condemning its practitioners is political double-speak.[36] It is pseudo-intellectualism. When and if party leaders, for example, refuse to condemn individual anti-Christians, they are effectively saying that they might have an intellectual problem with anti-Christianity, but actual anti-Christians are no problem at all.

Discussion Questions

(1) Do some of our politicians live in an insulated bubble world, driven by agenda-based narratives, the news cycle, and the promise of utopias? Give examples of political rhetoric (double-speak and news-speak) that support your answer.

(2) If item (1) has merit, what does this say about how political leaders can even theoretically act in the practical interests of the electorate who voted them into power?

THE KNOWING MORE THAN YOU KNOW OR CAN KNOW FALLACY

We start with an interesting example on a popular issue.

Example No. 1

In the debate on whether the border wall will stop some drugs from coming into the United States in areas between authorized ports of entry, the claim of one side of the argument is that 80 percent to 90 percent of illegal drugs come through the ports of entry. Therefore, there is no need for a border wall between ports of entry. This claim makes several fallacies—some logical and others economic-based.

The therefore part of the claim is a non-sequitir. Even accepting the speculative 80 percent to 90 percent estimate, why does the remaining 10 percent to 20 percent not count? Furthermore, does the amount of drugs smuggled not matter? Why not? How would anyone actually know the percentage of all illegal drugs at ports of entry and between ports of entry? To do so, one would have to know each and every instance of illegal drug smuggling attempts. But, like Social Security, Medicare, and voter fraud, some cases are unknown. That is one reason that they are successful. They go undetected.

Perhaps the statement means that 80 percent to 90 percent is the success rate of the detection of illegal drug smuggling at ports of entry? The issue just discussed applies here as well. In order to know the success rate one has to know the total number of attempts, and then divide one by the other. Some drugs clearly do get in illegally even at ports of entry (otherwise why would drug smugglers go to ports of entry?), and we do not know how much. The detection rate does not tell us that statistic because it does not apply to the non-detected attempts. So we cannot say that the rate at non ports of entry is 10 percent to 20 percent.

How do we know the percentage of all illegal drug smuggling that occurs not only at ports of entry but between ports of entry, where the argument is that a wall might help deter them by increasing their detection rate? Who is monitoring that activity? In fact, a tactic of cartel drug lords is to distract border agents with illegal immigrants attempting to cross, so that they do not notice the full scale of their drug activity.

Furthermore, if resources to detect drug smuggling are concentrated only at ports of entry, that itself will *incentivize* drug smugglers to avoid such ports and focus on areas between ports of entry. Basic modern economics shows that the argument considered here crumbles under the weight of its own assumptions and partisan rhetoric. Incentives matter, even though they are rarely mentioned by the rhetoric. Why? Because their consideration debunks the rhetoric, whose main goal is to survive and persuade.

What we know:

(1) Drugs are illegally smuggled into the country both at ports of entry and between ports of entry. Otherwise, we get a false dichotomy.

What we do not know:

(1) The percentage of illegal drug smuggling attempts that are not detected is not known, by definition. Therefore, the total number of attempts and the proportions of that total both at and between ports of entry are unknown and unknowable.

The purveyors of such rhetoric versus fact-based claims may think they know everything and drug smugglers know nothing. Rhetoric dictates to always make sure you state your claims and numbers with absolute certainty in order to make them therefore *sound* credible and persuasive. However, rhetoric is still rhetoric, whether it is expressed as absolute truth or not.

FALLACY OF CONFUSING RATES WITH STOCKS OF UNDERLYING QUANTITIES

This fallacy is very common. *Stocks* of a commodity are the actual numbers of units of that commodity under consideration at a given time. Rates are the *flows*, the changes in the stocks of the commodity over a time period under consideration. For example, the total number of jobs available in a country at a point in time is just that. The change in the total number of jobs over a month divided by the initial total is the rate of change of the total number of jobs.

CASE STUDY NO. 7: MINIMUM WAGE LAWS

Suppose the government declares that the federal minimum wage rate must be increased. Why? Because it is the only moral thing to do. Claiming moral authority without defining or earning it is another rhetorical (evidence-lacking) tactic of partisans who claim that minimum wage workers, and therefore all workers, will obviously have higher total earnings. What could be more obvious?

This makes good rhetoric but confuses rates with total wages and it ignores the responses of employers, whose labor costs have just gone up. Those employers are also workers striving to make a living. Unfortunately, public policy is not so simple as manipulating a single variable (the rate), and may actually worsen the lot of those it is designed to help. That, even by the morality posture, would be morally suspect.

> What could be the responses of employers to an increase in the minimum wage?
>
> (a) They could shut down business. Then all its present employees would earn a 0 percent wage rate, unless they could find other employment. They could also apply for unemployment benefits if they met the requirements.
>
> (b) They could reduce the labor force. Then the dismissed employees would suffer wage loss, unless they could immediately get another job, which is unlikely because all employers are in the same boat, thanks to the federal mandate.
>
> (c) The remaining minimum wage employees could have their hours cut. The decline in hours could easily offset the higher minimum wage. This is because total wages is the product of the wage rate and the number of hours worked.
>
> (d) They could *substitute* capital for labor, mechanizing some or all minimum wage tasks by robots or machinery that could do the job. Not only is this plausible; it has already happened in the manufacturing sector, and continues as certain restaurants are already actively pursuing this tactic.

Further, this mandate also does not consider the opportunity costs (see chapter 8) associated with minimum wage legislation. It targets the most unskilled members of society by making them unable to get legal jobs. It also incentivizes employers to be discriminatory because, with the excess supply of workers available at the minimum wage (they cannot be employed at rates below it), employers can not only cherry pick the employment base, they can also use non-employment criteria to do so. One such criterion is color and another is age.

One might argue that employers are already doing so, but this ignores the fact that, if so, they are cherry picking the employment base *across* wage rates. In the absence of minimum wages, employers will choose the best candidates for each given wage rate based on their criteria. In the presence of minimum wages, all those who might have been employed below but not at the minimum wage or higher are eliminated from the employment base. This includes those who have never been employed, for which entry level jobs are critical to their lifetime employment potential. The most skilled will be hired at the minimum wage or above, not the least skilled.

The latter group could have been hired at their marginal productivity (below the minimum wage) but the government in its alleged wisdom, foresight, and superior morality (all rhetorical unsubstantiated characteristics) forbids it. Thereby, the government is promoting discrimination against and criminality for those who, without the interference of government, could have entered the labor market. Now that their legal opportunities are reduced, thanks to the federal mandate, why be surprised that they choose crime and that the inner cities of major American cities become gang zones? Economic opportunity is restricted by minimum wage laws.

Policy wonks and their supporters should take note of the consequences of their policies and refrain from dressing them up with fake, rhetorical morality claims to make them sound acceptable. Note that, under plausible reaction functions of employers, minimum wage workers end up earning lower total wages—including those corresponding to the wage rate of zero. Thus the fallacy is thinking one can manage the world with a single variable. Total wages, as indicated above, involve two variables and multiplying them.

Note that these unintended consequences are nonetheless fully predictable—and have been predictable since minimum wages became popular. As discussed, wage and price controls have been tried for many centuries in multiple societies. The net result is that they have never worked.

Here is another example of discussions that confuse rates with absolute quantities.

CASE STUDY NO. 8: ILLEGAL IMMIGRATION AND THE RELEVANCE OF RELATIVE CRIME RATES

Before we can tackle a complex policy problem we will have to clearly define the objective(s) of policy solutions. We do not have a chance of solving such problems unless we do so. We will simply end up being enmeshed in the rhetoric of competing partisan views, and confirmation bias will decide.

We just saw that focusing on wage rates does not necessarily help even all minimum wage earners, despite the rhetoric stating that it does. That is in part because wage rates do not represent total take home wages. Only if we hold everything constant (hours worked, employment status, for example) do they have a chance of being even theoretically effective.

In the real world other things are not constant. They are interconnected. A change in one variable, the minimum wage rate, will be met by changes in other variables (hours worked and workers employed). Raising the minimum wage rate may very well cause unemployment.

Not to mention that wages do not represent the total funds of workers. The Marxist term (ca. 1858 but still part of modern-day rhetoric) "working class" can qualify for government assistance if they fall below specified subsistence levels.[37] This is an important point in discussions of poverty levels. You have to add in government transfers to earned income to get an idea who is really living in poverty and who is not.

Now consider the illegal immigration crime rates discussion. Much of that discussion is dominated by partisan claims and counterclaims. It is also confused by a lack of definition. Asylum seekers are not the same as migrant workers. The former have the right to seek asylum in the first country they reach. The latter have no right to employment, as in many countries. Their acceptance or rejection is based on domestic labor market conditions. The moral hazard problem is that both categories have incentive to claim they are asylum seekers.[38]

Claim No. 1: Crime rates of illegal immigrants are higher than those of legal immigrants.

Counterclaim No. 1: Crime rates of illegal immigrants are lower than those of legal immigrants.

This is one criterion for evaluating the desirability of the entry of illegal immigrants into a country, through open borders for example, but it seems like a partisan stretch (and it is). Nor is it even particularly relevant. Claim no. 1 and counterclaim no. 1 are neither a necessary nor a sufficient condition for an immigrant's admission or non-admission. Again, we are in the realm of dichotomous one variable thinking. In that world, choosing the one variable is problematic, at best.

Here is another single variable that could equally-well be chosen—legality. Illegal activities should not be encouraged or incentivized in a country that values its own laws. Immigration is an activity that can be one of two things, legal or illegal. Open borders, sanctuary cities, and withholding criminal activity information from law enforcement, all encourage illegal immigration of criminals because they lower its relative and absolute cost, thereby incentivizing the activity.

Now, let us return to illegal immigration crime rates. The goal of a rational immigration policy must (?) include, at a minimum, the minimization of total crimes caused by potential immigrants. In fact, numerous countries do background checks on individuals applying legally for immigration. Those who do not pass those checks are not admitted, just as for the case of acquiring guns legally. Is it hypocritical of the partisans to simultaneously demand strict gun control laws and lax laws for entry into the country?

The case for illegal immigrants is entirely different. Just as illegal gun owners do not have to pass any background checks by evading the entire legal system, so too do illegal immigrants bypass the procedures of legal immigration. Should they nonetheless be admitted based on the questionable relevance of statistics about their relative crime rates?

The discussion about non-detected drug smuggling applies here as well. How do we know the true crime rates of illegal immigrants, given that we do not have the total number? The number of illegal immigrants in the United States is an object of speculation. Are all illegal immigrants going to be open about their status, given that it is illegal and that the penalties are deportation, fines, and incarceration?[39]

Given that we cannot know the total number of illegal border crossings, we cannot calculate the percentage of those doing so who already are criminals. What we can approximate is the total number of illegal immigrants who have been caught, indicted, and either incarcerated or deported. Just as we can only approximate *detected* drug smuggling.

We cannot even approximate the crime rate of legal immigrants because that too would require the detection of all crimes committed by legal immigrants. What we can do is look at the incarceration rate and the deportation rate for detected crimes committed by legal immigrants. We also have to hope that there are no illegal immigrants in that pool.

This is why statistics on legal and illegal crimes generally pool the two groups. This makes the whole task of making disaggregated claims as above moot. But, let us suppose that such calculation is possible anyway. Then look at the underlying logic.

Suppose that the crime (homicide) rate for legal immigrants is one per thousand. That is, one homicide committed for every one thousand legal immigrants. Now, suppose that illegal immigrants have the exact same crime (homicide) rate, one per thousand illegal immigrants. Should we rest easy that their admission will not raise the crime rate because we have achieved the goal of equality in the form of proportionality? That assumption did not work for labor markets and it will not work here either.

Suppose we have ten million legal immigrants in the country. That amounts to ten thousand homicides. Should we admit another ten million illegal immigrants by not enforcing immigration laws? Why not? If we did, they too would commit an additional ten thousand homicides, the same rate per thousand for all immigrants, but now twice the number of homicides.

We have kept the homicide rate constant, but doubled the total number of homicides. It does not take much to see that the total number (just as for wage rates) is the relevant variable, and not the rate. The focus on rates has been a red herring distraction, because if we actually followed its rhetoric, we would have twice as many deaths. We would have incentivized homicidal crime.

Furthermore, we probably cannot do much more to prevent homicides by legal immigrants, except not to incentivize them, just as minimum wage laws incentivize crime by the most unskilled by reducing their economic opportunities. However, ever single homicide committed by an illegal immigrant is preventable by preventing their admission, particularly if it is known that they committed crimes in their own country. Preventing all preventable deaths is a minimum necessary requirement for a viable immigration policy, and rate equalization does not achieve that requirement.

Now suppose that illegal immigrants have a lower homicide rate than do legal immigrants. Then are not illegal immigrants highly desirable? Would admitting them, if this is true, lower the homicide rate across legal and illegal immigrants? Despite the fact that the goal of rate minimization is misconceived (except in the one case of a zero rate) we can analyze the logic in this question.

Suppose we have ten million legal immigrants in the country. That amounts to ten thousand homicides. Should we admit another ten million illegal immigrants if they commit homicide at a rate of 0.5 per thousand? Now the total number of homicides would be fifteen thousand (instead of twenty thousand) and there would be on average 0.75 homicides per thousand, a lower homicide rate.

If our goal was to reduce the homicide *rate* the best thing we could do is deport all of the legal immigrants and replace them by illegal immigrants. Since this is not feasible, the admission of illegal immigrants once again results in five thousand additional preventable deaths.

In only one scenario would the rate focus be appropriate and that is when the illegal immigrant homicide rate is zero per thousand. Then no preventable deaths would result from their admission. (This is precisely what many countries try to do in their admission policies.) Of course, this scenario is unlikely as it is in the interest of a country to expel its criminals. They are costly and do their home country little good. So we would expect a criminal component in the immigrant population trying to get admission into a country.

For one thing, they may be evading capture in their own home country. For another, the rewards to crime may be much higher in wealthy districts of wealthier countries, such as Long Island and San Francisco in the United States. Indeed, high profile crimes have occurred in precisely those, and other, districts. Those high profile crimes were fully preventable, especially when you consider that some of these criminals were deported and then re-entered the country numerous times.

Discussion Questions

(1) What is the economics (not the rhetoric) of sanctuary city policies?

(2) Do such policies contribute to an increase or decrease in crime in the United States? Why or why not?

(3) How do we begin to measure the indirect consequences of such policies? They are claimed to reduce crimes that allegedly would have occurred in their absence. What evidence supports this claim?

(4) Does the legal failure of states to report to ICE and prosecute criminal illegal immigrants mean that potential illegal immigrants are incentivized to commit crimes?

(5) Would this incentive structure increase or decrease criminal illegal immigration to the United States, particularly to sanctuary cities?

(6) Is this another example of where the proportionality measure, a weak measure of the never defined fairness criterion, may not be appropriate?

(7) Is preventing preventable deaths perhaps more relevant, particularly since actual human lives are involved as opposed to abstract and ambiguous concepts?

(8) Should state and local governments implement policies that save the rhetoric at all costs—despite the potential deaths induced by these policies themselves?

NOTES

1. For more on Karl Popper's discussion of falsification, see his *The Logic of Scientific Discovery* (Abingdon-on-Thames: Routledge, 1959), chapter 4.

2. Back then we had center of the universe deniers just like we have "anthropogenic climate change deniers" (rhetoric designed to shame and marginalize opponents) today in the scientific community. Just as the evidence decided whether the earth was the center of the universe, so too will the evidence—not the labels and shaming tactics—decide on the issues associated with the anthropogenic climate change hypothesis.

3. Karl Popper, *The Poverty of Historicism* (Abingdon-on-Thames: Routledge, 2002).

4. Note the ambiguity in the anthropogenic climate change debate, again an example of dichotomous thinking. The question is: assuming it is properly defined, exists, and is measurable, what *proportion* of total climate change (long term) does it explain, and therefore, how likely are reductions in man-made carbon emissions to impact it?

5. Robert L. Schuettinger and Eamonn F. Butler, *Forty Centuries of Wage and Price Controls: How Not to Fight Inflation* (Washington, DC: Heritage Foundation, 1979).

6. See Thomas Sowell, *Basic Economics: A Common Sense Guide to the Economy*, 4th ed. (New York: Basic Books, 2011), 39–65, esp. 64 for other examples.

7. Peter Wilson, "Venezuela's Season of Starvation," *Foreign Policy Group* (*FP*), June 19, 2016, https://foreignpolicy.com/2016/06/19/venezuela-maduro-food-shortages-price-controls-political-unrest (accessed November 22, 2019).

8. This may have something to do with the labor market discrepancies between black and white workers that we have been discussing in chapters 3 and 4.

9. Ryan Bourne, "Do Minimum Wage Increases Raise Crime Rates?" *CATO Institute* (blog), March 18, 2019, https://www.cato.org/blog/do-minimum-wage-increases-raise-crime-rates/ (accessed December 4, 2019).

10. Thomas Sowell, "Lessons From the Past," *Townhall*, Jan 28, 2019, https://townhall.com/columnists/thomassowell/2019/01/28/lessons-from-the-past-n2540365 (accessed January 26, 2020).

11. George Hawley, "The Demography of the Alt-Right," *Institute for Family Studies (IFS)*, August 9, 2018, https://ifstudies.org/blog/the-demography-of-the-alt-right (accessed December 29, 2019).

12. Daryl McCann, "Alt-Right vs Alt-Left," *Quadrant Online*, March 22, 2017, https://quadrant.org.au/magazine/2017/03/alt-right-v-alt-left (accessed December 29, 2019).

13. See Adam Smith, *An Inquiry into the Nature and Causes of the Wealth of Nations* (1776), ed. Edwin Cannan (London: Methuen, 1904); and Library of Economics and Liberty, "Adam Smith (1723-1790), *Library of Economics and Liberty*, n.d., https://www.econlib.org/library/Enc/bios/Smith.html (accessed November 22, 2019).

14. New York Post editors, "Mueller's Conclusions Expose Disgrace of Obama's Spy Chiefs," *New York Post*, March 26, 2019, https://nypost.com/2019/03/26/muellers-conclusions-expose-disgrace-of-obamas-spy-chiefs (accessed November 22, 2019).

15. John O. Brennan, quoted from an *MSNBC* video interview, posted by Wojciech Pawelczyk, March 29, 2019, 9:08 a.m., *Twitter*, https://twitter.com/PolishPatriotTM/status/1110211940104704001/video/1 (accessed November 22, 2019).

16. Katie Pavlich, "New and Rare Durham Statement Shows IG Report Doesn't Come Close to Telling the Whole Story," *Townhall*, December 9, 2019, https://townhall.com/tipsheet/katiepavlich/2019/12/09/durham-we-disagree-with-the-igs-findings-on-how-the-investigation-into-trump-officials-started-n2557706 (accessed December 10, 2019).

17. John O. Brennan (@JohnBrennan), posted March 17, 2018, 5:00 a.m. to @realDonaldTrump, *Twitter*, https://twitter.com/johnbrennan/status/974978856997224448?lang=en (accessed November 22, 2019). Why does this exact description not apply to Mr. Brennan himself if evidence is produced that he was lying? This is a hypothesis that is currently being tested. Investigators must know that they too may be investigated and potentially prosecuted because that is one way to generate some accountability.

18. See table 1. in Lennart Schön, "Sweden—Economic Growth and Structural Change, 1800-2000," *EH-Net, Economic History Association*, n.d., https://eh.net/encyclopedia/sweden-economic-growth-and-structural-change-1800-2000 (accessed December 5, 2019).

19. Gary S. Becker and Guity Nashat Becker, *The Economics of Life: From Baseball to Affirmative Action to Immigration, How Real-World Issues Affect Our Everyday Life* (New York: McGraw-Hill, 1997), 265–66.

20. There is a causation issue here as well.
21. Kyle Pomerleau, "How Scandinavian Countries Pay for Their Government Spending," *Tax Foundation*, June 10, 2015, https://taxfoundation.org/how-scandinavian-countries-pay-their-government-spending (accessed December 5, 2019).
22. Andreas Bergh, "Embracing Capitalism: The Real Success of Sweden's Universal Welfare State," *Elgar Blog from Edward Elgar Publishing* (blog), September 9, 2014, https://elgar.blog/2014/09/09/embracing-capitalism-the-real-success-of-swedens-universal-welfare-state (accessed December 5, 2019).
23. Nima Sanandaji, *Debunking Utopia: Exposing the Myth of Nordic Socialism* (Washington, DC: WND Books, 2016). There are many other studies available.
24. Nima Sanandaji, "The Nordic Democratic-Socialist Myth," *National Review*, July 26, 2016, https://www.nationalreview.com/2016/07/nordic-democratic-socialist-model-exposing-lefts-myth (accessed December 5, 2019).
25. See chapter 9.
26. U.S. Census Bureau, Thom File, Social, Economic and Housing Statistics Division, "Voting in America: A Look at the 2016 Presidential Election," May 10, 2017, *Census Blogs*, https://census.gov/newsroom/blogs/random-samplings/2017/05/voting_in_america.html (accessed November 22, 2019).
27. Maurie Backman, "How Bad Is Social Security's Fraud Problem? Nobody Knows," *Motley Fool*, May 21, 2017, https://www.fool.com/retirement/2017/05/21/how-bad-is-social-security-fraud-nobody-knows.aspx (accessed November 22, 2019); and Coalition Against Insurance Fraud, "Healthcare: Recoveries & Improper Payments," *Insurance Fraud*, March 2019, https://insurancefraud.org/fraud-stats/ (accessed November 22, 2019).
28. Heritage Foundation, "Election Fraud Cases [by state]," 2019, https://www.heritage.org/voterfraud/search (accessed November 22, 2019).
29. Brendan Morrow, "How Many Popular Votes Did Clinton & Trump Win in Each State?" *Heavy*, December 19, 2016, https://heavy.com/news/2016/11/how-many-popular-votes-did-hillary-clinton-donald-trump-win-2016-election-state-by-state (accessed November 3, 2019).
30. Jessica McBride, "Popular Vote 2016: How California Drove Hillary Clinton's Lead," *Heavy*, November 18, 2016, https://heavy.com/news/2016/11/popular-vote-results-2016-clinton-trump-2012-2008-vs-electoral-college-california-uncounted-ballots-new-york-update-totals-final (accessed November 3, 2019).
31. Hans A. von Spakovsky, "The Electoral College: A Safeguard for Stable Elections," *Heritage*, October 2, 2017, https://www.heritage.org/election-integrity/commentary/the-electoral-college-safeguard-stable-elections (accessed November 3, 2019).
32. Sarah Friedmann, "What Is a Certificate of Ascertainment? It Provides a Link between the Popular Vote & the Electors' Votes," *Bustle*, November 3, 2016, https://www.bustle.com/articles/191177-what-is-a-certificate-of-ascertainment-it-provides-a-link-between-the-popular-vote-the (accessed November 3, 2019).
33. Peter Klimek, Yuri Yegorov, Rudolf Hanel, and Stefan Thurner, "Statistical Detection of Systematic Election Irregularities," *Proceedings National Acad-*

emy Science USA (PNAS) 109, no. 41 (October 9, 2012): 16469-73, https://dx.doi.org/10.1073%2Fpnas.1210722109 (accessed November 22, 2019).

34. See Robert Higgs, *Against Leviathan: Government Power and a Free Society* (Oakland, CA: Independent Institute, 2005).

35. Richard Bessel, *Nazism and War* (New York: Modern Library Chronicles. 2004); and Robert S. Wistrich, *Hitler and the Holocaust* (New York: Modern Library Chronicles. 2003).

36. George Orwell, "Appendix: The Principles of Newspeak," *Nineteen Eight-Four: A Novel* (London: Secker and Warburg, 1949; repr. New York: Penguin Books, 1990), http://orwell.ru/library/novels/1984/english/en_app (accessed November 22, 2019).

37. Karl Marx and Friedrich Engels, "Manifesto of the Communist Party: I. Bourgeois and Proletarians," n.d., *Avalon Project*, Yale Law School, Lillian Goldman Law Library, 5, https://avalon.law.yale.edu/19th_century/manone.asp (accessed December 3, 2019). The *working class* was a term used by Marx for his proletarian class. The word *subsistence* is used on page 4 and throughout the document.

38. To understand the asylum process and the different categories of asylum seekers, see: Emily Larsen, "Fact Check: Are 80% of Asylum Court Cases Not Approved?" *Daily Signal*, July 05, 2018, https://www.dailysignal.com/2018/07/05/fact-check-are-80-of-asylum-court-cases-not-approved (accessed December 3, 2019). Even in the category of asylum seekers, in 2017 there was an asylum grant rate of 20.22 percent judged by U.S. judges to be illegitimate, based on application of U.S. laws in U.S. courts. Note that this was only among the cases *that were adjudicated*. The denial rate was not 79.78 percent. It was 33.51 percent. How can this be in a world of rhetorically driven dichotomous thinking? The reason is the large category of *asylum others* that had a decision of abandonment, not adjudicated, other, or withdrawn. See the nuanced data table that gives much more than a single number that can be politicized. See also Executive Office for Immigration Review (EOIR), "Asylum Rates," April 16, 2018, https://www.justice.gov/eoir/file/1061586/download (accessed December 3, 2019).

39. Sanctuary cities make it illegal to ask a person about their citizenship. That way, they will presumably be (more?) open with local police about criminal activities of which they are aware, even though there is no data to suggest that they are. Openness is not an easily observable quality and may invoke mind-reading. An alternative to all or nothing sanctuary cities thinking are the awarding of the U nonimmigrant status (U visas) preventing deportation for those who want to cooperate with police. See also U.S. Citizenship and Immigration Services, "Victims of Criminal Activity: U Nonimmigrant Status," 2019. https://www.uscis.gov/humanitarian/victims-human-trafficking-other-crimes/victims-criminal-activity-u-nonimmigrant-status/victims-criminal-activity-u-nonimmigrant-status (last updated June 12, 2019).

Chapter Six

Evidence

What It Is, What It Is Not

We have discussed and illustrated some important fallacies in detail. From a partisan tactical point of view, these provide the basis for evidence-lacking, agenda-driven rhetoric, false arguments, faux morality claims, and shaming tactics designed to force targets to prove their innocence (which is logically impossible).[1] There are numerous ways arguments can be false and we have discussed some of them.

Now we turn to the alternative to rhetoric, and that is *evidence*. Evidence needs to be collected and handled carefully. Unfortunately, data analysis is also plagued by deep-seated fallacies. The observer is often vested in their chosen evidence and this opens the door to *cherry picking* based on *confirmation bias*, which we will now discuss.

CONFIRMATION BIAS

According to Shahram Heshmat, "Confirmation bias occurs from the direct influence of desire on beliefs. When people would like a certain idea or concept to be true, they end up believing it to be true. They are motivated by wishful thinking. This error leads the individual to stop gathering information when the evidence gathered so far confirms the views or prejudices one would like to be true.

Once we have formed a view, we embrace information that confirms that view, while ignoring or rejecting information that casts doubt on it. Confirmation bias suggests that we do not perceive circumstances objectively. We pick out those bits of data that make us feel good because they confirm our prejudices. Thus, we may become prisoners of our assumptions."[2]

Therefore those with an agenda, and who need the rhetoric to support it, will be happy (confirmed) when they find the slightest shred of evidence that appears to support their agenda. Then they will conclude their biased research and declare to the world that their 'findings' are now elevated to the status of facts. A common World War II Nazi propaganda technique is to repeat them over and over (propagandize them) to make them stick. Modern day echo chambers also do that very well.

Discussion Questions

(1) Hypothesis: if you are going to accuse other people of being Nazis (or discriminatory) use Nazi propaganda techniques and repeat it over and over (see also the Tu Quoque hypocrisy fallacy below).

What is the repeat the lie Nazi propaganda technique?

(2) Are the dubious ethics of "the ends justify the means" (attributed to Machiavelli's *The Prince*) rhetoric used by some dictators while simultaneously starving their own people to death?[3] Give historical and current examples.

(3) Look up 'dictator' and see if Maduro in Venezuela fits the definition.

Also examine his self admission: "On Friday, September 8, Maduro said during a mandatory televised address that his government would 'achieve economic peace, prosperity, and price stability' by any means necessary.

I want to do it nicely, but if I have to do it the bad way and become a dictator to guarantee [low] prices to the people, I will do it," he added."[4]

(4) Can the government guarantee 'low' prices to the people through price controls? Why or why not? are prices 'low' when there is hyper-inflation as in Venezuela? Look up the inflation rate for Venezuela on fred.stlouisfed.org or statista.com.

(5) Such dictators make sure to *say* that they are merely acting in the interests of "The People" as in the quote in item (3). Is this collectivist rhetoric enough to excuse their actions?

(6) Why do some global leftists automatically come to the defense of Latin American dictators such as Maduro? is anti-Americanism involved?[5] Is Maduro a social justice warrior simply because he utters social justice rhetoric?

(7) Does the news media echo chamber engage in evidence denial and refuse to call out such leaders, because that would conflict with their support of the narrative of the alleged wonders of socialism and the corresponding alleged evils of a free market?

(8) Is the word "dictator" banned by the politically correct rhetoric movement (an offshoot of cultural Marxism) in the United States? If so, is this attempted

thought control designed to support Marxist agenda? Is it an example of the choice between saving lives and saving the rhetoric?

(9) Comment on the article "The Origins of Political Correctness" in the endnote.[6]

Confirmation bias has numerous ill effects including illusory correlation. This last phenomenon is confusing correlation with causation, a very common error that affects policy decisions in a negative way.

Note that collectives, run by individuals, can adopt confirmation bias as a business strategy by catering to people who want their bias confirmed by the "experts." *Smear campaigns* are a popular partisan strategy. The definition is "a campaign to tarnish the reputation of a public figure, especially by vilification or innuendo."[7]

As Jeff Nilsson points out in his 2012 article in the *Saturday Evening Post*, such campaigns have been used since the dawn of politics and certainly in American politics,[8] despite the attempt by partisans from both sides of the aisle to dismiss them out of hand as "conspiracy theories."[9] As noted earlier, not every alleged "conspiracy theory" is false ex-ante. They may be investigated in the same way as hypotheses are tested with evidence, if there is any, not with rhetoric in the form of confirmation bias.

Internet astroturfing is a related rhetorical agenda-based technique. Jerry Zhang, Darrell Carpenter, and Myung Ko define it as: "In the present study we defined online astroturfing as the dissemination of deceptive opinions by imposters posing as autonomous individuals on the Internet with the intention of promoting a specific agenda. It can be motivated by political, business, or military agendas and initiated by automated mechanisms or human actors."[10]

Smear campaigns can be run by political operatives with deep pockets and serve to attempt to lower the opposition's poll numbers in the court of public opinion, and to utterly discredit them. Mollie Hemingway and Carrie Severino, *Justice on Trial*, present and examine the modern example of the alleged targeting of Brett Kavanaugh.[11]

His very public interrogation made for riveting viewing (and huge profits for the media echo chambers), with grandstanding by partisans who thought they were protecting Roe versus Wade and who speculated that Kavanaugh would try to overturn it. The latter is a speculation based on the knowing more than you know or can know fallacy.

Further, politicians like Kamala Harris and Cory Booker could and shrewdly did use these hearings as photo ops to leverage their Presidential runs. That did not help Kamala Harris who has withdrawn from the race. Cory Booker's record may be examined by looking at his tenure as the mayor of Newark, New Jersey. He dropped out of the race on January 13, 2020.

Since we have little visual evidence of Stalin's kangaroo court hearings, it is important to preserve the historical record of the kind of abuses of power possible by special interest groups in the United States of America. It is also a prime example of the persuasive power of rhetoric in the court of public opinion. As to the evidence-based approach, no credible evidence of Brett Kavanaugh's alleged crimes was ever presented, as documented by Rachel Mitchell, Nominations Investigative Counsel of the United States Senate Committee on the Judiciary.[12]

That smear campaign also seems to have been based on turning the American justice system on its head by promoting partisan values expressed by sloganeers in the form of rhetoric such as: "victims do not lie" and "prove you are not guilty." Did the smear campaigners realize that such slogans *had* to be invoked to make the Kavanaugh smear campaign work, since the lack of evidence did not support the allegations? Further, did Christine Blasey Ford have a hidden agenda (according to her lawyer Debra Katz) based on partisan politics?[13] Did she perjure herself about her alleged travel phobias?[14]

Discussion Questions

(1) Based on the evidence, were the Brett Kavanaugh hearings a smear campaign? Provide reasons for your answers.

(2) Was Brett Kavanaugh judged guilty in the court of public opinion during and after the hearings? Consult polling data, if available.

(3) Did the Brett Kavanaugh hearings simulate a true court scenario in the American justice system, or was it a media spectacle? Give reasons for your answer.

We can learn much about rhetoric and how its purveyors operate from this example of confirmation bias. Despite the lack of evidence, Christine Blasey Ford's staging by her partisan lawyers, victimology pretense, lack of credibility, and her documented lies, some purveyors of the narrative continue to maintain that Brett Kavanaugh was guilty and got away with it. Talk is cheap, so one could equally well say that Christine Blasey Ford was guilty of false allegations and got away with it. In the absence of real evidence, confirmation bias would dictate towards which side one leans. Can we use the logic of evidence to dig ourselves out of this conundrum?

There are two null hypotheses here:

Null Hypothesis A: Brett Kavanaugh was guilty of crimes against Christine Blasey Ford, or

Null Hypothesis ~A: Brett Kavanaugh was not guilty of crimes against Christine Blasey Ford.

Null Hypothesis B: Christine Blasey Ford was guilty of falsely accusing Brett Kavanaugh, or

Null Hypothesis ~B: Christine Blasey Ford was not guilty of falsely accusing Brett Kavanaugh.

If we want to be scientific then a null hypothesis must be falsifiable. Neither *Null Hypothesis A* nor *Null Hypothesis B* can be empirically and conclusively disproven, because their negations are both negatives. Better choices of *Null Hypotheses* are ~A and ~B. Both are falsifiable, ~A by providing evidence of such crimes and ~B by providing evidence of false accusations. Note that neither ~A nor ~B can be empirically and conclusively proven, but falsifiability is more important.

However, acceptance (non-falsification) of *Null Hypothesis* ~A means that we cannot reject the hypothesis that Brett Kavanaugh was not guilty. In other words, he is innocent. Further, it precludes *Null Hypothesis* ~B because it means that the allegations made by Christine Blasey Ford were false and her alleged evidence does not exist. This is to say, B must not be rejected.

~A is the negation of A. Therefore to insist that *Null Hypothesis A* (Kavanaugh guilty) is *still* true, even though there is no credible evidence to support it, is to reject due process and substitute for it confirmation bias and the rule of the mob.

That is the trade-off that the dichotomous thinking of the purveyors of the rhetoric ignore. To them, one's identity is more important: victims are *always* credible, the accused are *never* credible. (Both Stalin and Hitler's kangaroo courts used similar rhetoric, in conjunction with truth inversion, to silence their opponents and perpetrate their extermination.) The view described is identity politics (neo-Marxism)—which is Marxist class warfare in yet another incarnation. But, to date, this is not the law in the United States of America.

Rhetoric is all about *tactic* as opposed to evidence. But it does a fine job of pretending that it cares about the truth and evidence. It usually tries to disarm its opponents by putting them on the defensive; prove your case, cite your evidence, why is this? why is that? Then its purveyors invoke the potshot fallacy and the nirvana fallacy. Nothing less than a perfect system, with no exceptions, will work. As long as there is any alleged discrimination in America, the country is doomed and it must immediately be dismantled. No plan is needed for what to do after the "revolution."

But, hypocritically, the same impossible standards do not apply to the purveyors. All they have to do is repeat the rhetoric. Prove me wrong is the mantra. That is, prove that which is impossible to conclusively prove. Their case, supported by the rhetoric, is usually never clearly or consistently stated, and it begs the question that its alternative system is invariably better than that of the opposition.

No amount of counter evidence will convince some plagued by confirmation bias, evidence denialism, and dichotomous thinking. To them Marxism, for example, and its offshoots such as "Democratic Socialism," constitute a quasi-religion that, by definition, is superior to free enterprise on moral grounds alone and not by its results. As Ocasio-Cortez states: "If people really want to blow up one figure here or one word there, I would argue they are missing the forest for the tree," she responded. "I think there's a lot of people more concerned about being precisely, factually, and semantically correct than about being morally right."[15]

Discussion Questions

(1) Is the implied dichotomy between facts and morality a false one?

(2) Is the appeal to morality a fallacy? which one?

(3) Does merely *stating* one is morally superior make it true? or, does that claim require evidence?

(4) Even if one is morally superior, does it follow that all of one's policies are—even if they contradict both argument and evidence and hurt groups of people? Or, is that a non-sequitir? And which other fallacy?

(5) Have demagogues throughout the centuries used this costless appeal to morality ploy to justify their atrocities, including the wholesale starvation, imprisonment, and murder of millions? Cite the historical record.

(6) Which side does Ocasio-Cortez prefer: rhetoric or evidence?

(7) Has Ocasio-Cortez been investigated for ethics violations in her campaign?[16]

(8) Is Ocasio-Cortez guilty of hypocrisy in using modes of transportation in direct contradiction to the green new deal, which would impoverish millions? (see chapter 8, n20).

(9) Why should anyone take anyone's words at face value? Is that the appeal to authority fallacy?[17]

Morality claims/grabs do not establish the blanket morality or viability of specific policies—nor does moral authority theft. Does the alleged superiority of (neo)-Marxist systems have anything to do with the evidence, historical or otherwise? When presented with the failures of their system, one common counter is the rhetoric that it has never been tried (in its pristine textbook form, as if that is possible).Where is the ideal world and where are the ideal people needed to make Marxist systems, including cultural Marxism, work? F. Hayek has addressed this question in detail.[18]

Believers in the rhetoric are recruited by the zero cost grant of automatic, unearned moral superiority—from which they conclude that only they deserve to rule the great unwashed masses. Deniers are not tolerated because centralized power systems are very fragile and allow minimal diversity of thought. That is also why they tend to become totalitarian (see chapter 10).

The whole gambit of countering rhetoric with logic, evidence and the non-rewritten historical record is like arguing with someone about religion. It is far better to have the purveyors present their case and evidence and have it evaluated for exactly what it is worth. But they resist doing so, because their rhetoric could then be exposed as rhetoric by the evidence or lack thereof to support their case. Thus rhetoric stands in stark opposition to evidence, and rhetoric must deny evidence that contradicts it—in order to save itself. There is a huge cost to be paid in whether rhetoric or evidence wins this existential battle. Human lives literally hang in the balance.

CHERRY PICKING

A consequence of confirmation bias is *cherry picking* the data in order to make it look like the hypotheses in question are supported by *all* of the data rather than by *some* of the data, another serious error. This error, of course, is related to the fallacy of composition, falsely extrapolating from a part of the data set to all of it. A non-random part of a data set is not necessarily representative of the whole data set, which will likely support entirely different conclusions.

The *Logically Fallacious* website defines "Cherry Picking":

> When only select evidence is presented in order to persuade the audience to accept a position, and evidence that would go against the position is withheld. The stronger the withheld evidence, the more fallacious the argument (also known as: ignoring inconvenient data, suppressed evidence, fallacy of incomplete evidence, argument by selective observation, argument by half-truth, card stacking, fallacy of exclusion, ignoring the counter evidence, one-sided assessment, slanting, one-sidedness).[19]

In other words, the act of collecting data is not neutral to the facts; nor does it uniquely prove every possible hypothesis and speculation. Not all evidence is created equal, there is circumstantial evidence and there is direct evidence, not to mention the ever present *interpretation* of the data. For every opinion you can find, there is some data that will probably support it.[20]

Example No. 1

A good example of cherry picking and twisting the data is when some elected officials want to demonstrate their stellar (relative) performance. Note that "performance" can be properly measured, and, it can also be mis-measured based on cherry picking. As a specific example, ex-President Obama used private sector job creation over a specific period to compare himself to his predecessor. Here is his statistical artifact:

1. In measuring private sector job creation be sure to choose the time point with the *lowest* private employment as the starting date. That way you will manufacture the highest job "creation" numbers.
2. Make a false comparison between the period in item (1) to the *whole* period of your predecessor. That is, remove from the opponent the advantage that you manufactured for yourself in item (1).

The error in item (1) is an example of cherry picking the data, and the error in item (2) is making a false comparison. These two errors invalidate the analysis as well as its conclusions about relative job performance.

Discussion Question:

(1) Read the article, Eugene Kiely, "Obama's Economic Sleight of Hand" in the endnote and find the errors indicated above.[21]

PROOF BY "COMMON SENSE"

Common sense is often used as rhetoric to make and justify claims lacking evidence. It is a useful piece of rhetoric to those who have neither evidence nor proof. An example is "common sense gun control." By slapping the words "common sense" on to policy proposals, the hope is that such proposals are suddenly and magically proven and accepted—in the absence of any evidence. Further they are allegedly superior of course to other non-common sense proposals that provide detailed analyses of the costs and benefits. Rhetoric has no need for any of the latter. The fallacy here is false dichotomy. Common sense, without evidence, is nothing more than confirmation bias.

Example No. 1

This example has already been expanded upon in the material in chapter 4 on the U3 unemployment rate and its interpretation. This example will illustrate how much and what kind of work is needed to get at the facts, while cherry picking is relatively easy, but simply supports the rhetoric and leads to false conclusions.

For example, it is common sense to think that the official government unemployment rate (called U3, the government publishes six measures known as U1-U6 [22]) is *always* a valid measure of unemployment and therefore of employment. What could be more commonsensical? When U3 goes down employment must go up.

Because of the way that "employed" is defined by the U.S. Bureau of Labor Statistics (BLS), the U3 rate going down does not necessarily mean that employment is going up. The official government definition of "unemployed" was given in chapter 4 and is summarized here: "People are classified as unemployed if they do not have a job, have actively looked for work in the prior 4 weeks, and are currently available for work."[23]

Herein lies the problem. If you are jobless and not looking for a job as defined by the BLS then you are *not counted* as unemployed. Therefore, the actual number of unemployed people must contain these *discouraged workers* as well, not just the ones the BLS chooses to measure in the always quoted U3. The BLS considers discouraged workers as non-workers who are out of the labor market when it computes U3. Other measures, U6 as discussed, adjust for this under-counting.

Therefore, the fact that U3 decreases can signal one of three things:

1. More people "employed."
2. More *exits* from the labor force.
3. A combination of (1) and (2).

One way to measure exits from the labor force is to look at the Labor Participation Rate (LPR) of prime-aged workers (ages 25 to 54 years). Looking at prime-aged workers avoids the usual problem due to students and retirees voluntarily exiting the labor market. When the LPR is going down, U3 cannot automatically be used to signal more employment.

Unfortunately for the rhetoric, the LPR for prime working aged workers was going down partially due to job exits both by discouraged and employed workers for the seven or so years after the 2008-2009 recession ended (see fig. 6.1).[24] Therefore, that U3 was going down could not be fully attributed to employment increasing (unemployment decreasing) because part of the U3 decline was caused by exits. Declaring it to be so is a non-sequitir.

Was employment as a percentage of the population going up over that period, as suggested by the U3 measure? To address this we need to go beyond dichotomous single variable thinking and look at what happened to the *employment-population* ratio when U3 was going down.

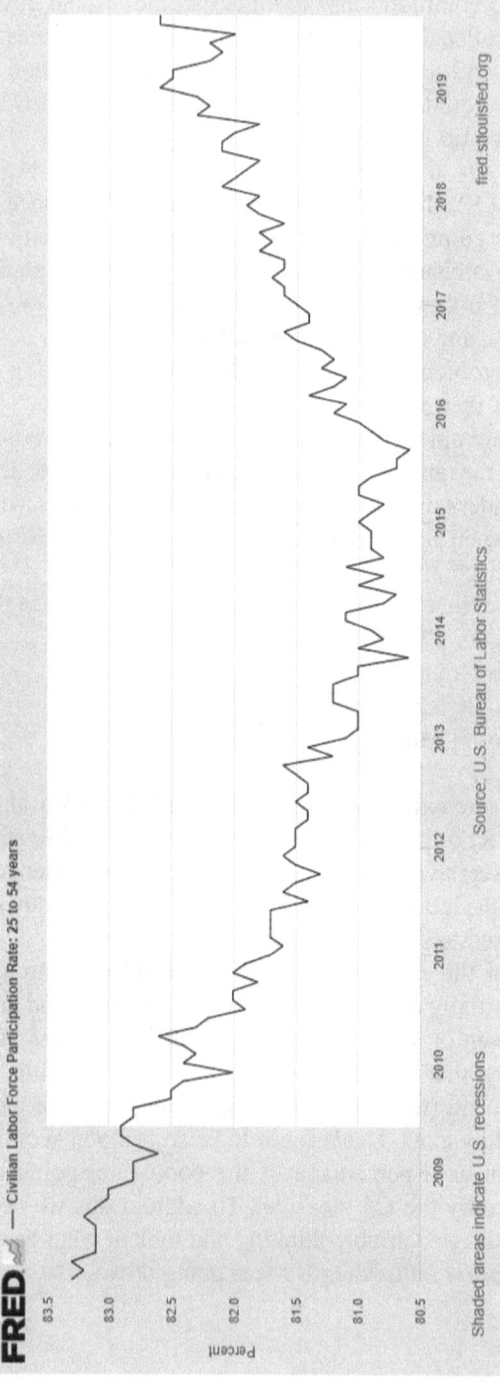

Figure 6.1. U.S. Civilian Labor Force Participation Rate, Ages 25-54 years.
Source: U.S. Bureau of Labor Statistics, Civilian Labor Force Participation Rate: 25 to 54 years, retrieved from FRED, Federal Reserve Bank of St. Louis, https://fred.stlouisfed.org/series/LNS11300060 (accessed November 4, 2019).

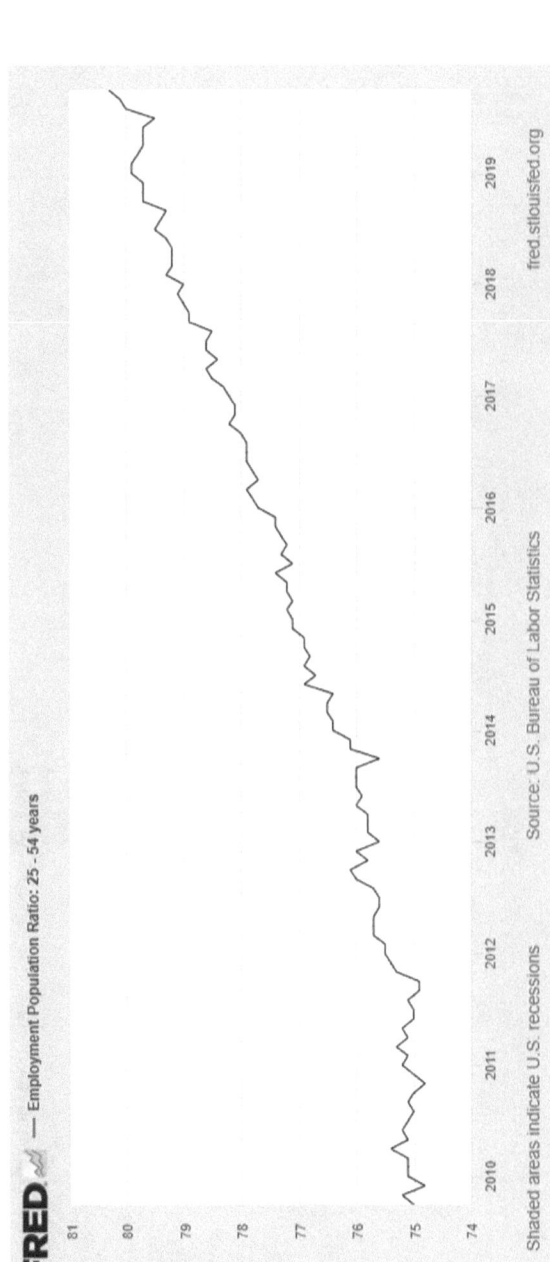

Figure 6.2. U.S. Employment-Population Ratio, Ages 25-54 years.
Source: U.S. Bureau of Labor Statistics, Employment-Population Ratio: 25-54 years, retrieved from FRED, Federal Reserve Bank of St. Louis, https://fred.stlouisfed.org/series/LNS12300060 (accessed November 4, 2019).

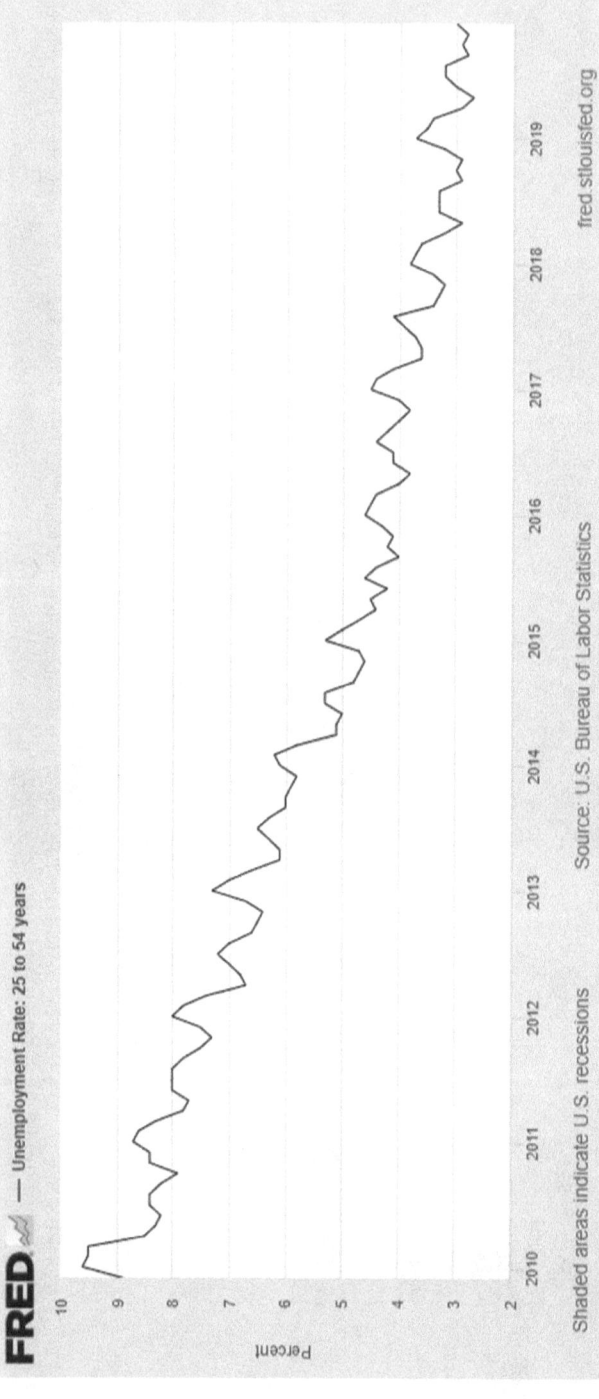

Figure 6.3. U.S. Unemployment Rate U3: Ages 25-54 years.
Source: U.S. Bureau of Labor Statistics, Unemployment Rate: 25-54 years, retrieved from FRED, Federal Reserve Bank of St. Louis, https://fred.stlouisfed.org/series/LNU04000060 (accessed November 4, 2019).

From figure 4.2 we already saw that whites (16+) clearly did not benefit in terms of the employment-population ratio from U3 declining over the period. Blacks (16+) did benefit. Both black and white *prime age* workers did benefit, with blacks benefitting more (see Table 4.3).

More generally, the aggregate prime working age population did not benefit from after the recession until about October 2011 (see fig. 6.2). It is known that employment is a *lagged* variable but the lag does not explain the 2+ years of stagnation. Also note that, as of 2014, the Labor Participation Rate for the aggregate prime working age population started to remain relatively constant, then it increased (see fig. 6.1).

To this we add the U3 rate for the prime working age population see figure 6.3.

The theory behind how the U3 rate can be going down while employment is static or even decreasing is again the LPR as presented in chapter 4. The basic identity follows.

Employment-Population Ratio

= (1-U3) x Labor Participation Rate.

This equation then becomes the *relevant* common sense, not the common sense of rhetoric. Therefore it is the *combination* of the two (not one) variables, 1-U3 and LPR, that determines whether employment relative to population goes up or down.

The data also shows this. While the unemployment rate U3 was decreasing over the period discussed, it was offset by exits as reflected in a declining LPR. Figures 6.1, 6.2, and 6.3 are consistent with this equation and this interpretation.

The rhetoric and its partisans rely on incorrect common sense by only looking at the single variable (causal reductionism fallacy) U3, which is an ambiguous signal of unemployment,[25] and then tells us a tale with a false conclusion based on an incorrect comprehension of the data.[26] Alternatively, partisans (including some media pundits), and government officials must look at discouraging exits, not ignore them.[27]

CORRELATION IS NOT CAUSATION

This is the classic *Post Hoc Ergo Propter Hoc Fallacy*: "if one event follows another in time then the first one must have caused the second." What could be more obvious and again commonsensical? It is also called failure to distinguish correlation from causation.

So, if I take my umbrella to work and it rains then my umbrella *must* have caused the rain. Or, if it does not rain, then my umbrella *must* have caused it *not* to rain. In other words, the alleged causation is non-existent. This fallacy often occurs in partisan discussions designed to prove the direct association between policies and outcomes. And by false implication, the superiority of the partisan's policies are rarely defined in enough detail to make their hypotheses testable.

Example No. 1

Every downward blip in the stock market (but never an upward blip, hence cherry picking) is falsely attributed to one's political opponents.

Example No. 2

Each and every warm weather pattern (but never the cooling ones, more cherry picking) is attributed to "climate change," which is conceptually different from weather changes. Another error here is failure to distinguish between *short term* phenomena (the weather) and *long term* phenomena (climate change).

Example No. 3

"Capitalism" is noted as the cause of all the world's problems (but never its positive effects like pulling mankind out of poverty), with socialism the obvious solution (ignoring the millions executed, those sent to re-education camps, and/or those starved to death by their own socialist leaders). Rhetoric never needs reasons or evidence—nor does it provide them.

Here is more on another example which we have already discussed in another context in chapter 5.

Example No. 4

The Nordic countries are often used by certain partisans as *proof* that their welfare state works. The implication is that the adoption of welfare state policies *caused* the allegedly desirable outcomes in those countries. Welfare states tend to have high taxes and high unemployment, neither of which *cause* prosperity.[28]

Welfare states create incentives to be unemployed because, if you meet the requirements, the government will support welfare cases. This creates a perverse incentive. Further, the relative returns can make it preferable not to work or seek employment. Unemployment goes up. High taxes are a cost to consumers and producers who jointly create prosperity, usually measured in terms of real GDP per capita growth rates. Taxes are a wealth re-distributionist tactic not a wealth generating tactic. Further, debt is simply deferred taxes so future generations can be encumbered by tax liabilities to pay that debt off.[29]

What does create growth and prosperity if not government? We can quote from Karl Marx himself:

> The bourgeoisie, by the rapid improvement of all instruments of production, by the immensely facilitated means of communication, draws all, even the most barbarian, nations into civilisation. The cheap prices of its commodities are the heavy artillery with which it batters down all Chinese walls, with which it forces the barbarians' intensely obstinate hatred of foreigners to capitulate. It compels all nations, on pain of extinction, to adopt the bourgeois mode of production; it compels them to introduce what it calls civilisation into their midst, i.e., to become bourgeois themselves. In one word, it creates a world after its own image.[30]

And we can also quote from Frederick Engels:

> Marx stresses the bad side of capitalist production, but with equal emphasis clearly proves that this social form was necessary to develop the productive forces of society to a level which will make possible an equal development worthy of human beings for all members of society. All earlier forms of society were too poor for this.[31]

The partisans are unaware that an alternative to their rhetoric is the possibility that welfare state countries would do even better *without* a welfare state model. Maybe this explains why all the Nordic countries have embraced capitalism, an inconvenient fact noted by Stefan Karlsson.[32] At work here are many effects that will be correlated with, but do not necessarily either individually or in aggregate cause the desirable outcomes. Not to mention the undesirable outcomes, such as welfare dependency which is usually ignored (cherry picking).

The ability to distinguish between correlation and causation is one of the most important skills needed to understand the world. Most of the alleged causation is correlation, so policy wonks who insist on making the correlation-confused-as-causation fallacy will likely recommend massive government boondoggles.

Example No. 5

Both guns and gun-free zones (the absence of guns) are correlated with gun homicides. Which of the two is the root cause of such homicides, or is that question a false dichotomy? This is a question asked in view of the false dichotomy of the dichotomous thinkers. Guns do not cause gun homicides. Only humans can do that. Neither do gun-free zones cause gun homicides. But they do incentivize them.

Will an attack be more or less likely to occur in an area where people are able or unable to protect themselves? Will individuals need the same level of guns as the bad guys in order to protect themselves? If not, will the bad guys have an incentive to attack and overpower the good guys, knowing they will be unable to adequately defend themselves?

Gun homicides are caused by humans using legally and illegally obtained guns of course. Note the false dichotomy of one or the other. But only legally acquired gun acquisition can even theoretically be limited and that will incentivize a black market consisting of illegal guns, which cannot be controlled so easily (or at all)—despite heroic claims to the contrary. The net result? More guns will be in the wrong hands and more gun crimes will be perpetrated against the innocent populace unable to defend itself.

The right to protect oneself against the government is a constitutional right in the United States.[33] Understanding gun control requires not only understanding economics, but also reading history. For an enlightening history of gun confiscation and its consequences Stephen P. Halbrook makes essential reading.[34] Totalitarian states have two major objectives which are to control the information flow and to disarm the populace. Both of these are needed for the state to secure its unassailable power over the populace.

Discussion Questions

(1) If gun control legislation is tightened or expanded, will the net effect be that it disarms legal gun owners and thereby incentivizes more gun crimes by illegal gun owners? why or why not?

(2) If gun control legislation is tightened or expanded, will the government become more empowered? If so, in what way? If not, why not?

(3) How do we account for the gun crimes, if any, that would have happened but did not happen had expanded gun laws been in place?

(4) How many *known* gun crimes would have been prevented if the gun control laws of partisans had been in place?

(5) How many *known* gun crimes have been actually stopped by armed civilians defending themselves and others?

(6) How many gun crimes have been stopped by the prospective perpetrator knowing that people were armed and ready to defend themselves?

As evident, legal gun "control" is a complex issue and it does not easily fit into a one variable model (like many real world issues) that is easily exploited by the rhetoric, promoted by media outlets, and then implemented by government officials—despite the lack of agreement of millions of people. Nor is there a unique allegedly "moral" solution, despite the rhetorical claims. The appeals to "common-sense" gun control and to cherry-picked data are equally suspect. As always, the rhetorical approach will end with people deciding on the basis of their confirmation bias and speculation elevated to the status of "facts."

Crime Prevention Research Center documents that laws restricting the legal acquisition of guns are remarkably ineffective across the globe, as shown by proper, non-partisan time series data analysis. Cross-sectional studies across countries are typically flawed. The definitions are not even the same across countries so such comparisons are of apples to oranges and nothing can be concluded from them.[35]

There is also the issue of aggregating all gun deaths into a single category. This confuses the issue because it includes both gun homicides and gun suicides. For the record, a suicide is when an individual takes their own life *voluntarily* and a homicide is when someone takes someone else's life *against their will*. Surely there is a big difference? When people think about "gun deaths" in the context of gun control laws, do they think of homicides, not suicides? Lumping the two together under "gun deaths" and then testing the hypothesis that more gun laws reduce gun deaths (which people may think means gun homicides) is rhetoric and data manipulation at its best. Why?

Suppose the data shows that total gun deaths do decline after more gun laws are introduced. The question is how to interpret that result. Is it because gun homicides have declined? Or, is it because gun suicides declined? Or, because one or the other, but not both declined? One cannot tell from the test based on the aggregated data. This gap gives the rhetoric an opportunity to create innuendo, thereby generating implied conclusions in the minds of the populace that are not valid based on the aggregated data.

According to Center for Disease Control data for the years 2001 to 2017, the average percentage of suicides by firearms was 61 percent, while the average percentage of homicides by firearms was 39 percent, measured relative to the sum of firearm suicides and firearm homicides.[36] Therefore, the largest component of total gun deaths is gun suicides, and its existence will tend to have a larger impact on the correlation, if any, between total gun deaths and a measure of gun control laws. Jacob Sullum gives a good summary in the endnote.[37]

If we look for correlation between the *total* number of deaths (gun homicides plus gun suicides) and some measure of the number of gun laws, finding a statistically significant correlation tells us nothing about the correlation between gun homicides and gun suicides individually and our gun laws measure. In order to find those correlations, we have to disaggregate the data. And note that it is not any correlation. It has to be *statistically significant* correlation and, even if it is, it is still not causation.

What does the evidence say? By evidence we mean appropriate disaggregated data sets, legitimate statistical testing performed by professional statisticians, and correct interpretations of the statistical significance of the results. For an introduction to this evidence, to the numerous issues associated with using crime data properly, and to some results, Crime Prevention Research gives an excellent discussion. They find:

> We now break down firearm deaths into two categories: firearm homicides and firearm suicides. While more gun laws mean fewer of both kinds of deaths, only the relationship for firearm suicides is statistically significant. The relationship between the number of gun laws and firearm homicides in this estimate is very small. The effect of the number of gun laws explains about 3% of the variation in firearm homicides.[38]

Thus firearm suicides, not firearm homicides, "drive" the relationship between firearm death rates (the sum of firearm suicides and firearm homicides) and more gun laws. The relationship between firearm homicides and more gun laws is statistically insignificant. An unwary reader subject to the rhetoric might easily conclude that more gun laws reduce firearm homicides. That conclusion is not supported by the data in this study. The fallacy here is the fallacy of division; what is true of the whole (the aggregate) is true of the part.

Unfortunately, the focus on firearm homicides and firearm suicides is a politicized straw man. What we should be concerned with is whether more gun laws are correlated with a statistically significant increase or decrease in *total* (firearm plus non-firearm) suicides plus homicides. Which direction is the correlation and how much does it explain? To quote the same study for this data, more gun laws means more deaths, not fewer deaths:

> Once one accounts for the average pre-existing differences in homicide and suicide rates across states and the average annual changes in those deaths from year-to-year, stricter gun laws are associated with more total deaths from homicides and suicides. Increasing the index of the gun laws in a state by 20 percentage points (about one standard deviation) is associated with an increase in the total death rate (homicides plus suicides) of 0.4 per 100,000 people.[39]

Since the topic of this section is "Correlation Is Not Causation," and its goal is not to take a partisan position on gun control à la the false dichotomy that one must choose between supporting or not supporting it in the forms dictated by the partisans, I suggest reading the article in the endnote. It describes the economic notion of substitutability and its application to this case.[40]

CASE STUDY NO. 9: CLIMATE CHANGE

In the introduction I discussed the rhetorical tactic of deluding people into thinking that there are only two sides to every (major) issue, and then forcing/shaming them to "take sides." I also pointed out that this is the false dichotomy fallacy. Climate change rhetoric is no different. You either believe in climate change 100 percent (believer) or you believe in it 0 percent (denier). This ignores all the positions possible between 0 percent and 100 percent. As an example, there are the lukewarmers.[41]

We will not be pretending to test the anthropogenic climate change hypothesis here. That can only be done in light of the theory and the evidence. Computer models, such as those of the IPCC are not empirical evidence—but are nonetheless judged by their ability to predict/project correctly.[42] Instead, we will restrict ourselves to formulating a falsifiable null hypothesis, comparing it to the one currently in vogue, and looking at the logic of some of the basic arguments. We will use the technology we have developed in the previous chapters, and will be revisiting this topic in case study no. 10, the "green new deal" in chapter 8. Here we provide the infra-structure for that discussion.

In order to benefit from the discussion, the reader is cautioned to not take a predetermined position on the truth or falsity of climate change claims before reading the following. A good exercise is to challenge any confirmation bias you may have by asking if there is evidence—and asking does it support it or not? It is not our goal to solve the issue once and for all (see the Introduction).

Linear Correlation

The topic of this section is "Correlation is Not Causation" so it is time to discuss causation directly. In order to understand the difference between correlation and causation we first have to understand what linear correlation is. Then, recognizing that linear correlation can be *spurious* illustrates that it is not causation.[43] Linear correlation is simply a measure of the *linear* co-movement between two variables. It measures how they *move together*—and that includes moving in opposite directions, or not at all. Moving together in a linear fashion is a very different concept than causation. Linear correlation is, in general, neither a necessary nor a sufficient condition for causation—although many think that causation means there must be linear correlation. Finding an example where there is both high linear correlation and causation proves nothing. Each such example can easily be matched with one where the opposite is the case.

Causation has at least two real characteristics and one dubious one. First, P *causes* Q means that you would never have Q were it not for P, ~P implies

~Q. This states that P is a *necessary* condition for Q; Q implies P. Note that P implies Q (P *sufficient* for Q) does not mean that P *causes* Q. The reason is that a sufficient condition need not also be necessary. The result Q can occur *without* the sufficient condition P (see the discrimination, non-proportionality discussion in chapter 2).

Second is the temporal sequence: P must precede Q. This is a *necessary* condition for causation. But it is not sufficient—merely correlating two series where the precedence order is consistent with causation does not prove causation. This is an example of concluding too much from the data. If the precedence order is incorrect then the series cannot support causation. But merely being in the right order does not establish causation.

This confusion occurs when the temporal order of global temperature and human CO_2 emissions is studied. If the study shows that human CO_2 emissions precede global temperatures, it does not follow that human CO_2 emissions *drive* (cause) global temperatures. The only thing it does show is that that is *possible*. If the temporal order is temperature precedes human CO_2 emissions, it does *not* follow that temperature *drives* human CO_2 emissions. (It does follow that human CO_2 emissions cannot cause temperature.) Both statements falsely attribute causation to correlation.

Third is the dubious one and it involves computer generated climate models. While such models use empirical data, they are not usually considered empirical evidence. It is hard to see how computer models could establish causation in the absence of any scientific argument. Causation involves a descriptive process and is established by theory, and then the implications of the theory are tested using observations (empirical data). Finding the best predictive model is a separate step involving numerous statistical issues. And it is a rocky road from theory to prediction, let alone accurate prediction. For an interesting discussion of the difference between prediction and explanation see the endnote.[44]

Some think that everything rests on prediction, not "just" description, and that predictiveness is the acid test of theory and gives it real world credibility. Alternatively, lack of predictiveness reduces its credibility. For example, if the claim is made that computer climate models do not 'work' in explaining the past (hindcasting) and predicting the future (forecasting) without including an allegedly causative variable P—human carbon emissions—then the same computer models better 'work' after including P.[45]

But what of scenarios where prediction is not possible? According to the IPCC: "In sum, a strategy must recognize what is possible. In climate research and modeling, we should recognize that we are dealing with a coupled non-linear chaotic system, and therefore that the long-term prediction of future climate states is not possible."

In this case the ordinary concept of prediction of individual climate states falls to the wayside and it has to be revised. The IPCC goes on to say: "The most we can expect to achieve is the prediction of the probability distribution of the system's future possible states by the generation of ensembles of model solutions. This reduces climate change to the discernment of significant differences in the statistics of such ensembles."[46]

Note that causation does not imply linear correlation—since the causation could be *nonlinear* as in weather and climate systems, and ordinary linear correlation would be zero in this case—*if* there are no trend lines for linear correlation to detect. Causation says nothing *in general* about the linear co-movement between variables—because P can cause Q but there can be zero linear co-movement between them.

Conversely, if P and Q are linearly correlated, then a causal relationship is not generally implied. Further, no matter how strong the association as measured by the linear correlation, linear correlation still does not imply causation. Many series are highly correlated with each other but have no causative relationship. Are global temperatures driven by US postal charges?

Let us apply these three criteria to climate change (aka global warming (GW)). Consider the hypothesis that human carbon emissions (P) caused the bulk of global warming during the 20th century (Q) (more precisely stated below by the IPCC).[47] Since causation means the cause is the necessary condition, this translates into "the bulk of global warming during the twentieth century (Q) implies human carbon emissions (P) existed"—because without human carbon emissions there would not exist the bulk of global warming during the twentieth century.

Note that the IPCC hypothesis in the next subsection is specific to the second half of the twentieth century, because there were documented periods of global warming in history prior to it. Over such periods, human carbon emissions (HCE) is not a *necessary* condition or even a condition at all. Factors *other* than HCE must have caused GW and these are usually called 'natural' variation—anything man-made is labeled as unnatural. The Medieval Warm Period (900 A.D. to 1300 A.D.) is an example as is a period in the first half of the twentieth century.

By stating that only the bulk of GW was caused (over the period chosen) by HCE, the IPCC admits that the *minority* of GW over that period and over the rest of the twentieth century was caused by factors other than HCE. Of course, to know how much GW was allegedly caused by (not just correlated with) HCE one has to know the total global warming effect of *all* C02 emissions and of all other factors, including positive and negative feedbacks. Unfortunately, sources of natural climate variation are not well understood nor are they even disentangled from HCE. We encountered the same problem when discussing illegal immigrant crime rates.

Second, do human carbon emissions always precede global temperature changes? If not, then HCE cannot be a cause of GW. The data indicates the global temperature precedes HCE by approximately eight hundred years so HCE cannot cause global warming.[48] This is an issue that illustrates the common error already discussed. Suppose that someone produces a graph that CO2 comes first. Then believers tend to run with it, propelled by the support to their confirmation bias. That is, they then present the correlation graph—demonstrating correlation only—as proof of causation as discussed earlier. Everyone is so excited that they then forget that correlation still does not establish causation. This is a very rhetorical approach. It is also the post hoc ergo propter hoc fallacy. This argument also applies if the graph indicates temperature comes before HCE.

Turning to the third requirement for supporting causation are the computer models. If they accurately predict after being fine tuned to the historical data then we can make an argument for including them as "evidence." If they do not then their incorporation as the main human cause of climate change (warming) is suspect.[49] The interpretation of the data requires climate scientists and therefore I add references in the endnote. There is a wealth of views and discussion.[50]

The ACC Hypothesis

First note that as to causation, there is no reason that climate change should fit into any effectively one variable model (the causal reductionism fallacy). The IPCC (Intergovernmental Panel on Climate Change) claims that the bulk (more than fifty percent, majority rule) of global warming from 1951 to 2010 was *caused* mainly by the single variable: human carbon emissions. It then extrapolates that forward as a logarithmic trend (subject to feedbacks) using computer models. The IPCC states:

> It is extremely likely that more than half of the observed increase in global average surface temperature from 1951 to 2010 was caused by the anthropogenic increase in greenhouse gas concentrations and other anthropogenic forcings together. The best estimate of the human-induced contribution to warming is similar to the observed warming over this period.
>
> Greenhouse gases contributed a global mean surface warming likely to be in the range of 0.5°C to 1.3°C over the period 1951 to 2010, with the contributions from other anthropogenic forcings, including the cooling effect of aerosols, likely to be in the range of −0.6°C to 0.1°C. The contribution from natural forcings is likely to be in the range of −0.1°C to 0.1°C, and from natural internal

variability is likely to be in the range of −0.1°C to 0.1°C. Together these assessed contributions are consistent with the observed warming of approximately 0.6°C to 0.7°C over this period.[51]

The policy implication is that drastically reducing human carbon emissions (effectively reducing production and its wealth) would reduce climate change to "acceptable" levels. This assumes that the 1951 to 2010 data is representative of future yet-to-be revealed data (a stability assumption) and that such future data can be extrapolated forward using the IPCC's computer models. Here we run head on into the fallacy of composition; what is true of part of a data set is true of the whole data set. Note that *marginal* effects are important in C02 mitigation strategies and that the relationship between increasing HCE and increasing global temperature is not linear. It is logarithmic which means that the same amount of HCE has a *decreasing* effect on GW.[52] I mention this rarely stated fact because there is a popular false impression, including among policy makers, that the alleged effect is linear.

Furthermore, periods with little or no human carbon emissions or production also correlate with alleged global warming, so carbon emissions cannot be the only or even the primary cause over those periods: the Medieval Warm Period (MWP),[53] and the warming period in 1915 to 1945 before man-made C02 emissions increased. Further, temperatures *fell* during the 1940 to 1970 period while C02 emissions were increasing, and there is also the hiatus in global warming of 1998 to 2014 while human carbon emissions were increasing.[54]

During those twentieth century periods HCE must have been swamped by non-anthropogenic causes. The swamping could result in warming, non-warming, or neither. Why? The answer is that if anything over fifty percent is the primary cause of GW then the only way it ceases to be the primary factor is when HCE is a causative factor below fifty percent. In those cases, other factors must now be the causative factors driving the outcome. Therefore, there is no reason to believe that the 1951 to 2010 allegedly HCE caused global warming will not be swamped again. It also looks like there is evidence denial here (not by the IPCC who acknowledge the cooling period) because the years 1998 to 2010 were part of the cooling, not warming, period.

In order to delineate the exact climate change hypothesis and its scientific viability, we note that it is not clearly stated so we have to dig it out. The role of the IPCC is a starting point:

ROLE 2. The role of the Intergovernmental Panel on Climate Change (IPCC) is to assess on a comprehensive, objective, open and transparent basis the scientific, technical and socio-economic information relevant to understanding the scientific basis of risk of human-induced climate change, its potential impacts and options for adaptation and mitigation. IPCC reports should be neutral with respect to policy, although they may need to deal objectively with scientific, technical and socio-economic factors relevant to the application of particular policies.[55]

In plain English, its role is premised on the assumed existence of alleged "human-induced climate change," and its alleged risks. Can we extract an underlying scientific, falsifiable null hypothesis that underlies the multi-billion dollar research agenda of the IPCC and is consistent with its self-defined role? [56] If so, we will call it the *Anthropogenic Climate Change* (ACC) hypothesis.

The null hypothesis is that, at a minimum, ACC exists. The primary mechanism is later spelled out: ACC is allegedly caused primarily by human carbon emissions and net positive feedbacks via the greenhouse effect. Therefore, the conclusion is that human carbon emissions are the primary cause of global warming (aka climate change).

It should also be noted that the ACC hypothesis (not a fact) is undeniable, by any evidence, according to some of its promoters. Note the incomplete description of the hypothesis. The minimal null hypothesis is that ACC exists. A further hypothesis is that it (global warming) was primarily (51%) caused over the period 1951 to 2010 by human carbon emissions. That is, HCE are the primary cause of global warming over the period 1951 to 2010 and indefinitely into the future unless we mitigate it (a separate issue).

Unfortunately this formulation of the null hypothesis is inconsistent with standard scientific method because it is not falsifiable, and falsifiability is a necessary requirement for scientific hypotheses—as opposed to articles of faith. The correct basic (unqualified) null hypothesis is the true null (no effect): ACC does not exist. Unlike the original null hypothesis this one is falsifiable by having the "believers" provide valid evidence disputing the non-existence of ACC. Again, the principle is innocent (no effect) until proven guilty (effects exist).

By its lack of falsifiability, the original positive claim of the null hypothesis removes it from the realm of science and its falsifiable hypotheses and puts it into the domain of dogma and propaganda. Hence the term "climate deniers" designed to win by intimidation and exclusion.

These tactics are not new. In the past, there were flat earth deniers and some lived to tell the tale. It is interesting to note that every attempt to overthrow the consensus wisdom in science (which political partisans then exploit to promote their agendas) has met with fierce resistance by the consensus defenders.[57]

The term "climate deniers" is rhetoric meant to label and marginalize anyone who disputes the unfalsifiable form of the null hypothesis. Such individuals will never be successful—because a negative cannot be empirically and conclusively proven. By putting the null in the form that there is ACC, opponents are disabled. No amount of evidence will convince proponents of the positive version of the ACC null hypothesis, because even if evidence that ACC does not exist could be presented, it would never close the case. There would always be the possibility that it does exist, despite evidence to the contrary.

This is analogous to declaring someone guilty of a crime (the null is guilty) by proving their innocence, an impossible task. The purveyors then amass evidence of guilt (alleged climate change) and use it to "prove" the null hypothesis, while the counter-evidence of the deniers has no impact. By reframing the null in negative form, it puts the burden on the accusers (climate change partisans) to provide evidence. If they have only rhetoric, they will not be happy with not being able to off load the burden of proof on to the climate change deniers.

Another Government Boondoggle?

The quest for drastically reducing human carbon emissions and thereby production and its wealth and the welfare of millions could very well be hypothesized to be yet another government boondoggle. The rhetoric and fear mongering of partisans is ever on the rise.

Christiana Figueres was the executive secretary of the United Nations Framework Convention on Climate Change beginning 2010 to 2016. As of 2016, Figueres, no longer has that role in the UN. She explains:

> This is the first time in the history of mankind that we are setting ourselves the task of intentionally, within a defined period of time to change the economic development model that has been reigning for at least 150 years, since the industrial revolution. That will not happen overnight and it will not happen at a single conference on climate change, be it COP 15, 21, 40–you choose the number. It just does not occur like that. It is a process, because of the depth of the transformation.[58]

And we were all led to believe that reducing human carbon emissions was needed to save the planet? It is, but from capitalism, not climate change. Human carbon emissions are of course related to production, which in turn is needed to keep people alive, generate food sources, and prosper. However, the implied connection between capitalism and global warming assumes that industrialization *caused* global warming. This is Michael Mann's hockey stick model which, even if true, does not establish causation.[59] See chapter 8 for further references.

As discussed, industrialization did not start in 1951, prior to which there have been other warming periods. Therefore, industrialization cannot be a necessary condition (without industrialization there would be no global warming) for global warming. Is it a sufficient condition? We will consider this in the new green deal discussion in chapter 8.

Figueres, a member of the socialist national liberation party of Costa Rica, repeats the rhetoric in the quote above by innuendo (who is the "we"? what "economic model"?) and this shows that she is not an unbiased top climate change official, but has a Marxist agenda. Perhaps this is why her quote was scrubbed from the unric site, where it was originally found.[60]

Is this a conspiracy theory? Perhaps. However, as discussed, *evidence*—not labeling—turns some alleged conspiracy theories into fact, and in others there is no there there. Another piece of evidence from the man behind the democratic socialist Alexandria Ocasio-Cortez is in the endnote.[61] Thus we have evidence in the form of two statements about the global warming hidden agenda from two insider partisans. Therefore it might be worthy of serious consideration that another government boondoggle is in process. And ClimateGate, which received zero exposure by the mainstream media's echo chambers, is also evidence.[62]

The attempt to always label only the opposition's arguments as debunked conspiracy theories (and never one's own of course), and therefore dismissable ex-ante is itself a piece of rhetoric and a non-sequitir. The debunking has to be provided, not just statements that they have been debunked with no evidence (another rhetorical tool). Rhetoric never likes to be exposed and doing so in this case weakens the scientific case for climate change, but strengthens the case for climate change as a tool for Marxist rhetoric, which Figueres adroitly exploits.

This is also a prime example of confusing correlation with causation, the topic of this section. And it ignores all warming periods pre-industrialization as well as the cooling periods post-industrialization. These were listed above and will also be listed in chapter 8 under the green new deal.

No evidence is provided by the partisans that their socialist alternative is better for the environment but rather, as rhetoric does, that is an assumption. In other words, it is the fallacy of begging the question. The evidence is the opposite, and so the hope is that no one will question the rhetoric, but just take it at face value, go with yet another instance of Marxist class warfare (this time between capitalism and the environment) and confirmation bias. Meanwhile, the evidence is that capitalism is cleaner than socialism because capitalism, unlike socialism, believes in property rights, and property rights protect the environment.[63]

MIND READING IS NOT EVIDENCE

Trying to trace from someone's words or actions uniquely back to their intent or what was in their minds at the time is a questionable method, especially when misused by pundits, unscrupulous partisan attorneys seeking fame, fortune, and media coverage, and agenda-driven opponents.

It involves mind-reading. It assumes prescience, knowledge that no one has or can have. Even the actor may not know what was "in their mind" at the time. Further, if you ask the person they may lie. Therefore how can we expect third parties to know the unknowable? This suspect theory does not uncover evidence even when it is attempted to make it look respectable by calling it "intent."

However, those who use rhetoric think it is a powerful tool to discredit their opponents and, by a non-sequitir, to support their own agendas. They usually confine themselves to attacking their opponents with this method, and never provide any argument or evidence to support their own policies, which we are supposed to accept without question, as in a totalitarian society.

The fallacy of mind-reading is related to psychobabble to be discussed. Briefly, psychobabble is the cheap, pseudo-scientific, fraudulent accusations of your opponent's mental health by those without the qualifications to offer such accusations (very common in the media and online).

SPECULATION EVEN BY "EXPERTS" IS NOT EVIDENCE

We already discussed the expert fallacy of composition: jack of one trade is jack of all trades. But experts in their own trade often offer their opinions and speculations outside of their areas of expertise—as if they have automatic value and constitute evidence. Without real evidence they do not. The rhetoric is: I am an expert on something so everything I say must be 100 percent valid.

If we look at the data on the accuracy of experts' forecasts and prognostications, we will find that the record simply does not support their alleged automatic value. A well-known Nobel prize winner in a field of economics, Paul Krugman, is a classic example of being wrong in his forecasts most of the time, while never adjusting to that evidence.[64]

Another classic example is the media's endless parade of unaccountable ex-government partisan experts, complete with prognostications on all sundry matters and axes to grind in front of journalists who never challenge their rhetoric. Trotting them out is based on the false notion that the government officials must know just about everything. The evidence suggests otherwise, as we note the constant flow of government gridlock and failure.

Take price and wage controls again for example. If the purveyors of this debunked economics know so much, why can they not control outcomes as they claim to be trying and able to do? Of course, there are real reasons they cannot (discussed below), but their speculative pretense is invalidated by their performance, which is the issue here.

Discussion Question

(1) Does the lack of accountability of "experts" incentivize bad policy?

Example No. 1

Bob Fredericks' 2019 article titled, "Michael Bloomberg says he won't run for president in 2020 but could beat Trump," brings up an interesting speculation.[65] Only the first part of his statement has any validity as a statement of intent (unless he was lying or changes his mind). Mr. Bloomberg's hypothesis is a prediction that is speculative, and cannot be tested unless he does run. It does make good rhetoric though.[66]

Mr. Bloomberg's rhetoric is akin to speculations such as: "Hillary Rodham Clinton could have won the 2016 Presidential election." Well yes, that is what elections are about. And that is precisely the hypothesis that was tested in 2016 with the existing election rules and voters.

What *would* have happened had the election rules and the voters been completely different is speculation, and is not answered by who won the popular vote, a red herring. The winning candidate, President Donald J. Trump, also said that he could have won that too had the popular vote been the rule. What we have here, on both sides, is rhetoric. You cannot simultaneously hold constant the opponent's election strategy and change the rules. Then declare yourself the real winner.[67]

Discussion Questions

(1) Children often cry "unfair" when they lose a contest. Saying you won the popular vote in a contest (based on winning the electoral college) is an example of such behavior. If you lose according to the rules should you just change or challenge the rules? Would an alternative approach be to not engage in any contest the rules of which you reject?

(2) Is it the nature of (political) rhetoric to know no limits in attempts to discredit their opponents? Give concrete examples of attempts to shame the opposition.

So What is Evidence?

Knowing what evidence is not goes a long way towards filtering out the non-evidence from the evidence. It is here that the scientific method proves very useful. First note that the endless array of speculative assertions are merely hypotheses, no matter how fervently their promoters try to promote them as fact. Some make no sense under the scrutiny of logic as shown.

So the assertions themselves have to be weeded out for fallacies. Once that is done, recognize that, in general, you cannot strictly prove a negative hypothesis. For some positive hypotheses, it looks like you can "prove" them. But data that supports these hypotheses in general does not prove them; it just shows that the data is consistent with these hypotheses and therefore they can provisionally be accepted (not rejected).

Note that a hypothesis is not a fact. It is simply "a proposition made as a basis for reasoning, without any assumption of its truth."[68] It is suggested (not proven) by theory and evidence. It is important to use all of the evidence, including that which does not support it, because that type of evidence is the acid test that can disprove it. No amount of supporting data bears any weight in the face of the counter example(s). An example is the flat earth hypothesis. It seems plausible to an earthling. Just because many believed it (the consensus opinion) that consensus does not make it true. It has been rejected and space ships were not needed to do so.[69]

Data has to be sampled correctly, that is randomly, so that it is not cherry picked. More data is better than less, provided it is correctly sampled. For example, if you assert that "President X was a good president," according to some measurable data, then take all the data over their term(s), otherwise there is cherry picking.[70]

Data when the a President is in office is better than when they are not. For, in the latter case, selective memory[71] and confirmation bias come into play. Also, there is the recency effect[72] which is that people tend to only remember the latest piece of data in making their judgments about the whole (fallacy of composition). If a President leaves office on an upswing (downswing), people will only remember that and excuse (accuse) them for (of) mistakes and misdeeds. It is far better to use all the data.

Data is also subject to *availability*. Contrary to the popular misconception, there is no online click that you can make that will give you the correct answer for everything you want to believe or investigate. There is a huge amount of misinformation and disinformation online, and the assumptions and the raw (unfiltered) source data are rarely given. So you have to know what you are doing, and have the critical skills to understand what assumptions are being made. And, you must know what you are looking for. In many cases, valid data is simply not available, and sometimes not even theoretically available, under ideal conditions. A good example is the earth's temperature data, an aggregate.

All data tends to have *noise* in them, therefore creating the problem of *filtering* the noise from the signal. How do we know that our conclusions are not based on the errors (noise) in the data?

Finally, it is important to know that many variables are usually involved in explaining social phenomena—not a single politicized one—and that all explanations are partial. You have to look at the *significant* variables, their interactions, and their relative explanatory power. Chapter 9 in this book on polling will give some insight on what to expect. Polls are very poorly understood, and equally poorly misinterpreted.

Data can be collected cross-sectionally or as a time series. So if you want to prove the null hypothesis (not fact) that "More gun laws do not *reduce* homicides," remember that you can only disprove it because a negative cannot be empirically and conclusively proven. Further, it is not enough to compare countries by their levels of (legal) gun controls. You have to look at the effect of gun controls in single countries *before* and *after* the implementation or increase in gun controls.[73]

There is massive rhetoric on this topic. A critique of John Lott's conclusions and his responses are in the endnotes.[74] Comparing countries is hazardous because they have different data definitions, making their results not comparable. In a 1998 interview with John R. Lott, Jr., by the University of Chicago Press, he notes:

> It is difficult to obtain comparable data on crime rates both over time and across countries, and to control for all the other differences across the legal systems and cultures across countries. Even the cross country polling data on gun ownership is difficult to assess, because ownership is underreported in countries where gun ownership is illegal and the same polls are never used across countries.[75]

Which Hypotheses Should be Tested?

To answer this question one has to appreciate the notion of scarcity and its cost. The fact is that, outside of utopia, resources are limited. As a current example, consider that before endless and expensive investigations into one's political opponents are instigated and special prosecutors are assigned, there has to be credible *evidence* of a crime—not simply a target to criminalize based on partisanship. Further, the unelected special prosecutor does not need to be given unlimited resources to carry on whatever they unaccountably do.

Discussion Questions

(1) Is the charge of "collusion with Russia" considered a high crime or misdemeanor under the U.S. Constitution? Why or why not?

(2) Is there now evidence consistent with the hypothesis that evidence for investigating this allegation may have been manufactured by the opposition?[76]

(3) Have those allegedly involved been investigated because evidence-manufacture is a crime?

(4) What was the underlying logic for the Russia collusion investigation of President Donald J. Trump and others?

(5) Is investigation iteration suspect?

(6) How does partisanship enter the equation as well as conflicts of interest?

(7) Is the above generic to the operation of government bureaucracies or is it an anomaly?

In brief, only hypotheses for which there is real evidence should be investigated, not ones based on the whims of unaccountable political partisans. We do not have unlimited tax payer resources to waste on government boondoggles, nor on ignoring evidence because of one's political leanings.

Like all investment decisions (see chapter 8), one has to choose between the alternatives. A good start is to take the existing evidence into account. If there is none, then the conclusion should be "nothing to investigate."[77]

Monitoring Evidence Claims

Now that we have learned how to distinguish the power of rhetoric from the logic of evidence, how do we evaluate the claims of pundits and partisans? We have to evaluate them based on them producing their arguments and evidence, rather than on the basis of what they say or how they say it. Sincerity in lying is of no value, except to the practitioners.

The theatrics and gesticulations of partisans is comical at best and wagging the finger at us, like the proverbial schoolmarm, provides zero support for their claims. Nor does the deflection to alleged moral superiority, or ad hominem such as the Nazi and discriminatory shaming tactic.

"How are we going to pay for your policies?" is a perfectly legitimate question, and not answering it suggests that the purveyor has no answer.[78] In brief, it is possible that purveyors have not thought through their proposals at the most basic level, feasibility, not to mention the unintended consequences. Why should we believe them when they barely believe their own rhetoric?

What we can and must do in the face of claims to evidence is to demand it. If those demands are ignored, then their claims must be dismissed. Further, if evidence claims are based on false premises then all the policy implications constitute a non-sequitur.

Those media pundits, partisans, corporate CEOs, government officials, Hollywood entertainers, special prosecutors, attorneys, and academics who seek to exploit their credentials for political gain and power get zero credit based on their positions alone. Neither their self-assured pontifications, repetitions, selective morality, hypocrisy, attempts to re-write history, nor any of their fallacious personal attacks (see chapter 7) serve to establish the facts.

Only the verifiable evidence counts. That is the standard for evidence. Real evidence can be recognized as such because it is verifiable by third parties with no stake in the outcomes. Unbiased theory (non-partisan science), history, and properly executed data analysis suggest the real facts.

NOTES

1. Learn Liberty, "Shaming Someone Doesn't Change Their Mind: People Are Prone to Believe What They Want to Believe," YouTube video, 1:57 min., February 1, 2017, https://www.youtube.com/watch?v=4qU7KVTAMIU (accessed November 23, 2019).

2. Shahram Heshmat, "What Is Confirmation Bias?" *Psychology Today* (on-line; blog), April 23, 2015, https://www.psychologytoday.com/us/blog/science-choice/201504/what-is-confirmation-bias (accessed November 23, 2019).

3. Caracas Chronicles Team, "ENCOVI 2017: A Staggering Hunger Crisis, in Cold, Hard Numbers," *Caracas Chronicles*, February 21, 2018, https://www.caracaschronicles.com/2018/02/21/encovi-2017 (accessed December 7, 2019).

4. Karina Martín, "Maduro Drops All Pretense, Vows to Become a Dictator to Ensure 'Economic Peace' in Venezuela," *Panam Post*, September 10, 2017, https://panampost.com/karina-martin/2017/09/10/maduro-dictator-ensure-economic-peace-in-venezuela (accessed December 7, 2019).

5. Simeon Tegel. "Why Do Many on the Global Left Still Support Venezuela's Maduro?" *NBC News*, October 26, 2017, https://www.nbcnews.com/storyline/venezuela-crisis/latin-american-leftists-defend-nicol-s-maduro-s-regime-n803866 (accessed December 7, 2019).

6. Bill Lind, "The Origins of Political Correctness," *Accuracy in Academia*. February 5, 2000, https://www.academia.org/the-origins-of-political-correctness (accessed December 25, 2019).

7. *Dictonary.com* s.v. "smear campaign," 2019, https://www.dictionary.com/browse/smear-campaign (accessed November 23, 2019); and *Collins English Dictionary* s.v. "smear tactics," HarperCollins, 2019, https://www.collinsdictionary.com/us/dictionary/english/smear-tactics

8. Jeff Nilsson, "The Long Tradition of the Smear Campaign," *Saturday Evening Post* (Weekly Newsletter), August 25, 2012, https://www.saturdayeveningpost.com/2012/08/tradition-dirty-politics (accessed November 23, 2019).

9. If everything an opponent states is a conspiracy theory, and hence is to be rejected out of hand, why worry about Russian interference in the 2016 election? Before the data is unearthed, any hypothesis can be labeled a conspiracy theory. In other words, the term "conspiracy theory" can be and is used as rhetoric.

10. Jerry Zhang, Darrell Carpenter, and Myung Ko, "Online Astroturfing: A Theoretical Perspective," *AMCIS 2013 Proceedings*, *bepress*, http://works.bepress.com/xiao_zhang/2 (accessed November 23, 2019).

11. Mollie Hemingway and Carrie Severino, *Justice on Trial: The Kavanaugh Confirmation and the Future of the Supreme Court* (Washington, DC: Regnery Publishing, 2019).

12. U.S. Senate, Committee on the Judiciary, Memo by Rachel Mitchell, "Memorandum: Analysis of Dr. Christine Blasey Ford's Allegations," September 30, 2018, https://static.politico.com/28/7f/80157df74b96bb352b10f8b7aa66/09-30-18-mitchell-memo-ford-allegations.pdf (accessed December 7, 2019).

13. Joe Saunders. "Christine Blasey Ford's Attorney Admits Protecting Abortion Was Part of Her Motivation," *Western Journal*, September 4, 2019, https://www.westernjournal.com/christine-blasey-fords-attorney-admits-protecting-abortion-part-motivation/ (accessed January 26, 2020).

14. Chris Murray, "Why Brett Kavanaugh Should Sue Christine Blasey Ford for Defamation," *Federalist*, October 17, 2018, https://thefederalist.com/2018/10/17/brett-kavanaugh-sue-christine-blasey-ford-defamation (accessed November 21, 2019).

15. Anderson Cooper, "Alexandria Ocasio-Cortez: The Rookie Congresswoman Challenging the Democratic Establishment," *CBS News, 60 Minutes*, January 6, 2019, https://www.cbsnews.com/news/alexandria-ocasio-cortez-the-rookie-congresswoman-challenging-the-democratic-establishment-60-minutes-interview-full-transcript-2019-01-06/?ftag=CNM-00-10aab7d&linkId=62017632 (accessed January 28, 2020).

16. Mairead Mcardle, "Conservative Group Hits AOC with Ethics Complaint," *National Review*, March 7, 2019, https://www.nationalreview.com/news/conservative-group-hits-aoc-with-ethics-complaint (accessed January 28,2020).

17. Logically Fallacious, "Appeal to Authority," *Logically Fallacious*, n.d., https://www.logicallyfallacious.com/tools/lp/Bo/LogicalFallacies/21/Appeal-to-Authority (accessed January 6, 2020).

18. See chap. 10, "Why the Worst Get on Top," 157-70, in Friedrich Hayek. *The Road to Serfdom: The Definitive Edition* (Text and Documents), ed. Bruce Caldwell (Chicago: University of Chicago Press, 2007).

19. Logically Fallacious, "Cherry Picking," *Logically Fallacious*, n.d., https://www.logicallyfallacious.com/logicalfallacies/Cherry-Picking (accessed November 23, 2019).

20. If provable data to support a claim cannot be found, a partisan tactic is to twist what is available to do so. To see this, research any number of statements made by

partisans and pundits alike. In other words, look for data (not opinion) to test their hypotheses, which are usually stated as facts with no sources.

21. Eugene Kiely, "Obama's Economic Sleight of Hand," *FackCheck.org*, June 15, 2012, https://www.factcheck.org/2012/06/obamas-economic-sleight-of-hand (accessed November 23, 2019).

22. U.S. Bureau of Labor Statistics, "Graphics for Economic News Release, HOUSEHOLD DATA, Table A-15. Alternative Measure of Labor Underutilization," 2018-2019, https://www.bls.gov/news.release/empsit.t15.htm (last updated October 2019).

23. U.S. Bureau of Labor Statistics, Glossary, "Unemployed Persons (Current Population Survey)," 2019, https://www.bls.gov/bls/glossary.htm#U (accessed November 22, 2019).

24. For an analysis of exits through 2005-2016 see Harley Frazis, "Employed Workers Leaving the Labor Force: An Analysis of Recent Trends," *Monthly Labor Review*, U.S. Bureau of Labor Statistics, May 2017, https://doi.org/10.21916/mlr.2017.16 (accessed January 10, 2020).

25. Jeff Poor, "Krugman Warns Not to Celebrate Last Week's Unemployment Data: 'It's Still Terrible,'" *Daily Caller*, April 3, 2011, https://dailycaller.com/2011/04/03/krugman-warns-not-to-celebrate-last-weeks-unemployment-data-its-still-terrible (accessed November 23, 2019).

26. Tony Pierce, "As Unemployment Falls to a Two-Year Low, Obama Says There's Still Work To Do," *Los Angeles Times*, April 1, 2011, https://latimesblogs.latimes.com/washington/2011/04/obama-unemployment.html (accessed November 23, 2019).

27. Steve MacDonald, "The Unemployment Rate vs. the Labor Force Participation Rate in 90-Seconds," *Granite Grok*, September 2, 2016, https://granitegrok.com/blog/2016/09/unemployment-rate-vs-labor-force-participation-rate-90-seconds (accessed November 23, 2019); Louis D. Johnston, "Why Falling Unemployment Doesn't Always Mean Rising Employment," *MinnPost*, December 7, 2011, https://www.minnpost.com/macro-micro-minnesota/2011/12/why-falling-unemployment-doesnt-always-mean-rising-employment (accessed November 23, 2019); and Matthew Johnston, "How Labor Force Participation Rate Affects U.S. Unemployment," *Investopedia*, June 25, 2019, https://www.investopedia.com/articles/investing/103015/how-labor-force-participation-rate-affects-us-unemployment.asp (accessed November 23, 2019).

28. Dan Mitchell, "The Rise and Fall (and Rise) of Sweden," *International Liberty*, November 3, 2016, https://danieljmitchell.wordpress.com/2016/11/03/the-rise-and-fall-and-rise-of-sweden (accessed December 5, 2019); and Dan Mitchell, "In One Chart, Everything You Need to Know about Big Government, the Welfare State, and Sweden's Economy," *International Liberty*, October 24, 2016, https://danieljmitchell.wordpress.com/2016/10/24/in-one-chart-everything-you-need-to-know-about-big-government-the-welfare-state-and-swedens-economy (accessed December 5, 2019).

29. John Stossel, "Governments Don't Create Prosperity: The Truth About Economic Growth," *Reason*, September 29, 2011, https://reason.com/2011/09/29/governments-dont-create-prospe (accessed November 26, 2019).

30. Karl Marx and Friedrich Engels, "Manifesto of the Communist Party: I. Bourgeois and Proletarians," n.d., *Avalon Project*, Yale Law School, Lillian Goldman Law Library, https://avalon.law.yale.edu/19th_century/manone.asp (accessed December 3, 2019).

31. See Tom Sowell, *Marxism: Philosophy and Economics* (London: George Unwin, 1985), 70-71.

32. For the case of Sweden, see Stefan Karlsson, "The Sweden Myth," *Mises Institute*, August 7, 2016, https://mises.org/library/sweden-myth?sms_ss=facebook&at_xt=4d91345528ba2b1c%2C0 (accessed November 23, 2019).

33. Dylan Moore, "How Gun Ownership Protects Citizens from an Abusive Government," *Federalist*, April 4, 2018, https://thefederalist.com/2018/04/04/guns-help-americans-protect-abusive-government (accessed January 1, 2020).

34. Stephen P. Halbrook, *Gun Control in the Third Reich* (Oakland, CA: Independent Institute, 2013).

35. Crime Prevention Research Center, "Comparing Murder Rates and Gun Ownership Across Countries," *CPRC* (Original Research), March 31, 2014, https://crimeresearch.org/2014/03/comparing-murder-rates-across-countries (accessed November 23, 2019).

36. WISQARS, "Compare Causes / States for Fatal Injury Data Visualization Tool," *Centers for Disease Control and Prevention*, n.d., https://www.cdc.gov/injury/wisqars/fatal.html (accessed December 29, 2019).

37. Jacob Sullum, "Do Strict Firearm Laws Give States Lower Gun Death Rates?" *Reason*, September 2, 2015, https://reason.com/2015/09/02/do-strict-firearm-laws-give-states-lower (accessed December 28, 2019).

38. Crime Prevention Research Center, "Do States with Stricter Gun Control Laws Have Fewer Gun Deaths? No. Do They Have Fewer Homicides and Suicides? Definitely Not," *CPRC* (Original Research), March 27, 2018, https://crimeresearch.org/2018/03/states-stricter-gun-control-laws-fewer-gun-deaths-no-fewer-homicides-suicides-definitely-no (accessed December 28, 2019).

39. Crime Prevention Research Center, "Do States with Stricter Gun Control Laws Have Fewer Gun Deaths?"

40. Eugene Volokh, "Zero Correlation between State Homicide Rate and State Gun Laws," *Reason*, Volokh Conspiracy, October 6, 2015, 12:32 p.m., https://reason.com/2015/10/06/zero-correlation-between-state (accessed December 30, 2019).

41. Patrick J. Michaels, "The 'BEST' Global Warming Science Goes Lukewarm," *Cato Institute*, August 2, 2012, https://www.cato.org/publications/commentary/best-global-warming-science-goes-lukewarm (accessed January 11, 2020).

42. J. W. Abbot et al., Preface in *Evidence-Based Climate Science (Second Edition)*, xiii-xiv, *Elsevier Science Direct*, September 23, 2016, https://www.sciencedirect.com/science/article/pii/B9780128045886050011 (accessed November 25, 2019); and David M. W. Evans, "I Was on the Global Warming Gravy Train," *Mises Institute*, May 28, 2007, https://mises.org/library/i-was-global-warming-gravy-train (accessed November 25, 2019).

43. See Joanne Nova, "Shock: Global Temperatures Driven by US Postal Charges," *JoNova*, n.d., http://joannenova.com.au/2009/05/shock-global-temperatures

-driven-by-us-postal-charges (accessed January 14, 2020); and Tyler Vigen, *Spurious Correlations* (New York: Hachette Books, 2015), http://tylervigen.com/spurious-correlations (accessed January 13, 2020).

44. Galit Shmueli, "To Explain or to Predict?" *Statistical Science* 25, no. 3 (2010): 289–310, https://www.stat.berkeley.edu/~aldous/157/Papers/shmueli.pdf (accessed January 21, 2020).

45. The IPCC was fully aware of its declining credibility as its predictions failed. What did it do? it changed the goal posts. Instead of predicting future climate states the new goal was projection of ensembles of states. See: Intergovernmental Panel on Climate Change (IPCC), "Climate Change 2007: The Physical Science Basis, *Contribution of Working Group I (WGI) to the Fourth Assessment Report (AR4) of the Intergovernmental Panel on Climate Change (IPCC)*, 2007, https://www.ipcc.ch/site/assets/uploads/2018/05/ar4_wg1_full_report-1.pdf (accessed December 17, 2019), the fourth report AR4, 943.

> *Predictability.* The extent to which future states of a system may be predicted based on knowledge of current and past states of the system. Since knowledge of the *climate system*'s past and current states is generally imperfect, as are the models that utilize this knowledge to produce a *climate prediction*, and since the climate system is inherently *nonlinear* and *chaotic*, predictability of the climate system is inherently limited. Even with arbitrarily accurate models and observations, there may still be limits to the predictability of such a nonlinear system. (AMS, 2000).
>
> *Climate prediction* A climate prediction or *climate forecast* is the result of an attempt to produce an estimate of the actual evolution of the *climate* in the future, for example, at seasonal, interannual or long-term time scales. Since the future evolution of the *climate system* may be highly sensitive to initial conditions, such predictions are usually probabilistic in nature.
>
> See also *Climate projection*; *Climate scenario*; *Predictability*.
>
> *Climate projection* A *projection* of the response of the *climate system* to *emission or concentration scenarios* of *greenhouse gases* and *aerosols*, or *radiative forcing* scenarios, often based upon simulations by *climate models*. Climate projections are distinguished from *climate predictions* in order to emphasize that climate projections depend upon the emission/concentration/ radiative forcing scenario used, which are based on assumptions concerning, for example, future socioeconomic and technological developments that may or may not be realized and are therefore subject to substantial *uncertainty*.

46. The Intergovernmental Panel on Climate Change (IPCC), "Climate Change 2001: The Physical Science Basis," *Contribution of Working Group I (WGI) to the Third Assessment Report (AR3) of the Intergovernmental Panel on Climate Change (IPCC)*, 2001, 774, https://archive.ipcc.ch/ipccreports/tar/wg1/505.htm (accessed December 17, 2019).

47. This is a hypothesis, not a fact, because to date no conclusive evidence has been provided for it. Computer models are used for fine tuning so it is stretching the definition of scientific evidence to include them. But we may if they correctly predict and hindcast.

48. Ole Humlum, Kjell Stordahl, and Jan-Erik Solheim, "The Phase Relation between Atmospheric Carbon Dioxide and Global Temperature," *Global and Planetary*

Change, 2013, https://doi.org/10.1016/j.gloplacha.2012.08.008 (accessed January 22, 2020); and Joanne Nova, "The 800 Year Lag in CO2 After Temperature—Graphed," *JoNova*, n.d., http://joannenova.com.au/global-warming-2/ice-core-graph (accessed January 14, 2020).

49. John Fyfe et al., "Making Sense of the Early-2000s Warming Slowdown," *Nature Climate Change* 6 (2016): 224-28, https://doi.org/10.1038/nclimate2938 (accessed January 21, 2020).

50. Judith Curry, "Spinning the Climate Model—Observation Comparison [Part I]," *Climate Etc.*, February 22, 2013, https://judithcurry.com/2013/02/22/spinning-the-climate-model-observation-comparison (accessed January 22, 2020); "Spinning the Climate Model—Observation Comparison: Part II," *Climate Etc.*, October 2, 2013, https://judithcurry.com/2013/10/02/spinning-the-climate-model-observation-comparison-part-ii (accessed January 22, 2020); and "Spinning the Climate Model—Observation Comparison: Part III," *Climate Etc.*, October 13, 2013, https://judithcurry.com/2013/10/13/spinning-the-climate-model-observations-comparison-part-iii (accessed January 22, 2020).

51. Intergovernmental Panel on Climate Change (IPCC), "Climate Change 2013: The Physical Science Basis," *Contribution of Working Group I (WGI) to the Fifth Assessment Report (AR5) of the Intergovernmental Panel on Climate Change (IPCC)*, 2013, http://www.climatechange2013.org/report/full-report (accessed December 17, 2019), see section D.3 Detection and Attribution of Climate Change (17); and for the future *estimated* impact, see section E. Future Global and Regional Climate Change (19) in the next UN report, AR6, is forthcoming in 2021.

52. Yi Huang and Maziar Bani Shahabadi, "Why Logarithmic? A Note on the Dependence of Radiative Forcing on Gas Concentration," *Journal of Geophysical Research: Atmospheres* 119, no. 24 (December 28, 2014): 13683-89, https://doi.org/10.1002/2014JD022466 (accessed January 14, 2020).

53. D. J. Easterbrook, "The Medieval Warm Period (900 A.D. to 1300 A.D.)," in *Evidence-Based Climate Science (Second Edition)*. *Elsevier Science Direct*, September 23, 2016, 137–60, https://www.sciencedirect.com/topics/earth-and-planetary-sciences/medieval-warm-period (accessed January 14, 2020).

54. Robert Tracinski, "Global Warming: The Theory that Predicts Nothing and Explains Everything," *Federalist*, June 8, 2015, https://thefederalist.com/2015/06/08/global-warming-the-theory-that-predicts-nothing-and-explains-everything (accessed November 25, 2019); Ronald Bailey, "Global Warming Hiatus Is Real." *Reason*, February 24, 2016, https://reason.com/2016/02/24/global-warming-hiatus-is-real (accessed November 25, 2019); Ryan Maue, "You Ought to Have a Look: Time for a New 'Hiatus' in Warming, or Time for an Accelerated Warming Trend?" *Cato Institute* (blog), May 25, 2017, https://www.cato.org/blog/you-ought-have-look-time-new-hiatus-warming-or-time-accelerated-warming-trend (accessed November 25, 2019); and Fyfe et al., "Making Sense."

55. Intergovernmental Panel on Climate Change (IPCC), "Principles Governing IPCC Work," 2013, https://archive.ipcc.ch/pdf/ipcc-principles/ipcc-principles.pdf (accessed December 17, 2019).

56. For those who wonder whether the data is available for every policy issue and an adventure in government accounting, see Maggie Koerth, "How Much Is the Government Spending On Climate Change? We Don't Know, and Neither Do They," *FiveThirtyEight*, February 8, 2019, https://fivethirtyeight.com/features/how-much-is-the-government-spending-on-climate-change-we-dont-know-and-neither-do-they (accessed January 26, 2020).

57. Alexander Bird, "Thomas Kuhn," *Stanford Encyclopedia of Philosophy*, Winter 2018, ed. Edward N. Zalta, https://plato.stanford.edu/entries/thomas-kuhn (accessed November 23, 2019).

58. A government boondoggle orchestrated by the anti-capitalism partisans. Here we have a rare opportunity to document a major UN climate change official stating the Marxist agenda behind the climate change hypothesis. The original link was removed from the source site. See Christiana Figueres, "UN Climate Change Warns That the World Economy Is Transformed Intentionally," *World Press* (blog), May 2, 2015, https://blogsl2n.wordpress.com/2015/02/05/the-top-un-climate-change-official-warns-that-first-time-the-world-economy-is-transformed-intentionally-christiana-figueres (accessed November 23, 2019). Figueres was appointed as the new Executive Secretary of the United Nations Framework Convention on Climate Change (UNFCCC) by UN Secretary-General Ban Ki-moon in 2010, and was reappointed for a second three year term in July 2013.

59. John O'Sullivan, "Breaking: Fatal Courtroom Acts Ruins Michael "Hockey Stick" Mann," *Prinicipia Scientifica*, July 4, 2017, https://principia-scientific.org/breaking-fatal-courtroom-act-ruins-michael-hockey-stick-mann (accessed November 25, 2019).

60. The original site for Christiana Figueres, "UN Climate Change Warns That The World Economy Is Transformed Intentionally," is https://unric.org/en/figueres-first-time-the-world-economy-is-transformed-intentionally. I have also seen it, before it was removed, as https://unric.org/en/page/2/?s=Christiana+Figueres+. Neither link is currently active.

61. Philip Klein, "AOC's Chief of Staff Comments Just Killed the Green New Deal," July 12, 2019, *Washington Examiner*, https://www.washingtonexaminer.com/opinion/aocs-chief-of-staff-just-killed-the-green-new-deal (accessed November 25, 2019).

62. Robert Tracinski, "ClimateGate: The Fix Is In," *Real Clear Politics*, November 24, 2009, https://www.realclearpolitics.com/articles/2009/11/24/the_fix_is_in_99280.html (accessed January 22, 2020).

63. Kevin D Williamson, "Capitalism Is Clean(er)," *National Review*, September 25, 2014, https://www.nationalreview.com/2014/09/capitalism-cleaner-kevin-d-williamson (accessed November 25, 2019); and Garrett Hardin, "Tragedy of the Commons," *Library of Economics and Liberty*, n.d., https://www.econlib.org/library/Enc/TragedyoftheCommons.html (accessed November 26, 2019).

64. Andrew Syrios, "Fact Checking Paul Krugman's Claim To Be 'Right About Everything,'" *Mises Wire*, June 10 2015, https://mises.org/library/fact-checking-paul-krugmans-claim-be-right-about-everything (accessed December 30, 2019).

65. Bob Fredericks, "Michael Bloomberg Says He Won't Run for President in 2020 but Could Beat Trump," *New York Post*, March 5, 2019, https://nypost.com/2019/03/05/michael-bloomberg-says-he-wont-run-for-president-in-2020-but-could-beat-trump (accessed November 23, 2019).

66. Since this writing Mr. Bloomberg entered the race on November 21, 2019 as a Democratic candidate for President of the United States of America. This offers an opportunity to test his hypothesis, and have him take responsibility for his hubris if he loses.

67. A common rhetorical shaming tactic is: (1) set yourself up as the judge and jury of all others, that is, steal credibility; (2) declare yourself the winner in all exchanges; and (3) wait for the inevitable defense by the shamed. As to item (1), the tactic is simply to steal moral authority as opposed to earning it. As to item (2), imagine if debaters in a debate or sports teams get to decide their own victory. Neutral third parties and the law are the alternatives. As to item (3), once "shamed," the shamed lose power and the shamers gain it. Then the shamed spend all of their time on worthless activities, such as defending themselves (prove you are not) while the shamers confirm (to themselves only) that they indeed are morally superior and therefore deserve to rule.

68. *Lexico* s.v. "hypothesis," 2019, https://www.lexico.com/en/definition/hypothesis (accessed November 23, 2019).

69. See American Physical Society, "This Month in Physics History," *APS News* 15, no. 6 (2006), https://www.aps.org/publications/apsnews/200606/history.cfm (accessed November 23, 2019).

70. Gallup. "Presidential Job Approval Center," n.d., https://news.gallup.com/interactives/185273/presidential-job-approval-center.aspx (accessed November 3, 2019).

71. Morningstar, "Course 407: Psychology and Investing, Selective Memory," 2015, http://news.morningstar.com/classroom2/course.asp?docId=145104&page=3 (accessed November 23, 2019).

72. Psychology iResearch, "Recency Effect," *IresearchNet*, n.d., https://psychology.iresearchnet.com/social-psychology/decision-making/recency-effect/ (accessed November 23, 2019).

73. The panel data does not contradict the correctly formed falsifiable null hypothesis that 'more gun laws do not reduce homicides" (see Crime Prevention Research Center, "Comparing Murder Rates and Gun Ownership Across Countries").

74. John J. Donohue, Abhay Aneja, and Kyle D. Weber, "Right-to-Carry Laws and Violent Crime: A Comprehensive Assessment Using Panel Data and a State-Level Synthetic Control Analysis," *National Bureau of Economics Research*, NBER Working Paper No 23510, November 2018, https://www.nber.org/papers/w23510 (accessed November 23, 2019); and Crime Prevention Research Center, "Responding To John Donohue's Responses to Our Evaluation of His New Study," *CPRC* (Original Research), July 12, 2017, https://crimeresearch.org/2017/07/responding-john-donohues-responses-evaluation-new-study (accessed November 23, 2019).

75. University of Chicago Press, interview with John R. Lott, Jr., 1998, https://www.press.uchicago.edu/Misc/Chicago/493636.html (accessed November 23, 2019);

and Crime Prevention Research Center, "Comparing Murder Rates and Gun Ownership Across Countries."

76. The Horowitz report on alleged Foreign Intelligence Surveillance Act (FISA) abuse has been released on December 9, 2019. See U.S. Department of Justice, Office of the Inspector General, "Review of Four FISA Applications and Other Aspects of the FBI's Crossfire Hurricane Investigation," [Redacted], comp. Michael E. Horowitz, December 9, 2019, https://www.justice.gov/storage/120919-examination.pdf (accessed December 10. 2019). The Durham Report, in progress, is investigating the evidence manufacture hypothesis. See Katie Pavlich, "New and Rare Durham Statement Shows IG Report Doesn't Come Close to Telling the Whole Story," *Townhall*, December 9, 2019, https://townhall.com/tipsheet/katiepavlich/2019/12/09/durham-we-disagree-with-the-igs-findings-on-how-the-investigation-into-trump-officials-started-n2557706 (accessed December 10, 2019). These are important investigations—based on evidence ex-ante—in order to hold upper level government officials accountable for actual (not simply alleged) abuses of power and corruption. See also Michael Goodwin, "Goodwin: Why are Democrats Acting Like They Have Something to Hide?" *New York Post*, October 26, 2019, https://nypost.com/2019/10/26/goodwin-why-are-democrats-acting-like-they-have-something-to-hide (accessed November 23, 2019).

77. One would think "taking the existing evidence into account," reasonable *before* spending millions (billions or trillions) of dollars of tax-payer money on government boondoggles, just to satisfy political partisans.

78. What is important here is that the media does it job and demands answers as opposed to being an echo chamber for amplifying partisan rhetoric.

Chapter Seven

Fallacies Based on Personal Attack

An accuser accuses an opponent of having a negative characteristic and/or of having performed misdeeds. The accused responds by the counterclaim that the accuser has exactly the same characteristic and/or has done similar misdeeds. This is known as the *'hypocrisy'* or *Tu Quoque* attack. Discriminators cannot accuse others of being discriminatory, liars cannot call out others as liars and so on.[1]

The Latin expression, *Tu Quoque*, translates as an appeal to hypocrisy. As a calling out of hypocrisy, this approach seems to be consistent with Western ethics. However, it has been extended beyond its applicability and appears as an excuse for bad behavior. In that format it is the fallacy that two wrongs make a right.

Example No. 1

When the United States calls out China for its human rights violations, China responds: At a daily briefing, Chinese foreign ministry spokesman Lu Kang dismissed the report as similar to those of previous years and "full of ideological prejudice." He said China hoped the U.S. would "also take a good look at its own human rights record."[2]

Fair enough, but human rights violations are—like most things—ranked on a relative scale, and the counterattack does not establish that they are not worse in China than in the United States. That claim would require evidence, not rhetoric. China cannot justify its failures to consider its own human rights violations on the basis that other nations have equal or worse violations. That is dichotomous thinking. Both are wrong.

Can one person or group of persons criticize others for moral imperfections without themselves being morally perfect? Perhaps, if the partisans tempered their self-righteous moral indignation in the face of the recognition that they may be guilty of exactly the same moral crimes that they accuse others of committing. *Tu Quoque* is more than anything a valid response to hypocrisy. As a way to deflect from the issues, bludgeon the opposition, and end all discussion it is deeply flawed.

Since this book is about rhetoric it is incumbent upon us to expose and discuss it. Machiavellian and Marxist tropes about the "ends justifying the means" in the name of "revolution" (all rhetoric) are also invoked, just like many dictators did. And the perennial favorite—alleged moral superiority—is used as cover for criminal behavior. Marxist partisans employ the *rhetoric of oppression* and assume that anyone who says they are a victim therefore must be one. This *begs the question* and invokes the knowing more than one knows fallacy, as well as dichotomous thinking and the fallacy of composition.

Examples abound:
- every person with a child in tow claiming asylum at the border must be a family unit,
- every leader (including terrorists) who mouths the correct Marxist freedom-fighting rhetoric must be a freedom fighter,
- the intensity with which one fights for a cause, either physically or otherwise, is a valid measure of the worthiness of the cause,
- all alleged victims must be believed especially if they are in the arbitrary category of the "unprivileged,"
- all members of the "patriarchy" are ex-ante guilty of crimes whether they commit any or not,
- any group that attempts to delegitimize a free enterprise state, particularly the United States, deserves unreserved support—regardless of whether they are terrorists or not,
- any group that attempts to delegitimize a communist/socialist state (particularly Cuba and Venezuela) deserves unreserved censure—regardless of whether those states are guilty of war crimes against civilians and/or their own people or not.

The whole rhetorical edifice is built on Marxist class warfare. Without the oppressed and the oppressors, that edifice crumbles—just as Nazism crumbles without anti-Semitism. The social justice movements also crumble because they too are built on class warfare. Without the warring classes there is no need for the savior class (the revolutionaries, social justice warriors).

It is all about the rhetoric and not about any evidence. As long as you utter the correct socialist buzzwords you are good as gold no matter how absurd, tried, failed, and damaging your policies are. Even dictators get a pass on that criterion.

From an economics perspective, this set of fallacies produces an industry of *free riders* who know they can get the support of the partisans merely by repeating correctly phrased rhetoric. Sinners become saints, saints become sinners, victims become perpetrators and perpetrators become victims. Truth inversion is the outcome. Rogue states and terrorists prosper and the rhetoric literally costs lives.

We have discussed the alt-right in chapter 5. It is assumed to be a mass movement, without evidence or question by the opposing partisans. Now we will discuss the alt-left, whose existence the same partisans deny. Rhetoric does not self-identify, preferring to hide and deny its own existence via the conspiracy theory rhetoric and the anti-white nationalism (vastly exaggerated) cover, and to do its damage under the radar. It also uses intimidation and ineffective shaming tactics that do not change peoples' minds.

Keri Smith writes defines the alt-left as: "When asked to define Alt-Left, I would describe it as a leftist but illiberal authoritarian ideology rooted in postmodernism and neo-Marxism that supports censorship, condones violence in response to speech, is obsessed with identity politics (much like the Alt-Right), and functions like a secular religion that gives its believers a sense of moral self-worth."[3]

The demographics of the alt-left are difficult to discern for the reasons listed. We can proxy the Antifa movement for it—but they hide their identities under pseudonyms, costumes inspired by the Nazis (Tu Quoque), and the like. Antifa seems to be growing and it may have achieved the status of a domestic terrorist group.[4]

Discussion Questions

(1) Members of Antifa admit they are biased. Why, according to them, is that bias justified? Is it because the other side is biased? So, do they state that their bias will "even out" the other side's bias? Upon what sociological or economic theory is the even out hypothesis based?

(2) Is item (1) the *Tu Quoque* fallacy? Does one evil justify another evil?

(3) Does responding to alleged bias with more bias, and violence, reduce the total amount of bias or violence ?

(4) Is calling people with alternative views "Nazis," then beating them up like Nazis would—while hiding their identities and wearing Nazi style uniforms—an example of hypocrisy (Tu Quoque)?

(5) Do the actions in item (4) have moral authority?

(6) Is the beating up part of item (4) a felony in the United States? If so, why is it tolerated in some major American cities by their mayors?

(7) Have some of our politicians resorted to the rule of the jungle supported by inflammatory rhetoric? If so, is this consistent with American laws? If not, why not?

SELECTIVE MORAL OUTRAGE

Moral outrage, demonstrated selectively is a form of hypocrisy used by partisans. The outrage is selective while purporting to be general. Partisans will cherry pick things they choose to be outraged at, based on the political mileage they can get out of them, and ignore all other outrageous behavior, including their own hypocrisy.

Selective moral outrage has several purposes: to prove the moral superiority of its purveyors by demonstrating their alleged sensitivity to social issues, and as a rationale to thereby remove the opposition. Ultimately, it demonstrates no more than cynical hypocrisy and the endless human desire to seize power using any method, including shaming the opposition, suppressing the freedom of speech of others, and outright violence. It is important to hypocritically appear white as the driven snow—while spouting the mandatory rhetorical buzz words and simultaneously demeaning the opposition. Modern masters of this technique are several of our Presidential candidates.

One problem remains. How do we know that the power grabbers are the saints, as they claim to be, and will do better and not form brutal totalitarian dictatorships as history has amply demonstrated? Why would they? Because as F. A. Hayek in *The Road to Serfdom* noted, that if a group of partisans is so power hungry, then the worst will rise to the top and will abuse that power once seized.[5] This has happened time and time again and it provides a reason to study history.

AD HOMINEM

The Latin term, *ad hominem*, is defined as attacking the person's character, not their argument. This very common fallacy is often applied to political opponents, but it says nothing about their policies. A better approach is: the policies, not the person. For example, one does not have to love a political leader to like some of their policies. The latter decision is based on the validity of their policies and not on one's personal feelings, confirmation bias, nor on the partisan rhetoric attempting to demonize or glorify the leader.

STRAW MAN ARGUMENT

Changing the person's argument by replacing it with an argument easier to refute (referred to as the straw man). Then refuting the straw man and falsely concluding that the opponent's original argument has been refuted. The straw man argument is basically a distraction technique.

Example No. 1

> *Argument*: We need a border wall to reduce the more unsavory aspects of illegal immigration, such as sex trafficking children, drug dealing, fraud, and homicide.
>
> *Counter Argument*: No, we do not support a border wall. A border wall will not solve all our problems. What we do need and support is comprehensive immigration policy.

The counter argument replaces the original argument with a far different one. It adds the qualifier "all our problems." Where did the original needs statement say or imply that it would? Further, a reduction is not an elimination (dichotomous thinking). The counter argument is a straw man. Nor does the original needs statement state that a border wall precludes "comprehensive immigration policy." This is another straw man and a false dichotomy.

A further economic and policy error here is the failure to distinguish between short-term immigration policy and long-term immigration policy. One can and should have a short-term solution without a long-term one. When one's house is burning down we try to put the fire out, not put out all potential fires—an impossible utopian goal. Denial of reality does not change that.

Discussion Questions

(1) The border wall debate is plagued by imprecision. What constitutes "working"?

(2) Does it fail to recognize the possible partisanship of its staunch opponents—who have a huge amount to lose if the invalid asylum seekers (not migrant workers) they want to admit are not admitted and hence cannot vote for them? Do borders that are not open threaten the voter base for certain partisans, specifically the Democrats?[6]

(3) Are partisans guilty of hypocrisy and moral turpitude when they talk about "family" separation at the border being the worst thing possible, while not acknowledging that not all alleged families actually are families? Is this the fallacy of composition: some are families implies all are families?

(4) Is it possible that there is gaming of the cross border immigration system? In particular, that there are cartel members trafficking children but posing as parents? Is the negation of this the claiming to know more than you know fallacy? or, is it evidence denial?

(5) Why do the preventable deaths caused by brutal gangs of illegal immigrants such as MS13 get ignored by certain partisans and the media echo chambers? Is that selective morality?

FALSE COMPARISONS

Just because someone arbitrarily compares A to B does not mean there is any automatic validity to the comparison. It is ex ante simply an opinion. There have to be valid reasons for the comparison. For example, comparing those who disagree with you to Nazis—simply because they disagree with you and/or your policies—is both a false comparison and a non-sequitur. Disagreement is neither a necessary nor a sufficient condition to make you a Nazi. The Nazis were guilty of horrendous crimes against humanity.[7] Few have matched them, though some communist/socialist dictators (no U.S. President) have tried to emulate the Third Reich.

Disagreeing with someone is not on the order of Nazi crimes, nor is the legal use of Presidential executive orders, Presidential executive privilege, nor many of the allegedly fascist or discriminatory things that people do. The very use of these words invokes false comparisons and is usually fully partisan, designed to stir up the base and get them to do whatever the partisans want them to do, in the name of selective moral outrage.

FALSE ANALOGIES

False analogies are those based on analogies that generalize from what people presumably think they know (sources) to areas they know little about (derivates). It saves the trouble of having to investigate the derivate by simply assuming it is just like the source.

Example No. 1

An example is the term "imperialism" whether real or imagined. This concept is then generalized to other areas to come up with novel terms such as "economic imperialism," a term that has no ex-ante meaning. What have we learned from the ill-conceived exercise? Economic imperialism (whatever that is), must be just as evil as ordinary imperialism. Why? Because we just analogized it to be so.

Example No. 2

Take the ever elusive and over-used term "social justice." Where does it come from? It is the juxtaposition of "society" with "justice," both abstractions. But "justice" is a concept that applies at the level of individuals and "social" is an aggregate—what "society" is about. Does it make automatic sense to juxtapose the two and extrapolate justice to the aggregate level? If so, what exactly does it mean? And how does it differ from individual justice? How and by whom is it implemented?

Some claim that it is just an analogy. We all know what individual justice is and we think we know what society is, so what is the problem? For one, who metes out social justice? It is usually the state because it has the power to enforce it. Then social justice is an asymmetric relationship between the state and the individuals, one fraught with the power of the more powerful state to abuse. Is it any wonder then that states that have organized around social justice have been so totalitarian? Examine the history.

For another, "social justice" could very well be a false analogy with neither meaning nor mechanism. It could be a mere figure of speech, rhetoric for special interest groups to use to steal moral authority and get their demands met.[8]

Discussion Questions

(1) What does "social justice" mean in practice? Is it used as rhetoric because it is rarely defined but is often invoked?

(2) Do social justice partisans consider the feasibility of its implementation in a free society?

(3) Do social justice partisans ever look at the history of their movement? In particular, that its implementation has been backed up by government force and mob rule. Of many examples: the street thugs who supported and implemented national socialism and the Stalinists who eliminated their enemies in the name of communism.

(4) Is Marxist ideology and its modern variants used to support social justice claims?

(5) Is social justice a falsifiable hypothesis ?

(6) Discuss the assertion made by Cathy Young: "Working to correct inequities is a noble goal—which explains the appeal of the "social justice" movement to many fair-minded people. But the movement in its current form is not about that. It elevates an extreme and polarizing version of identity politics in which

individuals are little more than the sum of their labels. It encourages wallowing in anger and guilt. It promotes intolerance and the politicization of everything. It must be stopped—not only for the sake of freedom, but for the sake of a kinder, fairer society."[9]

In contrast to the rhetorical approach, the data-based approach insists on testing properly formulated (falsifiable) and testable hypotheses with data, not accepting them outright.

NON-SEQUITURS

A non-sequitir is an argument wherein the conclusion(s) do not follow from the premise(s).

Example No. 1

"If someone alleged of a crime denies their guilt, then they must be guilty."

When stated this way, it is clear that denial of guilt does not imply guilt. The conclusion does not follow from the premise. In banana republics with kangaroo courts and in media echo chambers—where one is not allowed to defend oneself—this rhetoric is reality.

BEGGING THE QUESTION

Assuming the conclusion in the premise.

Example No. 1

"People who deny the truth of Marxism are simply dancing to the tune of their capitalist masters, as Marx understood so well."[10]

Re-phrasing: if you deny the truth of Marxism then you are being manipulated by your capitalist masters. In other words, "being manipulated by your capitalist masters" is a *necessary* condition for "denying the truth of Marxism." Anyone who was not so manipulated would readily acknowledge "the truth of Marxism."

Ignoring the fact that this may simply be propaganda, we will stick to the logical errors—which is what this book is about. As to "as Marx understood so well" that is mind-reading without a reference to the actual words of Marx. This kind of statement is typical of his followers, not of Marx himself.

This is an example of how the conclusion (dancing to the tune of their capitalist masters) is not a necessary condition for the premise (denying the truth of Marxism). There are many reasons, other than "dancing to the tune of their capitalist masters" for denying Marxism, one being the fact that his predictions were not borne out by actual events. Another is that no Marxist-based society has ever survived, let alone prospered.[11]

Perhaps the authors meant: "Those who believe in 'capitalism' deny the truth of Marxism." That is, reverse the premise and the conclusion. Then it states that "being a capitalist" (for whatever reason) is a sufficient condition for "denying Marxism," a far different statement. Since Marxism and capitalism are mutually incompatible on economic and historical grounds, this statement is most likely correct. Flipping it around is a common error and is invalidated by the distinction between necessary and sufficient conditions.

Example No. 2

When did you stop beating your significant other? The question assumes you are or have been beating your significant other. The correct way to state the question is by breaking it up so that it does not assume the premise (you beat your significant other).

(1) Did you ever beat your significant other?

(2) Did you stop yet?

Conclusion: if (1) is negative, then ignore (2).

PSYCHOBABBLE

"Psychobabble is speech that relies heavily on psychological jargon and expressions. It is often used by individuals who have little to no training in psychology. The word is derived from a combination of the words "psychology," or the study of the mind and behavior, and "babble," which is defined as to utter meaningless or unintelligible sounds. Even when used correctly, psychobabble is often difficult to understand and can obfuscate the meaning of even relatively simple ideas."[12]

Psychobabble is used as cheap, unaccountable, pseudo-scientific, fraudulent accusations of an opponent's mental health by those without the qualifications to make them (common online). This practice became so intense that people practicing psychobabble were sued for attempting to defame political candidates. The opposition tried this tactic on Barry Goldwater, 1964 Republican Presidential candidate, and it gave rise to the Goldwater Rule.

The American Psychiatric Association, in the Principles of Medical Ethics states, "On occasion psychiatrists are asked for an opinion about an individual who is in the light of public attention or who has disclosed information about himself/herself through public media. In such circumstances, a psychiatrist may share with the public his or her expertise about psychiatric issues in general. However, it is unethical for a psychiatrist to offer a professional opinion unless he or she has conducted an examination and has been granted proper authorization for such a statement."[13]

The fallacy and accompanying tactic, like the shaming tactic, continue to be used to this day: psychobabble the opposition. It is used when no rational argument is available and it is a form of ad hominem.

Example No. 1

Consider these statements: take your meds, you are mentally unstable, you have serious mental issues, you are not fit to govern, and an endless parade of variants—all equally defective.

Discussion Questions

(1) Where are the psychology degrees of those who perpetrate psychobabble? If they do not have any, does it then not follow that they are frauds and are thereby discredited?

(2) Would any psychology professional attempt to analyze someone online, whom they have never met?

(3) Who asked? Medical information, including psychological reports, is supposed to be private in the United States. Is psychobabble based on any hacked reports? or, is it rhetoric made up by the perpetrators?

FALLACIES BASED ON ALLEGED MORAL AUTHORITY

Fallacies that are based on alleged moral authority are related to the red herring fallacy. They change the focus from providing logical arguments and evidence to personal characteristics. As such, they are a deflection tactic. They save the purveyors from having to come up with actual valid, evidence-based arguments.

The rhetorical technique is simple. Just assume you are morally superior to the person or group you are trying to discredit. Then everything you say must be correct and everything they say incorrect on moral grounds. Of course, this is invalid. Arguments and policies are not correct based on the authors' moral authority. Numerous dictators, including Hitler, Mao, Castro, Stalin, and Maduro to name a few, have tried to use this ploy for centuries. It is also a basis for raw bigotry (see below).

CLAIMING MORAL AUTHORITY FOR SPURIOUS REASONS WITHOUT EARNING IT

In order to have moral authority you have to earn it, rather than steal it. Otherwise, everyone who says they have it can literally get away with murder on the basis of nothing more than their alleged moral authority. As stated, this is a favorite of demagogues with the power of force to back them up and destroy their opponents.

Before using this ploy, the practitioner must appear pure as the driven snow—because not being so is one way to invalidate the claim that they are morally superior. Another way to invalidate is to appeal to the lack of evidence fallacy. Alleged and actual moral superiority are not evidence. For example, many think that minimum wage laws are proof of moral superiority, enlightened social policies. This ignores their predictable negative consequences as discussed.

Example No. 1

Saying or implying by innuendo that all non-whites are, by definition, more moral than all whites—simply by virtue of the color of their skin—can be easily seen to be actually as opposed to allegedly discriminatory. Inventing an academic concept such as white privilege (apparently a perfect substitute for the over-used discrimination rhetoric) to support such statements is the begging the question fallacy. Is having good looks a form of privilege and if so, should Hollywood movie stars be punished for it? The search for sources of privilege (and hence grievances) is endless but none of those alleged sources constitute real evidence.[14]

Further, white privilege justifies a form of reverse discrimination and it suffers from the single variable explains everything fallacy which we discussed in chapters 2 and 3.[15] The unpublished paper referred to in endnote 7 of chapter 4 by Peggy McIntosh presents a list of privileges and then assumes—without any theoretical justification—that they are all the product of race, specifically the white race. This is the fallacy of causal reductionism.[16]

How is this academic construct in principle and in its application fundamentally different from Aryanism or Islamophobia? Is Mr. Farrakhan more moral than any number of white people? Are ISIS killers moral simply because they are not, on average white? Again, claims to morality must be based on *earned* morality, and reasons and evidence for policies, not simply claims to it for spurious reasons such as skin color, religion, or any of the identity politics categories.

Discussion Questions

(1) Do all whites already have "white privilege"? if so, do they deserve any "fairness"?

(2) Is "white privilege" another minor variation of Marxist class warfare?

(3) Is the construct "white privilege" an academic one to be used as a tactic to replace the "racism" rhetoric, and used to bludgeon opponents?

(4) Why are some academics, no matter how partisan, automatically given the discretion to lecture us on what we should want and prefer? is the assumption they may so lecture us the expert fallacy? and, is it the elitism fallacy? and, is it the unearned moral authority fallacy?

(5) Does peer review of academic concepts and research *guarantee* their validity? or, is evidence required? Same question for non-peer reviewed materials—such as predictions by academics.

(6) What role does the "elitism fallacy" play in agenda driven rhetoric?

(7) Who metes out "fairness"?

(8) What is cultural Marxism?

(9) Does (cultural) Marxism favor the workers and discriminate against the capitalists?

Example No. 2

Another example of the attempt to steal morality is finger pointing, hand waving, jumping on tables, gesticulations, eye rolling, and other theatrical moves. Do any of these have anything to do with moral authority? Are they necessary or sufficient conditions thereof? Examine the videos of Hitler. All demagogues employ these techniques because their person and policies do not stand on their own merits. Do the purveyors of these demagogic techniques think (or wish) that their viewers were small children?

MORALLY SUSPECT EQUIVALENCIES

Morally suspect equivalencies is a category of false comparisons combined with the added component of alleged superior morality. No evidence is required. The "all political opponents must be Nazis and fascists" mantra has already been discussed. Note the tactic here. The opposition is guilty until proven innocent, and they must prove to the self-proclaimed morally superior that they are not guilty (a negative that cannot be conclusively proven).

Discussion Questions

(1) Is the above totalitarianism and fully in the spirit of the Nazis and their kangaroo courts where the self-proclaimed racially superior (substitute non-white) judged the racially inferior (substitute white), and enforced their judgments by murder?

(2) What gives the accusers the "right" to dictate the rules of the game to their opponents? Is this done by shifting the burden of proving opponents guilty by demanding that they prove themselves not guilty? Is that a right at all or a violation of others' rights (see chapter 6, n67)?

VICTIMOLOGY

Victimology involves getting a blanket pass to disarm your opponents by falsely claiming that all of their arguments are victimizing you, or that you have victim status and are untouchable. Identity politics and pseudo scientific academic partisanship is based on this commonly used tactic. Unsupportable amoral and morally suspect principles emerge from the illogic, such as the shutting down of free speech on college campuses and embracing victimology and safe spaces. These devices are instrumental in keeping young minds indoctrinated by the rhetoric, in a dependency class, and easily manipulable by partisans to do their bidding. Is this last sentence a conspiracy theory?

The Fallacy of Composition

If you are white then you must be guilty of "white privilege" and must pay the price for it, no matter what generation you belong to. Assuming that "white privilege" can be defined and measured, the added assumption that all whites are a priori guilty of this manufactured sin is the fallacy.

Even if some whites (not all) are guilty of sins in the past and in the present (being born white is not a sin), why should their progeny pay a price in perpetuity to the alleged victim class? Not to mention that their claims have to be supported in the form of *specific* illegal acts, not some vague generality, as befits the Marxist class warfare rhetoric.

"Privileged" according to the purveyors means you have unearned advantages and, according to Marxist class warfare, others *therefore* do not (the zero sum game assumption). No evidence is provided to support this claim and no (economic) theory. The concept is not only discriminatory, but it is the essence of discrimination; denigrating an entire group of people for a characteristic they were born with.

Such tropes were used to murder millions of innocent people, again perfectly consistent with Nazi ideology. The other fallacy is that of hypocrisy: those who use this academic (therefore acceptable) discrimination are content to rail against the alleged discrimination of others, while being at least as discriminatory as those they accuse. Check the rhetoric of the most vocal accusers and then their own histories to confirm or deny this claim.

The Lionizing of "Victimhood"

This is a view that divides the people of the world into three categories: victims, perpetrators, and saviors (social justice warriors). It is based on Marxist class warfare: workers, capitalists, and self-declared revolutionaries (socialists). In its modern incarnation victims are further sub-divided into preferred victims and non-preferred victims, where preferred means preferred for political reasons.

This theory has been developed in transactional psychology by Dr. Stephen B. Karpman in his *A Game Free Life*.[17] Therein is a cure for the psychological disorder of victimhood. Consider the following.

The claims, no matter how egregious, of self-proclaimed preferred victims are to be accepted at face value, and require no evidence for the alleged crimes against them. Alleged victims *must* be believed. This makes for good rhetoric, but not everyone who calls themselves a victim is in fact a victim. The assumption that they are is dichotomous thinking, and it makes the alleged preferred victims a protected class—and presumably they are not subject to the usual laws. Of course, this is totalitarianism and it bypasses the rule of law.

Preferred victimhood is a well-rewarded industry and rent seekers can and will therefore game the system. Preferred victims are courted, financially rewarded, pitied, achieve instant fame, and are used as bludgeons against the political opposition by partisans. Since white males are guilty of the original sin of white privilege, according to this construct, only white females need apply. And the purveyors prefer minorities for the extra political mileage that they can extract from them.

Of course to say that all alleged "victims" are actual victims, without evidence, is the fallacy of composition. *Some* alleged victims are actual victims and some are not. How do we tell the difference? Ex-ante we cannot tell.[18] That is why we have a legal system as opposed to kangaroo courts. The only way to tell is on a case by case basis in a court of law where all of the evidence is considered in an unbiased manner. In other words, in the opposite of the court of public opinion, which is plagued by (confirmation) bias. Nor is there any system that is 100% correct all of the time. Some non-victims will pass as victims, and some victims will be dismissed as non-victims.

Preferred victimhood generates a form of rent-seeking as discussed (also see capitalism and socialism in chapter 10) by offering rewards to its practitioners. The rewards are proportional to the alleged crimes against the preferred victims. Therefore, people compete for the rewards and status associated with it. History is re-written by the partisans to support and generate unsupported claims. Re-writing history is a form of cherry-picking data and information to support a narrative.

Examples include trying to distance one's social justice movement from "fascism" by pretending that Hitler's ideology had nothing to do with social justice movements. This is contradicted by Hitler's own words where he clearly references both socialism and social justice (italics added) as foundational to his regime:

> Thus we can see the two great differences between races: Aryanism means ethical perception of work and that which we today so often hear – *socialism*, community spirit, common good before own good.
>
> Because it seems inseparable from the social idea and we do not believe that there could ever exist a state with lasting inner health if it is not built on *internal social justice*, and so we have joined forces with this knowledge and when we finally united, there was only one big question: How should we actually baptize ourselves?[19]

THE POT SHOT FALLACY

Critiquing every single policy, action, words of an opponent implies that you have better ones. For example, you can say "to me, capitalism is irremediable," as did Alexandria Ocasio-Cortez.[20] The words "to me" apparently excuse the speaker from having to justify their claim. No reasons given is a characteristic of rhetoric, illustrating that talk is cheap and dramatic talk even cheaper.

Opinion and personal preference are not arguments. They do not imply that any other system, for example, democratic socialism, is better. That implication, usually by innuendo, is a non-sequitur. Democratic socialism is also an infeasible concatenation of two mutually incompatible systems (see chapter 10) so it is also irremediable, making it not only not better but also not even an option.

Purveyors of this very common tactic are usually prone to the nirvana fallacy, where nothing quite measures up to utopia, by definition. Is utopia better? More to the point: is utopia possible? Why does history show us that utopias turn into dystopias with the complete loss of freedom of "the People" except for some of the autocrats?

NOTES

1. The fallacy here is that while your opponent might be a hypocrite, that observation neither justifies your bad behavior nor does it end the discussion.

2. Christopher Bodeen, "China Accuses US of Prejudice Over Human Rights Issues," *Washington Times*, March 14, 2019, https://www.washingtontimes.com/news/2019/mar/14/china-accuses-us-of-prejudice-over-human-rights-is (accessed December 17, 2019).

3. Keri Smith, "Yes, the Alt-Left Exists and It's Terrifying," *Foundation for Economic Education* (*FEE*), September 6, 2017, https://fee.org/articles/yes-the-alt-left-exists-and-its-terrifying (accessed December 29, 2019).

4. Documentation of the FBI declaring it as such is not publicly available.

5. F. A. Hayek, *The Road to Serfdom: The Definitive Edition* (Text and Documents), ed. Bruce Caldwell (Chicago: University of Chicago Press, 2007), 157–170.

6. It is not just the voter base that is affected. "The presence of all immigrants (naturalized citizens, legal residents, and illegal aliens) and their U.S.-born minor children will redistribute 26 seats in the House in 2020." See Steven A. Camarota and Karen Zeigler, "The Impact of Legal and Illegal Immigration on the Apportionment of Seats in the U.S. House of Representatives in 2020," *Center for Immigration Studies*, December 19, 2019, https://cis.org/Report/Impact-Legal-and-Illegal-Immigration-Apportionment-Seats-US-House-Representatives-2020 (accessed December 25, 2019).

7. Robert S. Wistrich, *Hitler and the Holocaust* (New York: Modern Library Chronicles, 2003).

8. F. [Friedrich] A. Hayek, *Law, Legislation and Liberty*, Volume 2, *The Mirage of Social Justice* (Chicago: University of Chicago Press, 1976); and see the essays on the topic "Is Social Justice, Just?" *Independent Review: A Journal of Political Economy* 24, no. 1 (2019).

9. Cathy Young, "The Pecking Disorder: Social Justice Warriors Gone Wild," *Observer*, June 11, 2015, https://observer.com/2015/06/the-pecking-disorder-social-justice-warriors-gone-wild (accessed January 23, 2020).

10. Texas State University, Department of Philosophy, "Begging the Question," *Texas State*, n.d., https://www.txstate.edu/philosophy/resources/fallacy-definitions/Begging-the-Question.html (accessed November 24, 2019).

11. Richard Pipes, *Communism: A History* (New York: Modern Library, 2001; repr. 2003).

12. GoodTherapy, "Psychobabble," *GoodTherapy* (blog), 2016, https://www.goodtherapy.org/blog/psychpedia/psychobabble/(last updated January 29, 2016).

13. American Psychiatric Association, *The Principles of Medical Ethics: With Annotations Especially Applicable to Psychiatry* (Arlington, VA: American Psychiatric Association, 2013), sec. 7, item 4, https://www.psychiatry.org/File%20Library/Psychiatrists/Practice/Ethics/principles-medical-ethics.pdf (accessed November 24, 2019).

14. Dennis Prager, "The Fallacy of 'White Privilege,'" *National Review*, February 16, 2016, https://www.nationalreview.com/2016/02/white-privilege-myth-reality (accessed December 31, 2019). See also the discussion in chapter 4, and specifically n7, which provides reference to the neo-Marxist hypothesis (not fact) of white privilege in an unpublished article by its originator, Peggy McIntosh.

15. Vincent Harinam and Rob Henderson, "Why White Privilege Is Wrong—Part 1," *Quillette*, August 22, 2019, https://quillette.com/2019/08/22/why-white-privilege-is-wrong-part-1 (accessed December 30, 2019).

16. Logically Fallacious, "Causal Reductionism," *Logically Fallacious*, n.d., https://www.logicallyfallacious.com/tools/lp/Bo/LogicalFallacies/64/Causal-Reductionism (accessed January 6, 2020).

17. Stephen B. Karpman, *A Game Free Life: The New Transactional Analysis of Intimacy, Openness, and Happiness* (San Francisco: Drama Triangle Publications, 2014).

18. Note that the rhetoric gives everyone who alleges victimhood a pass. That way no evidence is required.

19. Adolf Hitler, "'Why We Are Anti-Semites'—Text of Adolf Hitler's 1920 Speech at the Hofbräugaus," *Carolyn Yeager*, January 29, 2013, https://carolynyeager.net/why-we-are-antisemites-text-adolf-hitlers-1920-speech-hofbr%C3%A4uhaus (accessed January 26, 2020).

20. Michael Burke, "Ocasio-Cortez: 'Capitalism Is Irredeemable,'" *Hill*, March 10, 2019, https://thehill.com/homenews/house/433394-ocasio-cortez-capitalism-is-irredeemable/ (accessed November 24, 2019).

Part II

BASIC KNOWLEDGE FOR DECISION-MAKING AND EVALUATING POLICY

Chapter Eight

Making Good Decisions and Good Policy

Relative versus Absolute, Opportunity Costs, Marginalism

In this chapter we will present some basic concepts that can move the discussion away from rhetoric and towards economic realities and evidence. This chapter does not aim to be comprehensive. Rather, it defines and illustrates some basic economic and financial principles. One would hope that all elected government officials have this knowledge, which is basic to choosing social policy, but they apparently do not. Getting elected is more a question of rhetoric.

WHAT MAKES A GOOD DECISION?

Why even ask this question? Is the answer not obvious? Far from it. The reason is that decisions are choices from a set of feasible alternatives. As such, all choices involve both direct and *indirect* costs.

The direct costs are those involved in implementing the decision. The indirect costs are those created by selecting the particular alternative we choose—and thereby eliminating the alternatives. These are called *opportunity costs* (see below) and are typically usually ignored by partisans.

Looking just at direct costs does not ensure that we have made a good decision. We want to choose the best alternative because resources are limited, recognizing that our choice has at least temporarily eliminated the alternatives. By doing one thing, we cannot do all the other things we could have done. That is a cost as real as the direct monetary costs.

Example No. 1

This example illustrates that one must first identify the cash flows in analyzing whether it is good for the community that Amazon establish a headquarters in Long Island City. It is interesting to hear the main partisan opposing Amazon locating a headquarters in Long Island City, Alexandria Ocasio-Cortez, claim that the monies in tax subsidies to Amazon could now be used for other "more worthwhile" projects. This was partially due to Alexandria Ocasio-Cortez's rhetorical war to drive Amazon out of coming to Long Island City.[1] Examine her claims for fallacies such as false dichotomy, missing analysis of her allegedly more "worthwhile" projects, how they would "benefit the community" more than the Amazon opportunity, and why and how tax subsidies would be needed, available, and could be used. Was her position evidence or rhetoric-based?

The New York state tax subsidies in mind were *reductions* to the state taxes that Amazon would have paid if and only if it had established a location in Long Island City. They were predicated on Amazon running operations in Long Island City, and paying additional New York state and city taxes. If Amazon does not run operations in Long Island City then its non-operations in Long Island City generate zero incremental tax to New York state and New York City. So there is a complete loss of the taxes (net of the subsidies) that Amazon would have paid directly to New York State and New York City.

This is analogous to someone selling a product with a discount. You only get the discount if you buy the product. The seller does not pay it to you if you do not buy the product. Therefore, it is not available for anything else, since it does not exist.

You could reformulate this problem to make sense, which Alexandria Ocasio-Cortez did not do, but to do that you have to know what you are doing. The alternative use of tax subsidies is to "give them" (by reducing the taxes they pay) to some other tax-paying entity, presumably more worthy. This sounds partially right but it ignores the benefits (not just the costs) of having Amazon in Long Island City. The benefits have to be weighed against the costs.

If you give tax subsidies to some tax-paying entities what do you get for it? We will not get into the notion of ranking projects, which is discussed in every basic finance textbook. There is nothing morally superior about giving away something of value in return for nothing (value destruction).[2] The decision to ban Amazon was apparently based on anti-corporate rhetoric, not on solid decision making.[3] The moral of this example is: do not ignore the costs or the benefits when comparing projects.

RELATIVE VERSUS ABSOLUTE THINKING: THE NIRVANA FALLACY

Being aware of opportunity costs helps us to recognize the relative nature of our choices, which are not made automatic nor obvious by the cover of alleged moral superiority. When political partisans cannot justify their policies based on the economic support they have, they usually throw up their hands and appeal to their alleged superior morality, by which they mean their partisan preferences. What this may mean in the game of politics is that they—as a party—are ready to scrap everything done up to that point by their opponents, and steer the economy to disaster as a side-effect of their alleged superior morality, lack of basic reasoning skills, and questionable ideologies.

Examples for study and analysis include: price controls (for example, minimum wages), government subsidization boondoggles (for example, Solyndra), meddling in the housing market (for example, by forcing banks to lend to those unable to repay), regulation proliferation, tax policy, soak the rich schemes (old ideas from some of our Presidential candidates), monopolizing whole industries such as health insurance (under the false claim of government ability to lower future unknown costs and prices) and K–12—then mandating ideological indoctrination of school-age children by teaching neo-Marxist political correctness, un-settled science, anti-corporate ideologies, and pro-socialist ideologies. Conspicuously missing from the government's educational curriculum is teaching the ability to think independently about issues—without partisan entities telling children what to think and fostering the illusion that these entities have solved problems yet to be solved.

As already discussed, minimum wages are one example of a policy that appears to be (more?) moral, but which has consequences that are morally suspect. This does not seem to bother the partisans and provides a clue to their motivation: to get power and then get their way no matter what. They need to be asked: how can a "moral" policy have morally suspect consequences? In addition to being unsupportable by ordinary economic criteria and verifiable data.[4]

Opportunity cost is one example of an economic concept that serves to frame a rational economic-based discussion and policy based upon it. Underlying it is the question: relative to what do we evaluate policies? The distinction is relative versus absolute. The moralists usually talk in absolute terms implying, but not delineating, the unique absolute standard by which they judge all else. Economists take a much more limited task of discussing the comparable alternatives and choosing from among them. They recognize that there is no viable perfect utopian alternative.

A discussion of the failure of utopian schemes for running society is beyond the scope of this book. One can read the history of utopian experimental socialism (as if it is scientific, a hold-over from Marxist-Engels ideology[5]) and see whether communism/socialism (utopian-in-word-only-shell-games), for example, have ever produced the goods, so to speak.[6]

Treating people like guinea pigs and experimenting on them was popular among the national socialists and apparently equally popular in the eugenics movement in the United States, and among the Communists who wanted to perfect human beings. As Thomas C. Leonard, author of *Illiberal Reformers* notes, people have to first be reformed before they can give up their individuality and freedom, and then accept the state's controls over every aspect of their lives.[7] The notion that the state must not be given the power to implement and enforce such controls is one of the great lessons of modern history, lost on the partisans.

Comparing practical solutions to utopian ones and rejecting them because they do not live up to the perfection criterion is the *Nirvana Fallacy*, also known as the perfect solution fallacy or the perfectionist fallacy.

"Comparing a realistic solution with an idealized one, and discounting or even dismissing the realistic solution as a result of comparing to a 'perfect world' or impossible standard. Ignoring the fact that improvements are often good enough reason."[8]

The nirvana fallacy creates a false dichotomy between the perfect, but impossible, "solution" and *all* the feasible solutions. It lends itself to rhetoric because *any* feasible solution can easily be dismissed simply because it is imperfect. Under this fallacy, real world solutions (which are all imperfect) will always be defeated by the impossible "perfect" solution.[9]

For some practical devices that help in making real-world decisions, not just theoretical utopian fallacies, consider the following concepts.

OPPORTUNITY COSTS

Opportunity costs relate to decision-making under conditions of uncertainty. When faced with a decision, we should consider the alternatives of equal risk and—not view the decision in absolute terms. Considering the alternatives is needed and it gives us a relative, rather than absolute, perspective on our decisions. After all, at any point in time, we will get to choose only from the available alternatives. As in the nirvana fallacy, we could posit some ideal world relative to which we should compare the one we have. But then we would have to demonstrate: why it is "ideal" for everyone (not just for its proponents), how we get there, and how it is sustainable.

The opportunity cost of a decision is an *indirect* cost. It consists of the benefits forgone as a result of a given choice from the set of feasible alternatives. It is an indirect economic cost as opposed to a direct accounting cost. One way to think about opportunity costs is as foregoing the alternatives. In order that a decision be a good one, it has to earn its opportunity cost. If it does not, then one of the alternatives is a better choice by definition.

The concept of opportunity cost is very important for public policy for several reasons.

1. It counteracts the tendency to think in absolute terms by forcing one to think in relative terms. There are few feasible absolutes. The feasible alternatives are all evaluated relative to each other, not to some infeasible absolute standard, as the rhetoric implies.
2. It forces one to do *cost-benefit analysis*. This type of analysis explicitly recognizes the relative *marginal* costs and benefits of alternative courses of action. And, it lists them. Most real world decisions involve tradeoffs between their costs and benefits, as opposed to being unambiguously good or bad.

Example No. 1

Pollution: This issue has been addressed many times in the public domain. Some pollution seems inevitable if we also want economic growth. China and India are in precisely this position right now. Therefore, there is a tradeoff between pollution and economic growth. Carbon dioxide (CO_2) is part of the carbon cycle, which is necessary for life on the planet. Further, CO_2 is CO_2 whether it is anthropogenic or naturally occurring. There are not two kinds of CO_2, human carbon emissions and natural CO_2.

Example No. 2

Man-Made Carbon Emissions: Here we will augment the discussion in chapter 6. Leave aside the hypothesis that the man-made global warming scare may be a crisis manufactured by fear-mongering partisans backed by collective science in the service of partisan agenda.[10] The media is involved in spreading the word, not in the form of actual science, but in the form of rhetoric.

The United States, an advanced technological country, is not the main source of total (nor of highest per capita[11]) global carbon emissions,[12] which are hypothesized to be the *main* source of alleged "global warming." China, the United States, and India in that order, were the main generators of total CO_2 emissions as of 2016 (the latest by country data availability date).[13]

It is interesting that there is no standardized, comparable, publicly available data for 2018 to 2019, or even for the years for which there is data, given that this alleged crisis will allegedly end the planet in twelve years.[14] Apparently anthropogenic carbon emissions are quite difficult to measure: "Collecting these values for all countries in the world is extremely complicated and lengthy. There are no central reporting points, so the data must be calculated from other sources such as coal-fired power plants or oil company sales. This is not only tedious, but can only be done with great delays. The above data for C02 values come from the Carbon Dioxide Information Analysis Center and in most cases represent the year 2016."[15] Thus the data needed for a reasonable discussion is non-transparent and has a relatively high error rate.

Discussion Questions

(1) Would you expect the definitions and calculations to be identical across all countries (cross-sectionally)? Looking across space we have to know the non-trivial fact that the definitions and the numbers are comparable.

(2) Does a similar problem arises in cross-sectional analyses of gun control legislation?

(3) Check the per capita numbers and rankings for the United States for our two sites, Mundi Index and World Data Info.[16] Do they differ?

(4) What are the likely error measurement rates? See Mundi's "Limitations and Exceptions."[17]

(5) Is the U.S. government a neutral third party on this issue, and if so, can it manage the source data, such as it is, in a transparent manner? Or, may it be influenced by partisans potentially massaging the data (see ClimateGate) to fit their narrative?

(6) Does the politicization of this issue open the door to rhetoric because of the lack of timely data availability and non-transparency?

One view is that man-made C02 emissions, the result of production, are not pollutants.[18] Note that for every claim (mostly rhetorical) on this issue there are counter claims. My purpose here is not to document the entire rhetorical and scientific literature. Populous countries with relatively lower levels of real GDP per capita compared to the United States, such as India and China, who want to increase their production, are the main man-made C02 emissions sources. They are not too happy with the industrialized world, where the standard of living is a great deal higher, telling them to use cost-prohibitive inefficient fuels. There is a trade-off between carbon emissions and production.[19]

As to the hypocrisy fallacy, it is interesting to see the loudest leading-edge partisan, Alexandria Ocasio-Cortez, using, by choice, the highest polluting and carbon emitting forms of transportation as their mode of choice.[20] Why? Because those modes are the most *efficient* (lowest cost per unit of output), and the fastest (time-consuming). This is precisely the point for others as well. Why do partisans get to do what they tell millions of other people *not* to do?[21]

Some call the presumption that they do get to lecture us elitism. Then the expert fallacy is invoked. Unfortunately, even the "elites" are subject to the knowing more than they know or can know fallacy. They presume to know better than millions of people and are invariably on the "right side of history" (an untestable hypothesis involving future data). We will call this the elitist fallacy, recognizing its relationship to the expert fallacy.

CASE STUDY NO. 10: THE GREEN NEW DEAL: A TRUE CONSPIRACY THEORY?

The premise of this is the *Anthropogenic Climate Change* (ACC) hypothesis whose correct formulation was discussed in chapter 6. The "Green" New Deal is a misnomer and rhetoric based on a lack of understanding of C02 processes. It is also cherry picking by ignoring the positive effects. Reducing C02 emissions will make the planet less, not more, green. C02 increases plant productivity, with the consequent positive effects on agriculture, and thereby prosperity.[22]

This is one of the most politicized, cherry-picked, and propagandized issues, with the consequent lack of falsifiability of the positive hypothesis. The author of the pivotal hockey stick model that underlies the ACC hypothesis, Michael Mann, consistently refuses to share his data.[23] That landmark model has been independently debunked as in mathematical and statistical error,[24] cherry-picking by leaving out the Medieval Warming Period (MWP) (900–1300 AD), and implying the yet to be proven assertion that industrialization *caused* global warming (as discussed in chapter 6).

To summarize, there are four fallacies here: (1) ignoring the warming periods (warmer than modern ones), that occurred far before industrialization, in particular the MWP conveniently erased in the hockey stick analysis; (2) confusing *correlation* with *causation* (statistical models examine linear correlation); (3) the fallacy that a *single* factor is necessarily the primary variable that explains the correlation in the data (confused as causation) and is therefore the only important one (see the discrimination discussions); and (4) the appealing to authority fallacy.

A subset of climate scientists who support the hypothesis *must* be right. The often touted 97 percent consensus is based on a misuse of percentages (the number of such consensus scientists in the study was 77).[25] But it is invalid reasoning in any case. The dissenters, also climate scientists, *must* be wrong because they disagree. That reasoning would have excluded and presumably marginalized Einstein, Galileo, Ptolemy, Socrates, and others. Richard P. Feynman states, "Science is the belief in the ignorance of experts," from his address, "What Is Science?" to the National Science Teachers' Association convention, April 1966.[26]

Nonetheless, it is the job of the climate-change *deniers* to prove the positive hypothesis false, according to the purveyors. But, we know a negative cannot be conclusively empirically proven. It is far better to examine the evidence allegedly consistent—and particularly inconsistent—with the hypothesis; and its interpretation. We discussed the use of computer models in establishing causation through accurate forecasts in chapter 6. Evidence (data) in science usually refers to *observations* of physical phenomena which are then used to confirm or deny the theory and/or its implications. One of the flaws of computer-generated models is that they are black boxes to the public, the media, and most policy-makers. Therefore, their tuning can easily be manipulated and, of course, politicized.

The IPCC computer models also fail to even *backcast* properly. They fail to reproduce the temperatures of the MWP and of the hiatus, possibly because they minimize the role of solar activity and other natural sources. The goal of the rhetoric is apparently a model that implicates anthropogenic carbon emissions, which partisans can then use to promote their political agenda. There is also cherry picking, certainly in the rhetoric, in emphasizing extreme scenario cases and ignoring others. Finally, doomsday soothsaying is used as a rhetorical device by those who cannot predict the future. This is way beyond the scope of this book, but the logical implications are not.

The premise of the green new deal (GND) is the ACC. If that premise is false, or even questionable at best, then the policy proposals based on it are suspect. The result: no crisis, then no immediate action or even action at all is called for. The partisans know this, so they emphasize the alleged crisis and their forecasts of impending doom. That is, they propagandize it and use fear mongering.

A little historical perspective is in order. The GND is a utopian social experiment that takes its catchy name from the original New Deal, also a social experiment, imposed on America by Franklin D. Roosevelt and his army of government officials. As Jim Powell's *FDR's Follies* outlines, contrary to the grand myth, it did not get America out of the Depression, the crisis that triggered it. It extended it by several years, and is a classic example of the government's constant failure in micro-managing a free economy.[27] So the GND can take no halo effect by trying to leverage it.

On a more basic yet ignored level, let us apply the opportunity cost concept to it. Following Alexandria Ocasio-Cortez on Amazon, what else could we do with the trillions of dollars that the GND costs? Many worthy things, one of which is *not* doing the GND and investing in the foregone growth that it would cost. The GND would have a predictable *negative* effect on growth by curtailing industrial production—and the global poor would be most negatively impacted by this.

If the GND does not earn its opportunity cost (incremental foregone global GDP growth) then it should not be done. Why? Because its opportunity cost is a better option. And it is not as if the trillions of dollars needed to finance the GND is sitting in a pot of money somewhere (the Ocasio-Cortez fallacy).

The trillions would have to be *raised* by massive taxation and debt (deferred taxation). Not implementing the GND means other proposals that earn their opportunity cost could be implemented. Consumers and firms would be less taxed, and therefore could do more productive things (like growing the pie) with the resources freed up by not implementing another government boondoggle. We may now define a government boondoggle as a government project that does not earn its opportunity cost. To understand how government spending affects private spending, and many other topics of current importance, see the reference in the endnote.[28]

If we take just the human carbon emissions goals of the IPCC to prevent "catastrophic" climate change by 2050 or by 2100 a cost benefit analysis (that is what the opportunity cost does) can be done. Robert Murphy in "Using IPCC to Defeat UN Climate Agenda," does precisely this, uses marginalism, and is easy to follow. Using the IPCC data, he shows that the marginal costs of government intervention outweigh the marginal benefits in the IPCC's *worst-case scenario*. Marginalism is discussed in this chapter.

Energy costs would dramatically increase under carbon mitigation policies—as would taxes due to carbon emissions mitigation, not to mention the costs of many other components of the GND dependent on energy.[29] You do not have to be an economist to see why the *global* poor will be impacted relatively more than others; they spend a greater proportion of their income on energy.[30]

Discussion Questions

(1) Are the global poor the collateral damage of the GND?

(2) How could item (1) occur?

(3) What are the morality issues associated with item (1).

Growth enlarges the pie that the re-distributionists wish to place under government control. The alleged incremental benefits of the GND have to offset the opportunity costs (losses on foregone uses) to make it worthwhile. They have to also offset the future, incremental direct costs.

The partisans of GND provide no such cost-benefit analysis, from which we may reasonably hypothesize that they have none. Like FDR, they wish to force it on the people. Instead of using any kind of (economic) analysis, scare tactics will do just fine. We must do *something* because—if we do not—the earth will come to an end in twelve years. The *only* alternative to the GND is apocalypse in twelve years (the forecast horizon) projected with absolute certainty. Never do the purveyors consider *model risk*—the risk that their models are wrong. FDR did not either. They simply succumb to the fallacy that there is always a unique solution to every conceivable alleged problem and the government can "fix it" with our money. This is the classic *throw money at the problem* "solution" which politicians love. Does it work?

Many heroic assumptions are being made in the ACC debate.

Single Variable Assumptions:

- man-made carbon emissions are the *main* cause of alleged global warming in that they 'drive' temperature (correlation or causation?)[31];
- atmospheric water vapor is a greenhouse gas dominated in its effects on ACC by the trace element CO_2 with which it is correlated;[32]
- solar activity and solar cycles are insignificant contributors to global warming compared to man-made carbon emissions;
- Pacific decadal oscillation and cloud cover are not other key factors that account better for global temperature than human CO_2 emissions;[33]
- natural variation cannot account for alleged global warming;
- the earth has an optimal global temperature range, and even that the global temperature of the earth can be accurately measured and compared across millennia; and
- the earth cannot adapt (as it has done for millennia) without immediate global government action to fix ACC.

Economic Assumptions:

- there are no benefits to global warming (greening of the planet for example), which is allegedly a man-made threat and the greatest threat to humanity (rhetoric);
- government policy (generally a blunt tool) will be able to fine tune the earth's temperature through the single variable, man-made carbon emissions;

- the United States alone must take the lead in curbing carbon emissions (it has already done so) in order to avert the crisis, yet *global* warming is the premise (China, the United States, and India account for about 49% of global emissions[34]); as such, it would require other nations to curb carbon emissions, in particular China and India—who want the same standard of living enjoyed in the United States;
- there is a way to force the have-less nations to abandon or reduce cost effective production, which requires cheap fossil fuels;
- the benefits of man-made C02 emissions reductions outweigh the costs; and
- enough C02 mitigation is possible through national government action before the world ends in the number of years the partisans claim they know with 100 percent certainty.

Data (Cherry Picking) Assumptions:

- the Medieval Warming Period (MWP);
- the warming period in 1915 to 1945 before man-made C02 emissions increased;
- temperatures *fell* during the 1940 to 1970 period while C02 emissions were increasing; and
- the confirmed hiatus in GW 1998 to 2014.[35] Even the IPCC has admitted its existence and has lowered its warming projections accordingly.[36] Further, there are projections of a prolonged slowdown in global warming.[37]

Scare tactics and fear mongering have been used many times before to facilitate massive government interventions, based on the hypothesis that only the government and its army of government officials can save us from ourselves.[38] And, with the rhetoric never to let a serious crisis go to waste. As a few examples: the population explosion (never happened), Malthusian resource depletion due to growth (never happened), and more.[39] One way out of the fear trap is by accumulating actual knowledge and evidence.

For those wanting to pursue this highly politicized issue, the science of which cannot be evaluated by the lay person, see the sample references in chapter 6 and in the endnote.[40] Mine is a mere sampling. For every claim, there is a counter claim and the topic makes an interesting study in rhetoric versus evidence. Climate science is not an exact science and the science of ACC is far from *settled*, least of all by consensus, except by political entities and in the minds of believers.[41]

Rhetoric has effectively turned the phrase "climate change" into a religion and hence not falsifiable.[42] This is a great opportunity for rhetoric because climate science is highly technical and the ordinary person would not be able to assess it or its predictions, which have notable failures. Agenda-driven parties then exploit the expert fallacy because they are unable to assess them either, but they can assess the value of using scientists in order to promote their own agendas. Climate change rhetoric has also resuscitated an old fallacy about science, the fallacy of the consensus of a group of experts—assuming there is such a consensus.

CHANGE: INCREMENTAL VERSUS RADICAL (REVOLUTION)

It is fun to think that *revolution* can radically change the mythical aggregate called "society" and individual behavior for the positive overnight, without bloodshed and the violation of human rights. And to think that a more conservative *incremental* approach cannot, over time, improve the lives of millions of people. Fortunately, the evidence speaks otherwise.[43]

Revolutionaries tend to be mesmerized by their own very human rhetoric and hubris, lust for power and its perks, and ideology (particularly the nirvana fallacy). Therefore, they ask the rhetorical question: why question the costs and benefits of destroying one society in order to promote another? Why indeed.

Revolutionaries seem convinced that their ideas, assuming they have any about reorganizing society, are better—without evidence. This is the know more than they actually know or can know fallacy. They tend to assume they are morally superior (elitism), adopt dichotomous thinking, and propagandize as many others as possible to adopt their pre-revolutionary views. And, they do so sometimes by threatening a penalty of death.

Of course, after they seize power, getting rid of the classic enemies of the people (by which they mean the existing rulers and their agents) is much easier. Even the people can be controlled by starvation, re-education and "concentration camps," and torture and execution as needed. All of this is rhetoric in the name of the alleged higher good: the revolution. "The ends justify the means" is the guiding, morally suspect principle.

Looking at the data, most real advances have been incremental. After all, real advances, as opposed to mere rhetoric, are based on *new* knowledge and/or the novel use of existing knowledge. Neither are easy to come by. Many real advances, as opposed to social experiments seeking to control the minds of the populace (the domain of rhetoric), are based on technological advances.

Discussion Questions

(1) Who is a revolutionary?

(2) Does merely *saying* you are a revolutionary make you one? Or, do you have to do something actually revolutionary? Why or why not?

(3) Was Marx a revolutionary? Why or why not?

(4) What does "the ends justify the means" mean?

(5) Are partisans of social justice immediately rewarded by the free good of being deemed to be morally superior, regardless of whether they have earned any moral authority? That is, by merely supporting the revolution? why or why not?

(6) Is Antifa a domestic terrorist group or a group of social justice warriors as they claim? What evidence supports your answer?

(7) Why do all dictators and certain modern day entities incite violence to achieve the revolution, and then maintain strict control of the populace when in power?

(8) Is the incitement to violence against one's opponents consistent with a free society?

(9) How does one persuade people to accept one's policy ideas in a democracy?

(10) Is it possible to implement change in a free society without force?

WEIGHING INCREMENTAL COSTS AND BENEFITS: COST BENEFIT ANALYSIS

Suppose you want to buy a house or replace your car. These are major expenditures and most consumers will naturally do a considerable amount of research on them. That research will not be done in isolation, but will hopefully result in an informed decision based on the feasible alternatives. What other alternatives are there in the real world? No perfect house/car exists and how much would such an entity cost if it did?

Now imagine the problem of replacing one economy or society with another. If you are scratching your head, that is natural because there is no obvious meaning as to what that even means or how to achieve it, let alone whether it is a good thing. Part of the problem is the fallacy of treating aggregates as if they are individuals, such as cars and houses. They are not.

This particular fallacy is particularly dangerous because it automatically identifies the custodian of society with the *state*, which then becomes the guardian of the *public good*, another aggregate which can mean almost anything and can accommodate numerous agendas and their rhetorical claims. All manner of mischief to individuals (real people) has been done in the name of these allegedly morally superior empty euphemisms.

MARGINALISM

In doing a cost-benefit analysis, there are several operative concepts. One concept is known as *marginalism*.[44] This was discovered when Marx was alive, and it displaced his wage-labor theory economic constructs. The concept is critical and has many applications in public policy. One application is in determining the relevant costs and benefits associated with a decision and thereby policy appraisal. Briefly, the relevant costs and benefits are only the marginal costs and marginal benefits, marginal compared to the status quo, not to the *total* costs and total benefits.

Discussion Questions

(1) Whose money do the government officials spend? How much? Millions, billions, trillions?

(2) Look up government spending as a percentage of gross domestic product (GDP) over time to get an idea of the magnitudes in item (1).[45]

(3) Do government officials do a full non-partisan cost-benefit analysis before embarking on their projects?

(4) Do government officials make their economic justifications available to the taxpayers so they can vote on it?

(5) What is meant by the term "government boondoggles"?

(6) What mechanisms are in place to regulate the government and prevent it from allocating funds to more and bigger partisan government boondoggles?

Examples

Next, we will give some examples of marginal reasoning—without a complete cost-benefit analysis—applied to major proposals. We have already discussed minimum wage laws but will emphasize the marginal effects here. The way to determine whether something is a marginal effect is through *with/without analysis*. If an effect will occur when the project is accepted and also when it is not accepted, then it is not marginal. Otherwise, it is marginal.

We next illustrate the concepts by providing newsworthy examples of marginal costs and benefits. These include (1) health care insurance: private, public, or private-public mix?, (2) gun control and perverse incentives, (3) illegal immigration and sanctuary cities and, (4) trade and trade policy. Additional important topics, which we will not discuss due to space limitations, lend themselves well to marginal analysis. These are (4) government debt policy and (5) tax policy.

Marginalism applies very well to each of these major issues and to many more. A full cost-benefit analysis of each of these examples would take many pages and much research. Some of it is online, along with the partisan rhetoric of which there is much more. We hope the reader will get the basic idea and incorporate it and the opportunity cost idea into their own reasoning about public policy. These concepts will help the reader to cut through the rhetoric.

Health Care Insurance: Private, Public, or Private-Public Mix?

Government intervention and takeover of the health care insurance system has numerous marginal effects which have to be considered in analyzing them, as noted by Sally C. Pipes, *The False Promise of Single-Payer Health Care*, and Michael J. Boskin, *A Closer Look at the Left's Agenda*.[46] The rhetoric is much simpler because all it has to do is appeal to emotions.

"Let's get everyone covered" is the billboard slogan. The magic words sufficient for political purposes are "everyone" and "covered." They sound good but they also beg the real questions which are: what exactly does "covered" mean and at what cost? The devil is in the details of implementation and unintended consequences, as well as in prices. Government officials like to think that they can dictate prices for things they think they can control, but they cannot dictate the responses of human beings. That is why they try to force people to buy their product through the "individual mandate" for example, and their monopoly power. Private providers do not have these luxuries, are forced to compete (a good thing), and must meet the needs of consumers.

Just because you are formally covered does not mean you have timely access to quality health care, nor does it mean you are not paying for it, nor that you can get the procedures you need in a timely fashion. There are costs associated with dealing with the government's army of anonymous, unelected, and unaccountable officials shielded from competition of any kind—and with standing in endless lines to access your allegedly free health care. Standing in line has opportunity costs. None of this is pure theory, government health care insurance has been tried in numerous countries. So we can and should look at the historical experience.

Economists would tend to say that the most efficient (lowest cost) producer should produce a product in a competitive market. This rules out the government which has little incentive to reduce costs because those costs can always be passed on to the consumer, in this case to all taxpayers. The reason the government is even on the list is that, since it can tax everyone, it can in theory provide and force its one-size-fits-all model on everyone.

The private sector can tax no one (profits are the wages of entrepreneurs and are not a tax) and must compete to *earn* their business, something the government does not have to do because it has a monopoly and mandate power. It can literally force people, by penalty, to buy its products, the constitutionality of which is still being debated. The *Affordable Care Act* was later renamed *Obamacare* because it was anything but affordable to everyone and it included just such a provision. How this act was passed is interesting.[47] The GOP tax bill removed the individual mandate in late 2017. This is a victory for the freedom of individuals.

Of course, an evidence-based approach would ask how the government is able to make anything "affordable" except by declaring it so, as per the rhetoric-based approach. It would also ask "affordable" relative to what, and to whom?[48]

This discussion shows that one of the main marginal effects associated with the government's takeover of the health care insurance industry is the consequent loss of freedom to individuals. First, in being taxed to pay for it, then in being forced to buy it, since there are no alternatives. The government's army of officials is aware of these issues so invents things like *stealth taxes* to hide their taxation, not to mention outright falsification to get the uninformed public's buy in.[49] Then there are all the shell games it can play by giving "subsidies" to some financed by other taxpayers who are forced to pay for them. Recall that America was founded on the premise of "no taxation without representation."[50]

Are there any marginal benefits to government mandated health care insurance? Since it is based on restricting choice, the research one needs to do to find a private plan is reduced. You think you know exactly what you are getting, and cannot choose much anyway. Of course, like private premiums, taxes to finance health care insurance can and do go up. The government, as for any private producer, faces production costs and these change. Restricting output to reduce costs serves to raise prices and reduce access.

Another piece of partisan rhetoric is simply comparing health care spending cross-sectionally across countries, as if all countries provide the same levels and quality of health care and are directly comparable. We encountered this problem in the more gun control debate. If you spend twice as much on a better car than the median citizen, are you worse off? People's preference for health care *insurance* (not the same thing as health *care*) are diverse. One size of government health insurance and health care does not suit all. It just forces them to fit the mold, and again experience a loss of freedom to choose.[51]

Another loss of freedom is the marginal effect of the increased health care records on hackable servers. This incentivizes a black market (compare with gun control) of hackers who use persons' supposedly private health records to target them for product sales.

Another marginal effect is that, since the government (not they themselves people think) is "paying" for the health care services it is providing (think Medicare) it can and does restrict the coverage (think cataract surgery). It can and does tell doctors, who are paid by the government, how long they can spend with each in the huge queue of patients—thereby reducing the quality of their interactions and the chance of missing something important. Wait times are a drag on personal earnings and endanger lives. People die under single-payer plans, not because they have no health insurance (the straw man), but because it does not perform for the consumer.

Also, the paperwork demands of accounting to the government for costs wastes the medical resources of health care providers. The government is aware of costs, while not a cost minimizer. Finally, what reason is there to believe that the government has a comparative advantage in an industry about which it knows little? Nor does it have the power through ineffective price controls to make anything affordable, one of the biggest rhetorical propaganda ploys ever. Look at the record discussed earlier.

A modern example of the issues raised in the last paragraph is the housing crisis in California.[52] Lawrence J. McQuillan and Graham H. Walker note:

> But let's face it, here's what's really happening: First California passes laws that generate the crisis, then we declare a state of emergency to bypass those laws. But as a State of Emergency exemption, it's an ad-hoc fix. It doesn't address the systemic problem with the laws it sidesteps, and in fact it politicizes the whole situation further by allowing sensible construction only if political support for a formal Emergency can be cultivated.
>
> The homeless are indeed "victims of the system," but not the system that most people think of. They are not victims of a free market in housing, because California has built a regulatory system that killed a free market in housing at all but the top price levels. Middle-income Californians are squeezed by this, too, but the most vulnerable Californians are pushed out on to the streets. The bottom rungs of the housing market ladder—where economically marginal citizens could once afford a place to live—have effectively been removed by bad public policy.

Another marginal effect is the reduced *supply* of doctors who are dismayed by the thought of essentially becoming government officials versus practicing medicine. This increases the cost of health care by reducing the supply of health care providers and feeds the glut even more. In so far as a private system has less accounting to the government (for example, non-Medicare), the effect noted is a marginal effect. It also incentivizes a brain drain, where the most talented health care providers simply exit the system. That exit is not neutral, it reduces the overall quality of health care.

The main marginal (?) benefit to government health care is its alleged lower cost as a percentage of GDP. This claim is not adjusted for quality differences and uses notoriously unreliable cross-sectional data. As noted, gun control rhetoric suffers from the same defect. Note that the government *not paying* costs by restricting access (supply) means you are not eligible to get the services you may need. It is far from obvious that the cost of health care is reduced under the government relative to private health insurers. Why would it be? *Competition*, not monopoly, leads to lower prices for consumers. Why should the government be the lowest cost provider? Being the *only* provider begs the question as to whether it is the lowest cost provider.

Private health care allows you to buy and to pay for what you want and get, and private health care insurance covers much of it. "Medicare for All," is a conveniently fair sounding rhetoric brought to you by the partisans. What is fair about dying of a disease the medical care for which the government's army of officials determines you are not eligible? Or, how would you feel about waiting in line months or years for services, if you survive the wait that is? Do those scenarios sound fair?[53] Fairness usually degenerates into *partisanship* with the qualifier "fair for me and my group." It permits discrimination as well because fairness is in the eyes of the beholder.

The last thing we want is for politicians and the government's army of faceless, unaccountable government officials to have the power to determine what is fair and what is not fair, who lives and who dies. They have conflicts of interest and are not ethicists.

Here is another marginal effect: innovation (new cures, new technology, new drugs) are incentivized by profits. Therefore, public health care systems squelch innovation. The government, not the profit incentive, controls how much is spent on research and development. This is one unintended, but predictable, effect of price controls on drug prices. Less research on new life-saving drugs will occur under those regimes and the quality of drugs produced will also suffer because generics are cheap knock-offs of the real drugs.

Perhaps the government itself is partially responsible for raising drug prices through its regulations for drug approval? How? It is because such government intervention increases the costs of producing drugs that must pass the government's hurdles. If you doubt this, take a look at rent-controlled properties. Is it a big surprise that its caretakers are loathe to take care of them? The lower the supply price of a commodity or service, the less investment in it will be made.

Other marginal effects of a switch to a single payer health care system are the marginal costs and the marginal benefits. The alleged marginal cost (savings?) are never spelled out, and the assumption is that it is the same health care (not restricted relative to the current mix). Of course, to achieve cost containment, it would be restricted, and therefore, the comparison to the status quo is invalid.

Gun Control and Perverse Incentives

We already briefly discussed gun *control* in chapter 6 and the rhetoric that the government can control the proliferation of guns. This is a partisan title that begs the question: do gun laws actually control the prevalence of guns and gun homicides? Gun controls do not control *illegal* guns, just like prohibition laws in the 1920s did not control alcohol consumption (it increased). Can we have gun control without stiff prosecution of gun crimes resulting in, yes, incarceration?

The term "gun control" is like price controls with its history of utter failure. Gun control laws simply try to keep guns out of the hands of *some*, not all, people attempting to buy guns *legally*. Even when government regulation is effective, and it hardly ever is, the underlying demand for guns does not disappear.[54]

That demand will be supplied by the world-wide black market (not just neighboring states as the rhetoric claims), which will be more active the more the gun controls. The *total* number of guns, legal plus illegal, may even grow. More importantly, gun control laws shift gun ownership in a way that favors the criminals (who are *incentivized* to have relatively more guns), and disarms the law abiding (who now have relatively fewer guns).[55] The likely consequence is more gun crimes against the now more disarmed law-abiding. Consider the following economic argument.

If you make it more costly (direct plus indirect costs) to legally acquire guns for legitimate purposes such as self-defense, then legitimate people will buy fewer of them.[56] This is economics 101, demand is downward sloping unless completely inelastic.[57] The illegal users (criminals) know this and now have more incentive (because their targets are now relatively more disarmed), evade the ineffective gun control laws by acquiring their guns in the black market, and now target more law-abiding people. Gun crimes against legitimate people go *up* not down. The policy therefore more likely has the exact opposite effect of that intended, namely to protect innocent people. It arms the perpetrators and disarms the victims.

In summary, controlling who owns guns will just create a vigorous black market as it did in Australia, and criminals will bypass the regulations no matter how many regulations there are. According to the U.S. Department of

Justice "Special Report on Source and Use of Firearms Involved in Crimes: Survey of Prison Inmates, 2016" published in January, 2019: "Among prisoners who possessed a gun during their offense, 90% did not obtain it from a retail source. Among prisoners who possessed a firearm during their offense, 0.8% obtained it at a gun show."[58]

To meet the demand, illegal guns will be imported (not just across state lines), and relatively more guns will be in the hands of the bad guys, and relatively fewer in the hands of the good guys.

This is an economic argument and it needs to be addressed by policy wonks and the partisans. We do not have complete data for everything, such as undetected criminal behavior. So we must use all the tools at our disposal and that includes valid economic reasoning.

As to counter views, it is incumbent upon the holders of such views to demonstrate that they possess the required skills (including understanding basic economics) to make informed policy appraisals and to present valid counter arguments, and not just pretend they exist, use the relativism fallacy that all assertions are equally valid, and fail to provide any (counter) evidence. But rhetoric (disguised as counter "views") rarely does so, contenting itself with denying all theory and all data that contradicts its narrative. Then it slickly attempts to pass the burden of proof on to its opponents (prove me wrong) while sitting back and applying the pot shot fallacy. No amount of evidence is able to change the narrative (the nirvana fallacy).

Theory, history and evidence have shown that governments do not have the ability to prevent the formation and operation of black markets. Every regulation carries with it the incentive to bypass it, and black markets are an example of this. We have modern examples to illustrate this. Further, you cannot have "gun control" without vigorous *prosecution* of gun crimes. In complete contradiction to their gun control advocacy, some high profile politicians (including ex-President Obama), do not believe in stiff prosecution nor in incarceration. You cannot have it both ways.[59]

Discussion Question

(1) Is there any reason to fear the consequences of government bans on guns?[60]

Illegal Immigration and Sanctuary Cities

This issue is one of the hot button issues which is almost completely dominated by rhetoric and dichotomous thinking. One of the problems is that, before you can examine the marginal effects, you have to have the data, which is hard or impossible to come by. In a world without the actual data, partisan rhetoric dominates.[61]

Also there is the failure to apply the definitions, as well as illegality and gaming the system. An *asylum seeker* is not the same as an *economic migrant*, although the categories are not mutually exclusive. Who people declare themselves to be to gain entry to a country is not necessarily who they are. The "fallacy of composition" is rampant here: all immigrants are asylum seekers because some are.

Also the knowing-more-than-we-know-or-can-know fallacy and dichotomous thinking (false dichotomies). We do not know what we do not know. That includes knowing that we do not know. For example, how do we know that every family unit actually is a family unit? So the recent rhetorical charge of "tearing children away from their [alleged] parents" would be a *good* thing if the adult with a child is really a trafficker.

Nonetheless, we can discuss the marginal effects and let the purveyors back up their numerical speculations with real evidence, not rhetoric, to earn credibility. Here is another economic argument. It is in the interest of a country to get rid of its worst. That is, to export them. That is also why such countries do not want them back. They are expensive in many ways. For example, the British Isles sent its criminals to populate America. Why would other countries not do the same? The idea is cost reduction or minimization.

Therefore, one of the marginal negative effects of increased illegal immigration would be the increased numbers of criminals, including terrorists, entering the country. A country with laws basically wants legal immigrants. Another marginal effect of illegal immigration is their increased use of welfare resources. This is why the United States, Canada, and other countries demand that potential legal immigrants provide *proof* that they can support themselves, including references to others who will guarantee it. Working immigrants are fine, as needed, because they contribute to growing the economy and they pay taxes (which fills the government coffers). Both of these are marginal effects. Seasonal workers are a separate case in that they have a comparative advantage relative to local workers.

Among sanctuary cities' marginal effects are to incentivize criminal illegal immigrants to settle there. Where would you rather be if you were a criminal: in a sanctuary city or a non-sanctuary city? The alleged benefit of sharing information about criminals is counter to basic economics and, if it exists, it is not publicly documented. Further there is a special U nonimmigrant status (U visas) for those who do want to share such information.[62] The contention that sanctuary cities are safer than non-sanctuary cities (if true and there is no evidence that it is) confuses correlation with causation. All of the other variables contributing to relative crime rates have to be held constant. One cannot simply compare raw crime rates, assumed to be available. And where exactly are the government data (not the rhetoric) and comparisons available?

An interesting piece of rhetoric is that the *only* factor in not sharing crime information is an illegal immigrant's fear of being deported, presumably obviated by sanctuary city status. This is the *fallacy of uniqueness,* which is related to confusing correlation with causation. What about the fear of being murdered by gangs and cartel members for snitching on them?

We will let the reader investigate this issue further, using the marginalism tool as well as the other economic and data-based concepts discussed in this chapter. And, once again to cut through the fog of the rhetoric, no matter how many times and with what selective moral outrage it is repeated in the media's echo chambers.

Trade and Trade Policy

As Thomas Sowell in *Economic Facts and Fallacies* outlines, economics is a hot-bed for fallacies.[63] Trade in particular can be easily politicized with the standard protectionist rhetoric. In order to pave the way for a rational discussion of trade, we will have to do a little preparatory clarification. One source of major error is the failure to distinguish between accounting statements such as the national income identity and dynamic economic analysis. The national income identity states:

$GDP = C + I + G + (X - M)$ where

GDP=Gross domestic product (the nation's output),

C=Consumer spending on *consumer* goods and services, foreign and domestic,

I=Investment spending on *business* capital goods, foreign and domestic,

G=Government spending on *public* goods and services, foreign and domestic,

X=Exports, and

M=Imports

The first fallacy is *that imports* M *are a drag* on GDP because they get subtracted in the national income identity. However, the reason imports are subtracted is that they are *already counted* in C, I, G, and X, and the whole point of the GDP measurement is to measure *domestic* expenditure. C, I, G, and X include expenditures on foreign goods (imports).

Therefore, to get (*domestic*) GDP we *have to* subtract imports M in the equation. Since imports will then not be included in GDP they cannot affect it in the direct way indicated by the accounting identity.[64] We will also consider whether imports affect GDP in an economic sense and if so, how.

Another fallacy is generated by the brackets around X-M in the national accounting identity. The error here is that if imports do not matter then *ex-*

ports minus imports obviously do matter, as indicated in the identity. X-M is called the *trade balance*, also known as the *current account*. It is in deficit if we export less than we import or in surplus if, like China, they export more to the United States than they import from the United States.

Which is better, according to this fallacy? Well, if $X > M$ (exports exceed imports) then X - M adds a positive amount to the other terms (assumed to not change) *raising* GDP according to the error, while if $X < M$ the opposite happens and GDP is reduced. Therefore, in order to raise its GDP through trade, a country ought to try to maximize exports and minimize imports and enjoy a *more favorable* trade balance, which usually means a trade surplus. This is classic mercantilism. The alternative is to run a trade *deficit*, but deficits are allegedly bad because of the false analogy to government *budget* deficits which must ultimately be repaid. Trade deficits, according to this fallacy, are viewed as some kind of debt.

The mercantilists were business men and business men tend to think in terms of profits and losses. Imports are things we buy from foreigners. Therefore, the reasoning goes, they *cost us* dollars. Those dollars are viewed as *outflows* in a profit/loss statement. Exports are things we sell to foreigners. Therefore they *pay us* dollars. Those dollars are viewed as *inflows* in a profit/loss statement. If you run the country by analogy to a private business, then you might want to maximize profits. This would entail minimizing costs (imports) and maximizing revenues (exports), precisely the mercantilist point of view.[65]

Mercantilism sounds perfectly commonsensical but common sense is not always a good guide to the foreign trade policy of a country, nor is it static. The mercantilist view is predicated on the assumption that a country is analogous to a private firm and should be managed as such.

Discussion Question:

(1) Should a country be run like a firm? Why? Why not?

However, you cannot prove anything with tautological identities. Here is an example showing that, by rearranging the identity, a diametrically opposite policy implication follows. Take the national income identity GDP = C + I + G + (X − M) and move consumer spending (consumption), government consumption (spending), and private sector investment spending, C + G + I , to one side. Then

C + G + I = GDP + (M - X)

This says that total consumption (the end purpose of production), C + G + I, is equal to domestic consumption (GDP) plus consumption of

174   *Chapter Eight*

foreign imported goods M minus non-consumption of exports X. Namely it is equal to GDP plus imports minus exports (what we do not consume). Holding everything else constant, a country should therefore attempt to maximize imports and minimize exports. This is just the opposite of the mercantilist policy.[66]

Under this alternative view, it is not the *dollar flows* that matter, but rather the *commodity flows*. After all, that is what trade is about as in a barter system. Why we trade is the important question. When we trade we exchange our goods for the goods of another country, according to the terms of trade. We get imports in return for exports. Imports are now the benefit and exports are now the cost. Nonetheless, it is not possible to simply maximize imports and minimize exports.

The *merchandise* trade balance (current account) ignores the *capital* side of trade. That is reflected in the *capital account* and it balances the current account. What this means is that the *total* value of goods (including capital) that a country exports to a trading partner must be equal to the total value of goods (including capital) that the country imports from a trading partner. In effect when all trade is taken into account there is no trade imbalance.[67] An example of a capital account trade is the Industrial & Commercial Bank of China's lease of office space in Trump towers.[68]

How could it be that, in equilibrium, what we exchange with another country (exports) in return for what they exchange with us (imports) can be chronically different in value? If it were then one party would definitely be worse (better) off than the counterparty.

If we import more goods from another country than we export to them, then they end up with a surplus of dollars which would be invested in dollar denominated US capital (for example in financial assets like US Treasury bonds, and/or in real assets like US real estate). After all, something has to be done by someone with the US dollars.

Accounting for these transactions is in the US capital account. Thus, running a merchandise trade deficit is tantamount to running a US trade *surplus* in capital. This makes up for the deficit in the current account: we simply sell (export financial and real capital) to make up for the shortfall in the amount we export in merchandise. In this way total exports are equalized to total imports and the total trade positions balance.

In order to dig ourselves out from the fallacies of foreign trade we can ask in this brief summary: what determines the manufacturing trade balance of a country?[69] The national accounting identity does not say—because it is simply an accounting of C, G, I, M, and X as components of GDP.

The answer is the domestic savings (S), domestic investment (I) profile of the country, specifically S - I. This can be shown to be equal to the X – M.[70]

Countries that have more domestic investment opportunities than national savings have a manufactured goods trade deficit. Other countries that save more than they invest domestically have a manufactured goods trade surplus. Their respective S - I is one main reason they trade with each other.

If a country, say the United States, has a manufactured goods trade deficit with another country, say China, then domestic savings are insufficient to support our desired level of domestic investment. To make up the difference, the country with the deficit will sell some of its *capital* to the surplus nation. The country with the deficit has now been enabled to pursue its excess domestic investments. The country with the surplus has now found a home for its excess domestic savings. The total trade balance, capital plus current account, has been reduced to zero. Trade has benefited *both* parties (therefore trade is not a zero sum game) who voluntarily entered the exchange relationship.

As to jobs lost or gained from trade, the research indicates that a trade deficit (or a surplus) creates no *overall* job loss.[71] The *pattern* of trade (export versus import sensitive) definitely affects the *mix* of jobs (and the resulting winners and losers)—and this is a politically sensitive issue. Tariffs are a politicized issue as well, but they are essentially taxes and can be analyzed as such, with emphasis on their incidence.[72]

NOTES

1. Natalie Musumeci, "Ocasio-Cortez Finds Amazon's HQ2 in NYC 'Extremely Concerning,'" *New York Post*, November 13, 2018, https://nypost.com/2018/11/13/ocasio-cortez-finds-amazons-hq2-in-nyc-extremely-concerning (accessed November 24, 2019).

2. Unless you are a partisan and it gets you votes and the power to be unaccountable, and to enrich yourself and your cronies at the expense of others who foot the bill. It clearly is not morally superior in that case either. It is just based on pure self interest, nothing more.

3. Ludwig von Mises, *The Anti-Capitalistic Mentality* (Princeton, NJ: D. Van Nostrand, 1956; repr. Auburn, AL: Ludwig Von Mises Institute, 2008), available online at https://mises.org/library/anti-capitalistic-mentality (accessed November 25, 2019).

4. Moreover, why should we assume that any special interest group of partisans, and they alone, are morally superior? Where is any evidence to that effect other than their rhetoric to that effect ? In many cases their actions do not support their rhetoric when, and if, they are revealed as shameless hypocrites and self-seeking partisans. The reader can find numerous examples of the latter.

5. Bryan Caplan, "Utopian Experimental Socialism," *Library of Economics and Liberty*, 2012, https://www.econlib.org/archives/2012/10/utopian_experim.html (accessed November 25, 2019).

6. Richard M. Ebeling, "Socialism, Like Dracula, Rises Again from the Grave," *American Institute for Economic Research*, July 16, 2018, https://www.aier.org/article/socialism-like-dracula-rises-again-from-the-grave (accessed December 18, 2019); and Robert Heilbroner, "The World After Communism," *Dissent* (Fall 1990): 429–30; repr. rev. ed. "Socialism," *Library of Economics and Liberty*, n.d., https://www.econlib.org/library/Enc/Socialism.html (accessed November 25, 2019).

7. Thomas C. Leonard, *Illiberal Reformers: Race, Eugenics, and American Economics in the Progressive Era* (Princeton, NJ: Princeton University Press, 2016; repr. ed. 2017).

8. Logically Fallacious, "Nirvana Fallacy," *Logically Fallacious*, n.d., https://www.logicallyfallacious.com/logicalfallacies/Nirvana-Fallacy (accessed November 25, 2019).

9. See the book by Nima Sanandaji, *Debunking Utopia: Exposing the Myth of Nordic Socialism* (Washington, DC: WND Books, 2016), examines the nirvana myth applied to Nordic socialism.

10. Philip Klein, "AOC's Chief of Staff Comments Just Killed the Green New Deal," July 12, 2019, *Washington Examiner*, https://www.washingtonexaminer.com/opinion/aocs-chief-of-staff-just-killed-the-green-new-deal (accessed November 25, 2019).

11. Mundi Index, "C02 Emissions (Metric Tons per Capita)—Country Ranking," *MundiIndex*, 2014, https://www.indexmundi.com/facts/indicators/EN.ATM.CO2E.PC/rankings (accessed November 24, 2019).

12. Per capita versus total is an important distinction here. Total is the relevant units since total carbon emissions is the hypothesized variable.

13. World Data Info., "Greenhouse Gases Emissions by Country," *WorldData*, c. 2012, https://www.worlddata.info/greenhouse-gas-by-country.php (accessed November 24, 2019).

14. However, the EPA has an interactive site with data through 2017. See U.S. Environmental Protection Agency (EPA), "Greenhouse Gas Inventory Data Explorer," n.d., https://cfpub.epa.gov/ghgdata/inventoryexplorer (accessed January 24, 2020).

15. World Data Info., "Greenhouse Gases."

16. Mundi Index, "C02 Emissions"; and World Data Info., "Greenhouse Gases."

17. Mundi Index, "C02 Emissions."

18. William Happer, "C02 Is Not a Pollutant: Debunking a Global-Warming Myth," *Public Discourse*, December 1, 2009, https://www.thepublicdiscourse.com/2009/12/1037 (accessed November 26, 2019).

19. Robert P. Murphy, "Using IPCC to Defeat UN Climate Agenda," *Institute for Energy Research* (*IER*), September 23, 2014, https://www.instituteforenergyresearch.org/climate-change/using-ipcc-defeat-un-climate-agenda (accessed November 25, 2019).

20. Isabel Vincent and Melissa Klein, "Gas-Guzzling Car Rides Expose AOC's Hypocrisy Amid Green New Deal Pledge," *New York Post*, March 2, 2019, https://nypost.com/2019/03/02/gas-guzzling-car-rides-expose-aocs-hypocrisy-amid-green-new-deal-pledge (accessed December 18, 2019).

21. The defense of Alexandria Ocasio-Cortez that other politicians also use relatively high carbon emitting forms of transportation illustrates the Tu Quoque fallacy. It does not excuse her. The defense, a distraction, also ignores that some other politicians do not agree with her green new deal. The benefit of carbon emissions is increasing productivity (for one of many examples, not wasting time travelling) and it illustrates the tradeoff.

22. Is this a utopian social experiment implying socialism? See Kevin D. Williamson, "Capitalism Is Clean(er)," *National Review*, September 25, 2014, https://www.nationalreview.com/2014/09/capitalism-cleaner-kevin-d-williamson (accessed November 25, 2019). See also Claire Curtis, Ishmael Russell, and Lucas Russell, "Increasing Carbon Dioxide Levels Affect Plant Growth," YouTube video, 10:10, posted by G. Morwong, October 29, 2015, https://www.youtube.com/watch?v=0NFu4QBIXRw (accessed November 25, 2019); and CFACT editors, "Seeing the C02 Greening of Plant Earth," *CFACT*, March 8, 2018, https://www.cfact.org/2018/03/08/seeing-the-co2-greening-of-planet-earth/ (accessed November 25, 2019).

23. John O'Sullivan, "Breaking: Fatal Courtroom Acts Ruins Michael "Hockey Stick" Mann," *Principia Scientifica*, July 4, 2017, https://principia-scientific.org/breaking-fatal-courtroom-act-ruins-michael-hockey-stick-mann (accessed November 25, 2019).

24. See Richard Muller, "Global Warming Bombshell: A Prime Piece of Evidence Linking Human Activity to Climate Change Turns Out to be an Artifact of Poor Mathematics," *MIT Technology Review*, October 15, 2004, https://www.technologyreview.com/s/403256/global-warming-bombshell (accessed November 25, 2019); and Stephen McIntyre and Ross McKitrick, "Hockey Sticks, Principal Components, and Spurious Significance," *Geophysical Research Letters* 32, L03710, February 12, 2005, http://www.climatcaudit.info/pdf/mcintyre.mckitrick.2005.grl.pdf (accessed November 25, 2019).

25. Ian Tuttle, "The 97 Percent Solution," *National Review*, October 8, 2015, https://www.nationalreview.com/2015/10/climate-change-no-its-not-97-percent-consensus-ian-tuttle (accessed November 25, 2019).

26. Richard P. Feynman, "What Is Science?" to the National Science Teachers' Association convention, April 1966, reprinted in Richard P. Feynman, *The Pleasure of Finding Things Out: The Best Short Works of Richard P. Feynman*, ed. Jeffrey Robbins (New York: Basic Books, 1999; repr. 2005), 187.

27. Jim Powell, *FDR's Follies: How Roosevelt and His New Deal Prolonged the Great Depression* (New York: Three Rivers Press, 2003); and Gene Smiley, *Rethinking the Great Depression: A New View of Its Causes and Consequences* (Chicago: I. R. Dee, 2002).

28. Henry Hazlitt, *Economics in One Lesson* (Fiftieth Anniversary Edition) (Baltimore: Laissez Faire Books, 1996), 25–26.

29. Douglas Holtz-Eakin, Dan Bosch, Ben Gitis, Dan Goldbeck, and Philip Rossetti, "The Green New Deal: Scope, Scale, and Implications," *American Action Forum (AAF)*, February 25, 2019, https://www.americanactionforum.org/research/the-green-new-deal-scope-scale-and-implications (accessed December 18, 2019).

30. Bjørn Lomborg, "How Green Policies Hurt the Poor," *Spectator*, April 5, 2014, https://www.spectator.co.uk/2014/04/let-them-eat-carbon-credits (accessed December 18. 2019); and Craig Richardson, "The 'Green New Deal' Is a Prescription for Poverty," *Washington Examiner*, January 28, 2019, https://www.washingtonexaminer.com/opinion/op-eds/the-green-new-deal-is-a-prescription-for-poverty (accessed December 18, 2019).

31. D. J. Easterbrook. "Greenhouse Gases," in *Evidence-Based Climate Science (Second Edition)*. *Elsevier Science Direct*, September 23, 2016, 163–73, https://www.sciencedirect.com/science/article/pii/B9780128045886000094 (accessed November 25, 2019).

32. D. J. Easterbrook, "Water Vapor," in *Evidence-Based Climate Science (Second Edition)*. *Elsevier Science Direct*, September 23, 2016, 163–73, https://www.sciencedirect.com/topics/earth-and-planetary-sciences/water-vapor (accessed November 25, 2019).

33. J. [Jyrki] Kauppinen and P. [Pekka] Malmi, "No Experimental Evidence for the Significant Anthropogenic Climate Change," *arXiv* (Cornell University Open Access), July 13, 2019, https://arxiv.org/pdf/1907.00165.pdf (accessed November 25, 2019); and D. J. Easterbrook, "Pacific Decadal Oscillation," in *Evidence-Based Climate Science (Second Edition)*. *Elsevier Science Direct*, September 23, 2016, 395–411, https://www.sciencedirect.com/topics/earth-and-planetary-sciences/pacific-decadal-oscillation (accessed November 25, 2019).

34. Tyler Durden, "All the World's Carbon Emissions In One Chart," *ZeroHedge*, June 7, 2019, https://www.zerohedge.com/news/2019-06-06/all-worlds-carbon-emissions-one-chart (accessed November 25, 2019).

35. Robert Tracinski, "Global Warming: The Theory that Predicts Nothing and Explains Everything," *Federalist*, n.d., https://thefederalist.com/2015/06/08/global-warming-the-theory-that-predicts-nothing-and-explains-everything (accessed November 25, 2019); Ronald Bailey, "Global Warming Hiatus Is Real," *Reason*, February 24, 2016, https://reason.com/2016/02/24/global-warming-hiatus-is-real/ (accessed November 25, 2019); and Ryan Maue, "You Ought to Have a Look: Time for a New 'Hiatus' in Warming, or Time for an Accelerated Warming Trend?" *Cato Institute* (blog), May 25, 2017, https://www.cato.org/blog/you-ought-have-look-time-new-hiatus-warming-or-time-accelerated-warming-trend (accessed November 25, 2019).

36. See chapter 9, box 9.2, 769–72; and chapter 11, 1010–11, with particular emphasis on figure 11.25, on 1011, in Intergovernmental Panel on Climate Change (IPCC), "Climate Change 2013: The Physical Science Basis," *Contribution of Working Group I (WGI) to the Fifth Assessment Report (AR5) of the Intergovernmental Panel on Climate Change (IPCC)*, 2013, http://www.climatechange2013.org/report/full-report (accessed December 17, 2019).

37. Thomas R. Knutson, Rong Zhang, and Larry W. Horowitz, "Prospects for a Prolonged Slowdown in Global Warming in the Early 21st Century," *Nature Communications* 7, no. 13676 (2016): 1–12. https://doi.org/10.1038/ncomms13676 (accessed January 18, 2020).

38. Robert Higgs, "Fear: The Foundation of Every Government's Power," *Independent Institute*, May 17, 2005, https://www.independent.org/publications/article.asp?id=1510 (accessed November 25, 2019).

39. Mark J. Perry, "18 Spectacularly Wrong Predictions Made Around the Time of First Earth Day in 1970, Expect More This Year," *AEIdeas* (blog), April 20, 2017, https://www.aei.org/carpe-diem/18-spectacularly-wrong-predictions-made-around-the-time-of-first-earth-day-in-1970-expect-more-this-year (accessed November 25, 2019).

40. Daniel Greenfield, "The Environmental Apocalypse: The Movement to Destroy Human Civilization as We Know It," *Frontpage*, July 13, 2013, https://www.frontpagemag.com/fpm/198937/environmental-apocalypse-daniel-greenfield (accessed November 25, 2019); Benjamin Zycher, "Earth Day 2019: The Sixth Mass Extinction and the Imperative of Apocalypse," *AEIdeas*, April 22, 2019, https://www.aei.org/articles/earth-day-2019-the-sixth-mass-extinction-and-the-imperative-of-apocalypse (accessed November 25, 2019); and Robert M. Carter, "Why Scientists Disagree About Global Warming," *Heartland Institute*, November 30, 2015, https://www.heartland.org/news-opinion/news/why-scientists-disagree-about-global-warming (accessed November 25, 2019); Jonathan S. Tobin, "Doubling Down on Global-Warming Alarmism," *National Review*, October 11, 2018, https://www.nationalreview.com/2018/10/global-warming-ipcc-doubles-down (accessed November 25, 2019); Caleb Rossiter, "The Scientific Consensus On Global Warming Does Not Support the Green New Deal," *Federalist*, March 7, 2019, https://thefederalist.com/2019/03/07/scientific-consensus-global-warming-not-support-green-new-deal (accessed November 25, 2019).

41. To see this, look at the hundreds of papers that are published about climate change with claims and counterclaims, evidence and counterevidence, not to mention the papers that do not get published because they challenge the status quo.

42. Peter Ferrara, "The Disgraceful Episode of Lysenkoism Brings Us Global Warming Theory," *Forbes*, April 28, 2013, https://www.forbes.com/sites/peterferrara/2013/04/28/the-disgraceful-episode-of-lysenkoism-brings-us-global-warming-theory/#1d3664207ac8 (accessed November 25, 2019).

43. Michael McConnell and Steve Thompson, "What Is a Revolution?" *Alpha History*, June 20, 2018, https://alphahistory.com/vcehistory/what-is-a-revolution (accessed November 25, 2019); and David A. Bell, "Why Sanders Should Stop Talkin' 'Bout a Revolution," *Politico*, February 29, 2016, https://www.politico.com/magazine/story/2016/02/bernie-sanders-revolution-donald-trump-2016-213684 (accessed November 25, 2019).

44. Steven E. Rhoads, "Marginalism," *Library of Economics and Liberty*, n.d., https://www.econlib.org/library/Enc/Marginalism.html (accessed November 25, 2019).

45. U.S. Bureau of Labor Statistics, FRED, "Federal Net Outlays as Percent of Gross Domestic Product," 2019, https://fred.stlouisfed.org/series/FYONGDA188S (accessed November 25, 2018).

46. Sally C. Pipes, *The False Promise of Single-Payer Health Care* (New York: Encounter Broadside, 2018); and Michael J. Boskin, *A Closer Look at the Left's*

Agenda: Scientific, Economic, and Numerical Illiteracy on the Campaign Trail, (Stanford, CA: Hoover Institution, Stanford University, 2019), available online at http://hoover.org/sites/default/files/research/docs/a-closer-look-at-the-lefts-agenda-scientific-economic-and-numerical-illiteracy-on-the-campaign-trail.pdf (accessed November 25, 2019).

47. Gary Price and Tim Norbeck, "A Look Back at How the President Was Able to Sign Obamacare Into Law Four Years Ago," *Forbes*, March 26, 2014, https://www.forbes.com/sites/physiciansfoundation/2014/03/26/a-look-back-at-how-the-president-was-able-to-sign-obamacare-into-law-four-years-ago/#71ebfca526b7 (accessed November 25, 2019).

48. eHealth, "Health Insurance Price Index Report: 2018 Open Enrollment Period," *eHealth*, September 2018, http://news.ehealthinsurance.com/_ir/68/20188/eHealth%20Health%20Insurance%20Index%20Report%20for%20the%202018%20OEP.pdf (accessed November 25, 2019); and Robert Book, "Yes, It Was the 'Affordable' Care Act That Increased Premiums," *Forbes*, March 22, 2017, https://www.forbes.com/sites/theapothecary/2017/03/22/yes-it-was-the-affordable-care-act-that-increased-premiums/#796c4b0211d2 (accessed November 25, 2019).

49. David Zeiler, "Warning: Hidden Obamacare Taxes Will Cost You More Than You Think," *Money Morning*, August 5, 2012, https://moneymorning.com/2012/08/05/warning-hidden-obamacare-taxes-will-cost-you-more-than-you-think (accessed November 25, 2019).

50. The phrase "no taxation without representation" was a rallying cry of many American Colonists during the period of British rule in the 1760s and early 1770s.

51. Esteban Ortiz-Ospina and Max Roser, "Financing Healthcare," *OurWorldInData.org*, 2019, https://ourworldindata.org/financing-healthcare (accessed November 25, 2019).

52. Lawrence J. McQuillan and Graham H. Walker, "Housing, Human Dignity and 'State of Emergency,'" *Independent Institute*, October 25, 2019, http://www.independent.org/news/article.asp?id=12962 (accessed November 25, 2019).

53. David Gratzer writes, "My book's thesis was simple: to contain rising costs, government-run health-care systems invariably restrict the health-care supply," in "The Ugly Truth About Canadian Health Care," *City Journal*, Summer 2007, https://www.city-journal.org/html/ugly-truth-about-canadian-health-care-13032.html (accessed November 25, 2019).

54. Washington Examiner editors, "Gun Control Is a Fantasy. Start a Realistic Conversation About Preventing School Massacres," *Washington Examiner*, February 21, 2018, https://www.washingtonexaminer.com/gun-control-is-a-fantasy-start-a-realistic-conversation-about-preventing-school-massacres (accessed November 25, 2019).

55. Russell Roberts, "Incentives Matter," *Library of Economics and Liberty*, n.d., https://www.econlib.org/library/Columns/y2006/Robertsincentives.html (accessed November 25, 2019)

56. Craig A. Depken, II, *Microeconomics DeMystified* (Emeryville, CA: McGraw-Hill, 2006), see chapters 4 and 5.

57. David R. Henderson, "Demand," *Library of Economics and Liberty*, n.d., https://www.econlib.org/library/Enc/Demand.html (accessed November 25, 2019).

58. U.S. Department of Justice, Office of Justice Programs, Bureau of Justice Statistics, "Source and Use of Firearms Involved in Crimes: Survey of Prison Inmates, 2016," comp. Mariel Alper and Lauren Glaze, Special Report, January 2019, https://www.bjs.gov/content/pub/pdf/suficspi16.pdf (accessed January 3, 2020).

59. John R. Lott, Jr., "Weak Evidence For New Gun Control Laws," *Townhall*, July 23, 2018, https://townhall.com/columnists/johnrlottjr/2018/07/23/weak-evidence-for-new-gun-control-laws-n2502786 (accessed December 19, 2019).

60. Fox News, "Venezuelans Regret Gun Ban, 'A Declaration Of War Against an Unarmed Population,'" *Education News*, December 14, 2018, https://www.educationviews.org/venezuelans-regret-gun-ban-a-declaration-of-war-against-an-unarmed-population (accessed January 2, 2020); and Audrey D. Kline, "Gun Control in Nazi Germany," *Mises Daily Articles*, *Mises Institute*, May 9, 2014, https://mises.org/library/gun-control-nazi-germany (accessed January 2, 2020).

61. In fact, my hypothesis is that the volume and intensity of rhetoric varies inversely with the amount of available evidence. The reasoning is that evidence is a penalty (cost) for rhetoric. If you increase the penalty (more evidence), you reduce the production of rhetoric because the supply price for rhetoric decreases. Suppliers provide less (more) of a good the lower (higher) the *net* price they receive for it. A further hypothesis is that more rhetoric will be forthcoming from the political party *not* in power than the one in power.

62. U.S. Citizenship and Immigration Services, "Victims of Criminal Activity: U Nonimmigrant Status," 2019, https://www.uscis.gov/humanitarian/victims-human-trafficking-other-crimes/victims-criminal-activity-u-nonimmigrant-status/victims-criminal-activity-u-nonimmigrant-status (last updated June 12, 2018).

63. Thomas Sowell, *Economic Facts and Fallacies*, 2nd ed. (New York: Basic Books, 2011).

64. Pierre Lemieux, "Are Imports a Drag on the Economy?" *Regulation* (Fall 2015): 6–8, https://www.cato.org/sites/cato.org/files/serials/files/regulation/2015/9/regulation-v38n3-6_0.pdf (accessed November 25, 2019). See heading "Are Imports a Drag on the Economy?" 6.

65. It is also no surprise that it is the view of another businessman, the President of the United States Donald J. Trump.

66. David Gould and Roy J. Ruffin, "Trade Deficits: Causes and Consequences," *Economic and Financial Policy Review* (January 1996): 10-20, https://www.researchgate.net/publication/5029945_Trade_Deficits_Causes_and_Consequences (accessed November 25, 2019). A slightly more sophisticated analysis would say to maximize the dollar value of imports per dollar value of exports.

67. Herbert Stein, "Balance of Payments," *Library of Economics and Liberty*, n.d., https://www.econlib.org/library/Enc/BalanceofPayments.html (accessed November 25, 2019).

68. Kimberly Amadeo, "Capital Account, How It's Measured, with Examples," *Balance*, December 8, 2018, https://www.thebalance.com/what-is-the-capital-account-measurement-and-examples-3306266 (accessed November 25, 2019).

69. Alan S. Blinder, "Free Trade," *Library of Economics and Liberty*, n.d., https://www.econlib.org/library/Enc/FreeTrade.html (accessed November 25, 2019).

70. Define private domestic savings as: Y–C–T where Y is GDP, C is consumption, and T is taxes. Government savings is T - G. Adding the two we obtain total savings= (Y–C–T) + (T–G) = Y–C–G, which according to the national accounting equation is equal to I + (X–M) where I is private domestic investment. Therefore, (total domestic savings – total domestic investment) = X–M (the manufactured goods trade deficit or surplus). In brief S – I = X-M.

71. Pierre Lemieux, "Free Trade Isn't Killing Jobs," *Foundation for Economic Education* (*FEE*), October 16, 2017, https://fee.org/articles/free-trade-isnt-killing-jobs (accessed November 25, 2019).

72. Pierre Lemieux, "The Poverty of Protectionism and the Impact of Tariffs," *Library of Economics and Liberty*, n.d., https://www.econlib.org/the-poverty-of-protectionism-and-the-impact-of-tariffs (accessed November 25, 2019); and Katherine Mangu-Ward, "Tariffs Are Self-Imposed Sanctions," *Reason*, June 2018, https://reason.com/2018/05/01/tariffs-are-self-imposed-sanct (accessed January 3, 2020).

Chapter Nine

Certainty versus Uncertainty
Multiple Factors, Multiple Uncertain Outcomes, Polls and Their Interpretation

This chapter is related to the dichotomous thinking that tends to predominate in utopian discussions. Utopian schemes (green new deal, single-payer healthcare, Obamacare, socialism, communism, price controls, guaranteed free income, guaranteed free education, guaranteed free housing, guaranteed work for those willing to work) over promise relative to what the state can actually deliver in the real world and relative to the rhetoric.

These schemes result in massive cost overruns, the result of attempts to save the plans and the reputations of their purveyors at all cost to the public, whom the purveyors claim to represent.[1] Doing so earns them the reputation of bait and switch schemes, no matter how moral-sounding the intent of their purveyors, which alleged moral authority is not a sufficient condition for validity, implementability, or success.

The root problem in utopian schemes is to expect *certainty* in the real world of *change* and *uncertainty*. Utopian schemes are, by definition, perfection in action so they cannot be improved upon. This gives them their endearing static quality. But change happens and the best laid plans have to accommodate it. There is little to no learning in such schemes.

We have already indicated that there are usually multiple explanations of data, as opposed to the partisan cherry-picked ones.[2] The reason is that data is generated in the real world of uncertainty where phenomena are multivariable and hence complicated. To expect simple common sense solutions to inherently complex phenomena, like anthropogenic climate change,[3] or gun control is another fallacy.[4] Nor are there even unique solutions to some real problems. It is an assumption, that begs the question, that the government has any demonstrated ability to fix such problems. This is contrary to the vote-generating partisans.

The first step in dealing with uncertainty is simply to *recognize* its existence. Dichotomous thinking fails to do so.

NOISE VERSUS SIGNAL

One of the biggest problems in dealing with and interpreting real world data is distinguishing between noise and signals. This results in the fallacy of confusing noise with signals (responses to new information).

Example No. 1

The Stock Market: Not every blip in the stock market, for example, is the result of some event. That common idea confuses correlation with causation. A significant amount of stock market volatility, and many other economic variables including climate change, is pure white noise. A good introduction to the problem of distinguishing the signal from the noise in the stock market is outlined in Boris Marjanovic's article, "Don't Be Fooled by Stock Market Noise."[5]

The noise component in economic series is the *unexplainable* part. Only the signal contains new but not necessarily true information (in which case false signals could be created). Policy based on noise is unlikely to treat problems that are assumed to be the results of real variables.

Why the noise? One main reason is that we cannot measure anything with one hundred percent precision. Therefore there are errors in measurement. To quote the BLS:

> When a sample, rather than the entire population, is surveyed, estimates differ from the true population values that they represent. The component of this difference that occurs because samples differ by chance is known as *sampling error*, and its variability is measured by the *standard error of the estimate*.... A sample estimate and its estimated standard error can be used to construct confidence intervals; when these estimates are unbiased, the statistical properties of confidence interval "coverage" are known.[6]

An interesting real world test case is provided next. It is a good illustration of the difference between rhetoric and evidence and it also relates well to this chapter's topic and to search costs in a world of uncertainty.

CASE STUDY NO. 11: "CONFIDENCE" IN THE SPECIAL PROSECUTOR'S PRESS CONFERENCE OF MAY 29, 2019

How much evidence or lack thereof is needed before we declare someone guilty or innocent of a crime?[7] We already discussed some of this in chapter

3 in the context of proving guilt or innocence of a crime. That discussion was based on the impossibility of empirically and conclusively proving a negative. The justice system in the United States is based on *evidence*, not rhetoric or speculation. Everything hinges on the evidence, not the rhetoric. Therefore, the presumption is innocence, not guilt.

The statement by Robert S. Mueller III: "If we had confidence the President did not commit a crime, we would have said so," is a red herring and it is inconsistent with both the U.S. justice system and logic.[8] Why? Because it assumes you can prove a negative: "did not commit a crime." The standard of innocence is not might be *guilty* but requires evidence to establish guilt. Proving innocence is logically, and therefore practically, impossible. Robert Mueller's assertion represents a classic case of unaccountable government overreach.

The focus in this chapter is on uncertainty and information. Let us focus on the issue of *confidence*. We will ignore the fact that Special Prosecutor Mueller does not state his definition of confidence, thereby leaving it in the zone of rhetoric. What precisely creates confidence in the minds of special prosecutors and their staffs that crimes have *not* been committed? And how much confidence is needed in order to say something, as opposed to appealing to an industry of partisan speculators?

The answer, consistent with feasibility, is *lack of evidence* of crime. Just as evidence of crime helps to establish guilt, although defendants usually get to defend themselves, a lack of evidence of crime suggests lack of crime (innocence).That is the whole point of a prosecutor's investigation—to present evidence of guilt. No evidence of guilt means no crime, no indictment, and no prosecution. In the U.S. system, unless there is evidence of crime, the defendant is innocent. The fact that anyone, including special prosecutors, accuses someone else of guilt without evidence, is partisan political rhetoric.

Confidence may be in the minds of the prosecution but has no weight outside of the evidence. The appeal to confidence, outside of evidence, is rhetoric and it relies on confirmation bias. Of course, you cannot conclusively prove innocence so that creates the wiggle room exploited by partisans.

How could you ever be one hundred percent certain that no crime was committed, in the absence of any evidence? The answer is that you could not because there could always exist some evidence somewhere. If one hundred percent certainty were necessary to declare targets not guilty, few would be so declared. That is the essence of Beria's dictum, "show me the man, and I will show you the crime." What is necessary in the U.S. justice system is evidence of crime: no evidence, no guilt.

In the real world of uncertainty, we do not have perfect information; 100 percent certainty is generally not feasible. How long should we keep searching for evidence to support a hypothesis, say of the guilt of our political opponents? On the one hand, search is a costly project, so when the discounted value of the expected benefits of search outweighs the discounted expected costs at the margin, perhaps we should continue. On the other hand, lengthy searches resulting in no evidence suggest that a continued search is unlikely to come up with something new so it should be terminated. After all, there are other things to do with our limited resources (think opportunity costs).

Some of those afflicted by confirmation bias, like gamblers, will go to unlimited lengths to confirm it, despite the absence of evidence. Rhetoric will spur them on. Like gamblers defying the sunk cost fallacy, they usually end up in ruin.

There are several other fallacies, including confirmation bias, worthy of exposure in the current debacle. One is the fallacy of the expert: even though zero evidence is provided, the special prosecutor *must* have some information about the alleged guilt of his target. Too bad he refused to present his *additional* evidence (not rhetoric) which he would have done if he had any, and that he said there was no more evidence.

The evidence he does produce establishes innocence as per U.S. law. The knowing-more-than-you-know fallacy is operative here also as partisans scramble to make their case. Why should partisans be able to know more, or have more resources, than the special prosecutor? Not to mention that we the taxpayers have already paid for several investigations of the hypothesis, whose rationale apparently was not credible evidence.

POLLS

Here we will be discussing what polls are and how to read and interpret them. Polls are fundamental to the rhetoric industry because they enable speculators. Unfortunately, they are poorly understood and frequently misused. In order to understand how to read and correctly interpret polls, it is important to have a rudimentary understanding of what a poll actually is.

Out in the universe there is presumably a number representing the percentage of the likely voting population who say they are going to vote for a particular political candidate. That number is changing over time as voter preferences change. No one knows exactly what the percentage actually is at any given point in time—until the election results are in. The pundits do not know, nor do the journalists and the politicians.

But we can use statistics to try to *estimate* the percentage, a proportion. We cannot take a census of the entire population (of likely voters) because that would be far too costly, time-consuming, and difficult. Nor could we repeat the census to update the estimate on a timely basis. Therefore, we try to use the power of statistics.

By taking a *random* sample of the population in question, we calculate the needed numbers on the basis of that sample, provide the estimate and, most importantly, the measure of its *accuracy*. The latter estimate is usually called the *standard error* of the estimated proportion. The *margin of error* (MOE) of the poll is related to this and measures half the total width of a 95 percent *confidence interval* centered at the estimate of the proportion.

Charles H. Franklin, "The 'Margin of Error' for Differences in Polls," provides a good discussion with examples.[9] To summarize the discussion in his article, for a standard poll with n =1111, under standard assumptions the *standard error of the estimate* of the proportion is about 1.5 percent. And the MOE is about twice that, 3.0 percent. The *95 percent confidence interval* is from the estimated proportion -3.0 percent to the estimated proportion +3.0 percent.

Since no sample of the population will perfectly represent the entire population, we can expect our polling estimates to be *imperfect* estimates of the actual unknown proportion we are trying to discover. It is therefore as important to present the degree of accuracy of our estimate as it is to present the estimate itself. Knowing what polls represent allows us to set our expectations on what to expect from them. Polls have limitations and understanding those limitations is important.

There are different kinds of polls: *approval* polls and *horserace* polls being key examples. In an approval poll, we want to know the percentage of the overall population who approve (disapprove) of the individual. In a horserace poll, we want to know which of several (usually the two front runners) is leading and by how much.

Different kinds of polls have different standard errors of their estimates and margins of error, in theory and in practice. It is *much harder* to get a reliable estimate of the lead in a horserace poll than to get a reliable estimate of the approval rating of a political candidate, because the MOE is much higher in a horserace poll than in an approval poll. The media usually completely ignores this fact, implying by omission, that it makes no difference. However, ignoring information (called falsification by omission and/or ignorance) is a partisan policy. It relies on innuendo, proves nothing, and can have devastating results.

Given this very basic background on what polls are, we can now delve a little more into some basic statistical concepts upon which polls are based. One is *hypothesis testing* and the other is *confidence intervals*. All polls are based on an underlying hypothesis called the *null* hypothesis. The null hypothesis is the hypothesis which the poll is designed to test, by taking a random sample from the population. For a proportion, as discussed above, one null hypothesis usually made is that the sample proportion is equal to the true but unknown value of the proportion, say 0.50, for ease of exposition.

In practice, we cannot prove the null hypothesis, we can only test whether the data is or is not consistent with it for a given *confidence* level, say 95 percent. Here is where confidence intervals come into play. Confidence has a precise meaning in this context and they are key to understanding how to interpret polls correctly. Confidence intervals have to do with *statistical significance*, a concept well-suited to the world of uncertainty we inhabit. A confidence interval for a proportion, for example, is based on the probability distribution of the *sampling statistic*; the percentage of those surveyed who say they approve of a politician for example. It specifies a *range* of values wherein the true parameter is supposed to lie. In the usual parlance, 3 percent below the estimated sample proportion and 3 percent above the estimated proportion for a 95 percent confidence level.

Of course, we do not know the true proportion, which is the whole problem. But we can say we are "95 percent confident" (or not) that our null hypothesis is consistent with the data in the sense that if we repeatedly and independently *randomly* sampled the population and constructed corresponding 95 percent confidence intervals for each sample, then the true parameter will be in 95 percent of those confidence intervals.

For a single sample, if we find that the assumed proportion, say 0.50, is not in our confidence interval, then we can say much less. We reason it out logically, minus the confirmation bias. We took a single sample, therefore we are limited by that fact. We are testing the null hypothesis, say that the true proportion is 0.50, so our sample statistic is conditioned on that hypothesis. Our sample says the sample statistic is say 0.40. The confidence interval is from 0.37 to 0.43 if the null hypothesis is correct.

The test does not accept the null hypothesis because the hypothesized value of 0.50 is outside the one confidence interval, and we therefore reject it. But this will happen by chance alone 5 percent of the time if the null hypothesis is true. So we are making an error here; noise, rather than true voter preferences, is influencing our decision causing us to reject the true null hypothesis. At least we have admitted our error as has the test itself. The chance of rejecting the null hypothesis when it is true is 5 percent. This type of error is called a *Type I error* and it is built into the test through the significance level. The test, like the world, is imperfect and we have accepted that by qualifying our test.

Conversely, if we had collected a thousand independent random samples and found that the null hypothesis was rejected by 25 percent of them on average, we could be a lot more confident that noise was *not* the culprit. We could feel that *voter sentiment* was the contributing factor because the noise would be cancelled out to a great extent. We could restate our null hypothesis and reiterate the testing procedure.

Unfortunately, partisans driven by confirmation bias usually ignore the noise in polls when they confirm their bias and cherry pick the polls. A better solution is to use averages of polls.[10]

Testing the Lead In a Horse Race Poll

We start with a level playing field where it is assumed that the candidates are perfectly tied. That is, the proportion of likely voters who prefer candidate A is exactly equal to the proportion of likely voters who prefer candidate B. This assumption is the null hypothesis underlying the poll. We can never prove it, but we can attempt to disprove it and find out who is statistically significantly leading, if one candidate is so leading.

If the null hypothesis is correct then neither candidate has a lead, they are tied. We do some polling and find that candidate A is estimated at 47 percent and candidate B is estimated at 53 percent. Then B has an estimated lead of 6 percent over A. But is that estimated lead statistically significantly higher, or is it within the error bounds of the *correct* confidence interval?

The poll is re-sampled and now A is estimated at 53 percent and B is estimated at 47 percent. Thus A now has an estimated lead. We still do not know whether that estimated lead is statistically significant. That depends on the *confidence interval* for the *difference of proportions* between two candidates. We cannot use the MOE of plus or minus 3 percent as for approval polls because the flipping phenomenon shows that it is twice as large as for a single item poll, 6 percent in this case. That means the confidence interval is the estimated lead minus 6.0 percent up to the estimated lead plus 6.0 percent.

The conclusion is that the confidence interval for a horserace poll is approximately *twice* as large as for a single poll. Yet the partisans keep reporting the same MOE for both types of polls. The net result of this error is thinking that one candidate has a statistically significant estimated lead over another when the hypothesized lead (0%) falls out of smaller confidence intervals. This will of course happen more often the narrower the confidence interval (as for approval polls with MOE of 3%). Thus an alleged lead turns into an actual tie.

What this means in practice is that an estimated lead of a few percentage points in a horserace poll of two political candidates is meaningless. They are tied, despite the rhetoric. Only if the lead is above 6 percentage points can we say with 95 percent *statistical confidence* that one candidate has a statistically significant estimated lead.

This happened in the 2016 Presidential election polling. Odds are that this error will not be corrected by the 2020 election. A safe rule is to take whatever the usual press says is the MOE for horserace polls and multiply it by 2.0. See Franklin's "Margin of Error" noted above for more details.

PREDICTIVE OR DESCRIPTIVE?

Despite the politicization of each and every cherry-picked poll, there is evidence that, until close to the actual election, they fail to accurately predict. Their predictive ability increases as the election day arrives, but that does not mean they suddenly become *perfectly* predictive with 100 percent accuracy.

That is awfully hard to do in the world of uncertainty and with the multiple factors (some not captured in polling) behind human behavior. This is to be contrasted with utopian certain world rhetoric where everything is knowable in advance, under the assumptions that remove uncertainty. What, we may ask, happens to the five year plans when an unanticipated shock affects the economy?

NOTES

1. Adam Brinklow, "California High-Speed Rail Cost May Approach $100 Billion," *Curbed San Francisco*, March 12, 2018, https://sf.curbed.com/2018/3/12/17110190/high-speed-rail-cost-money-bullet-train (accessed January 3, 2020); Scott Shackford, "California's Bullet Train Project Doesn't Deserve Your Moist-Eyed Love Letters," *Reason*, February 14, 2019, https://reason.com/2019/02/14/californias-bullet-train-project-doesnt (accessed January 3, 2020); and David Ditch, "California's High-Speed Rail Failure Shows the Insanity of Green New Deal," *Daily Signal*, February 12, 2019, https://www.dailysignal.com/2019/02/12/californias-high-speed-rail-failure-shows-the-insanity-of-green-new-deal (accessed January 3, 2020).

2. Logically Fallacious, "Causal Reductionism," *Logically Fallacious*, n.d., https://www.logicallyfallacious.com/tools/lp/Bo/LogicalFallacies/64/Causal-Reductionism (accessed January 6, 2020).

3. When considering the subject of anthropogenic climate change, it could be a manufactured problem to facilitate a massive government boondoggle as discussed in chapters 6 and 8.

4. "Gun control" is a rhetorical two word buzz phrase that begs the question: the issue is not whether inanimate objects, guns, can be *controlled*, but rather, whether gun homicides can be mitigated by government regulation. Note the imprecision of the rhetoric, its leaving out important details, and its false over-promise, but emotional appeal.

5. Boris Marjanovic, "Don't Be Fooled by Stock Market Noise," *Seeking Alpha*, April 16, 2015, https://seekingalpha.com/article/3074086-dont-be-fooled-by-stock-market-noise (accessed November 26, 2019).

6. U.S. Bureau of Labor Statistics, "Calculating Approximate Standard Errors and Confidence Intervals for Current Populations Survey Estimates," November 2018, https://www.bls.gov/cps/calculating-standard-errors-and-confidence-intervals.pdf (accessed November 26, 2019).

7. C-SPAN, "Statement from Special Counsel Robert Mueller," YouTube video, 10:30, posted by C-SPAN, May 29, 2019, https://www.youtube.com/watch?v=3ah7mneJ32A (accessed November 26, 2019).

8. Tim Harris, "Mueller Makes First Statement: 'The Report Is My Testimony,' I Hope This Is The Only Time I Speak," *RealClear Politics*, May 29, 2019, https://www.realclearpolitics.com/video/2019/05/29/watch_live_special_counsel_robert_mueller_to_make_statement.html (accessed November 26, 2019). With that statement, Special Prosecutor Mueller revealed himself to be partisan and opened the door to rhetorical denials of the lack of evidence of crime he himself reported.

9. Charles H. Franklin, "The 'Margin of Error' for Differences in Polls," posted by *ABC News*, October 27, 2002, rev. February 9, 2007, https://abcnews.go.com/images/PollingUnit/MOEFranklin.pdf (accessed November 26, 2019).

10. See Robert Erikson and Christopher Wlezien, "How To Read The Polls—And Keep Your Sanity—In Two Easy Steps," *Washington Post*, June 8, 2016, https://www.washingtonpost.com/news/monkey-cage/wp/2016/06/08/how-to-read-the-election-polls-and-keep-your-sanity-in-two-easy-steps (accessed November 26, 2019).

Chapter Ten

Individual Preferences and Opportunities, and the State's Role

Capitalism, Communism, (Democratic) Socialism, and the Welfare State

We are going to be brief in this last chapter and note that each of these topics has generated numerous treatises and debates. Yet the definitions of these alternative economic systems are not always given, so the objective is to provide their distinguishing features. The reader can decide which system is *better*—based on the evidence—rather than going with rhetoric and confirmation bias.

Words matter. By never defining the terms of discourse and blurring the differences (for examples, democratic socialism versus socialism, fascism versus communism, capitalism versus the welfare state), temporary political advantage can be obtained. The citizenry then bears the costs when ambiguous ideologies and their buzzwords turn into law.

Before proceeding, this is a good time to pause to think about what you have learned in this book so far, and how to apply it. You can test your knowledge by trying to give criteria for how to compare economic systems.

INDIVIDUALISM VERSUS COLLECTIVISM

One of the key things that distinguishes economic and political systems is where they start and to what they give primacy. Whether the individual or the state is primary is a key feature. The contrast here is between individualism and collectivism. The primacy of the specific (individuals) versus the aggregate (a construct) is something to look out for in evaluating economic and political systems.

The individual (sometimes called the household for statistical reasons) is the micro unit. As discussed, the "People" is a convenient-to-politicize aggregate that really has little meaning. It is an abstraction: there are only individual people. You could say individuals *share a characteristic*, such as nationality, but that does not mean that the aggregate supersedes the individuals, nor that the aggregate has a single *will* that should be followed.

Even democracies do not capture this alleged property of group behavior. Not every person living in a democracy believes in the notion that the majority represents their opinion nor even that it should "*rule*."[1] Tyranny of the majority (or even of the minority) can easily emerge. Further, theocracies (a system of government in which a priest/religious leader rules in the name of God/a god) around the world reject the democratic model.

The notion that what is true of the whole (the aggregate) is also true of the part (the individual) is the *Fallacy of Division*.[2] This is one we have not discussed yet. Accepting the aggregate as representative of the parts (each and every individual) is an example of this fallacy.

By appealing to the *will of the people*, some revolutionaries think they can force agreement with their policies, before they actually get power. After the classic power grab, agreement often is literally enforced by force. What is amusing here is that two different partisans can come up with two opposing wills of the people and two completely different policy agendas. That is because the expression, "the will of the people," is a piece of rhetoric that, as is typical of rhetoric, can mean almost anything.

The will of the people is also mislabeled the *public good*, which can also practically mean anything, for political purposes. When was the last time any government official has been held accountable for failure to further the "public good"? We already discussed this issue in chapter 5 on the fallacy of treating aggregates like individuals.

When looking at political rhetoric it is good to remember that politicians sometimes represent their constituencies, the special interest groups (SIGs) discussed in chapter 1, that put and maintain them in power. They are beholding to them if they want to stay in power. Do SIGs represent the "will of the people" or rather, like distinct individuals, their own varying wills?

Let us consider the individual since it is hard to ignore them. The individual or individual household has its own preferences about what it wants, its goals, and how to realize them. Individuals have utility functions that try to capture the individual's welfare and changes to it—based on what creates their individual welfare.

In the real world of uncertainty, there is also risk to deal with, and different people have different degrees of risk aversion. Therefore, as long as we respect individual freedom, we must recognize that different people can and should have the freedom to behave, think, and act differently in pursuit of their varying goals. Some societies tend to be individualistic. Others support and enforce collectivism and strict obedience to it under the agency of the "state."

A social welfare function, if it existed, attempts to aggregate individuals into one big collective and replace individual utility functions by the societal one, assumed to exist. This social welfare function is said to be what matters because it allegedly takes into account the welfare of all people. But society is a construct and has no existence beyond or separate from the individuals who live in it. The fallacy, already discussed, is in treating aggregates as real as the individuals they aggregate.

Discussion Questions

(1) How do we collect evidence on what society "thinks"?

(2) How does society make decisions?

(3) What are the instruments of collective action?

(4) How well do the instruments in item (3) represent the interests of the people as opposed to the most vocal special interest groups (SIGs)?

Not only are there major theoretical issues in defining and identifying an aggregate, consistent social welfare function—which does not exist yet is alleged to be primary—but also there are numerous practical issues as well. That society itself has a will, like individuals, and must act to consistently *rank* social goals and maximize *social utility* is the fallacy of composition. It is an anthropomorphism of an aggregate.

Arrow's Impossibility Theorem, named for economist Kenneth J. Arrow, asserts and shows that the extension of utility from individuals to society is not possible under minimal conditions.[3] The goal of ranking social projects and thereby showing which benefit society the most is not possible. It is one thing to say there is a ranking, it is quite another to say that it is *most beneficial* to the "collective interest" and thereby, actually benefits society. The latter are rhetorical claims.

Remembering the relative principle that all choices are relative to each other and incur opportunity costs, the exact same principle applies to the aggregate. The impossibility of ranking social projects in a way that respects individuals' rankings is perhaps why SIGs vigorously *compete* for their own pet projects to be adopted.

The problem here is that the impact on the *social good* amounts to helping some SIGs and hurting others, an accepted principle of Marxist class warfare (MCW). The economic term for this is *Pareto inefficient*.[4] Yet partisans keep claiming that all their proposals express the "will of the American people."

This is rhetoric because the object being benefitted cannot be *identified*, nor planned. "That which we cannot know cannot be planned" (a statement attributed to Friedrich A. Hayek).[5]

The reason that we want to be able to rank projects is that alternative A can be inferior to alternative B in the social ranking. It makes us less better off or even worse off in aggregate than alternative A. This is not a remote possibility. Partisans regularly offer up such alternatives and individuals, from their view, recognize them as such because only individuals can rank alternatives according to their *own* individual preference rankings.

The issue is therefore usually politicized by SIGs because an aggregate ranking is not possible. At the SIG level, which is fundamentally still individualistic, one SIG can easily be made worse off by benefitting an opposing SIG. Hence, their rankings are mutually incompatible. We are led to the consensus problem which is a problem that majoritarian voting rules do not solve.

Discussion Questions

(1) Which is more important: clean air or clean water?

(2) To whom?

(3) Who decides and why?

The likelihood of dictatorship (rule by force) in centralized economies planned around the collective quickly becomes a real possibility, as history amply shows in the numerous attempts to *erase* "enemies of the state." In the Marxist philosophy:

> The proletariat will use its political supremacy to wrest, by degrees, all capital from the bourgeoisie, to centralize all instruments of production in the hands of the State, i.e., of the proletariat organized as the ruling class; and to increase the total of productive forces as rapidly as possible.[6]

This is the dictatorship of the proletariat. The possibility of dictatorship occurs even in democracies, where presidents use the power of the pen and the phone to impose their pet projects, without any vote whatsoever by those affected.

The same considerations apply to the aggregate construct of *social justice*, because justice is an inherently individualistic concept that the body of law is designed to protect. The extension to society is once again the fallacy of composition. Hence, we get SIGs competing with different mutually exclusive proposals to create and maximize social justice. But social justice is, like social welfare, both immeasurable and not rankable and these are minimal conditions for implementability. Perhaps this explains why it is so ephemeral and so often politicized?

The social justice rhetoric becomes the banner of MCW, a hallowed concept among partisans. Even the terminology reflects its violent disposition under the fallacy of unearned moral superiority in the term social justice *warriors* (SJWs).

Discussion Questions

(1) Hypothesis: That SJWs actually benefit *social welfare* is usually assumed—not proven—since it *cannot* be proven.

If it can be proven, how? If not, why can it not be proven?

(2) Is the hypothesis in item (1) an article of faith of SJWs? or, is it rhetoric?

(3) What is the fallacy of *begging the question*? And, how may it apply here?

CAPITALISM

Capitalism is a non-utopian economic system—not a religion—named by its opponents as such with the mandatory implied ad hominem, rhetorical sustained sneer (workers are good; capitalists are bad).[7] A more appropriate term for the twenty-first century is *a free-enterprise, free-exchange market* system, as opposed to a *centrally planned* system. It belongs to the individualistic, not the collectivist, category.

While capitalism is a non-utopian system, it is interesting to note that the evidence shows that it has benefitted individual human beings far more than its utopian rivals.[8] Having *ideals* does not necessarily generate a better system, nor one that can even achieve those ideals. That is another fallacy.

Every economic system has to address *what* to produce, *how* to produce, and *to whom* to distribute the fruits of production. This is true whether the economic system is any of the options, including (democratic) socialism, an illogical rhetorical construct. Not only that, it is perfectly reasonable to ask how and by whom utopian projects are going to be paid for, and expect to have a complete cost-benefit analysis—employing the opportunity cost notion. The same applies to free-enterprise, free-exchange market system projects.

A free-enterprise, free-exchange market system requires an orderly infrastructure and laws that preserve individual liberties. These include private property rights, such as discretion over one's own *human* capital. Individuals are not slaves to abstractions such as the state or to the collective, and are free to employ their labor services as they see fit. That is to say, in accordance with their own individual preferences as to what they, not others or the state, perceive as their personal happiness and the happiness of others. Therefore, the state has a role and it is simply to maintain individual freedoms, including freedom from state coercion.

Production goes to those who specialize in production, the capitalists. Just because some wish to seize the *means of production* from those whose capital assets are their private property, and then nationalize them, does not imply that they know what to do with them. That assumption, of course, is a non-sequitur. The means of production are not a given either. You have to figure out what to produce first and how to produce it.

Did the means of production to produce personal computers exist in the 1800s? Someone had to come up with a vaccine for polio before it could be produced. The discoverer of that vaccine was a capitalist. Human knowledge is a capital asset too, not just machines.

What the means of production will be depends on the capitalists first discovering them and investing their own private capital in them, at their risk, for which risk they need to be rewarded. The government has no advantage in production, nor does it invest its own capital. It spends other peoples' money and passes on the risk of loss (think Solyndra) to the taxpayers. To date, it has exhibited little success in picking winners to subsidize or losers to drive out of business.[9] Under a free-enterprise, free-exchange market system, the market makes those choices.

A free-enterprise, free-exchange market system recognizes property rights and that it is morally suspect to steal the works of others, make them slaves to the state, or dictate what they must do for the collective, an abstraction. Yet this is precisely the history of what has happened—under Stalin, Mao, and Castro, among others. The cost is millions of human lives.

Karl Marx and Friedrich Engels also recognized property rights in the assertion that workers were not paid their surplus value. It is interesting that they simultaneously thought that capitalists' property rights could and should be routinely violated, the reason being that they are the victimizers according to MCW rhetoric.

But what could workers actually do in the absence of capitalists, because they create the capital that workers use? Of course, workers are free to create their own capital under capitalism, factories for example. But then, alas, they would be capitalists. Better that the state expropriate the capital in their name and then risk squandering it in the name of the rhetoric. The assumption here is that the state expropriation of private capital somehow magically makes it collectively owned (an abstraction). Even if this were true in a practical sense, the history of collectively owned assets is not a pretty picture. One of numerous issues is the *tragedy of the commons*,[10] which is the empirical consequence of everyone owns everything means that no one owns anything.

At the same time Marx was writing, an economic theory called marginalism (discussed earlier in another context) was discovered.[11] It gave an economic foundation for wages which is marginal productivity. Capitalists increase the wages of workers by providing them with the capital needed to increase their marginal productivity (wages). Thus, a win-win situation between workers and capitalists arises, debunking the MCW zero sum game assumption.

Discussion Questions

(1) How much work would there be without the capitalists and their capital?

(2) What would wages be like in the scenario in item (1)?

(3) How does capital increase the productivity of workers (hint: personal computers).

(4) How does productivity affect wages in modern capitalist economies?

(5) Might Marx's labor theory of value be historically superseded?

A free-enterprise, free-exchange market system has markets where financial capital can be raised for consumption goods and final products, for raw materials, and for talent. The allocation system to buyers/sellers is through these markets where dynamic prices are formed and buyers/sellers voluntarily transact at these prices. These prices continuously respond to evolving information and they provide signals to both producers and buyers to guide their decisions.

There is no need to fix prices through minimum wage laws, rent control, or any government control mechanism. Fixing prices makes them insensitive to new information and therefore worthless as a guide to behavior. Prices guide the system to equating ever-changing supply and demand conditions, thereby avoiding surpluses and deficits (shortages, famine), a classic problem under government centrally planned systems.[12]

Transactions between buyers and sellers are *voluntary* and therefore generally make both sides better off, otherwise they would not engage in them at existing prices. This itself would make prices change until transactions do take place. This is another example of why the zero-sum game assumption is a fallacy. Therefore, MCW does not apply in a voluntary exchange economy.

Nor does it even apply to the relationship between the dubious worker (good) versus capitalist (bad) false dichotomy. After all, workers are capitalists too since they own their own human capital in a world were the state does not own everything and workers are not slaves to the state. Marx viewed workers essentially as slaves to capitalists because presumably capitalists own the "means of production" and workers do not. This shows that that idea rests on a false dichotomy. But then he realized the consequences of that idea, and declared the dictatorship of the proletariat and the temporary nature of the state on the road to utopia (though he denied it was such).

Capitalism is predicated on competition, as opposed to a centralized government monopoly (hence immune from competition) and immune from accountability. The next topic is profits, but first note that free-enterprise places responsibility for success and failure squarely in the hands of the entrepreneurs. There is no convenient someone-to-blame victimology fallacy here.

Profits (Much Maligned, Much Misunderstood)

What exactly are the profits that go to those who provide capital to a firm? Again, the worker versus capitalist conundrum is an anachronism and a false dichotomy. Workers profit from the operations of a modern firm. They provide human capital to the firm in exchange for wages, health-care insurance, and other benefits of employment.

Discussion Questions

(1) What are the sources of capital for a modern firm?

(2) Who are the owners of the modern firm?

The owners of a firm are the claimants to the residual earnings of the firm and are those who take on most of the risk of the firm. Residual means after every other claimant has been paid. These include the firm's bondholders, the government in the form of taxes, the wage-earners, suppliers, and all the other costs. What is left over goes to the stockholders, those who invest in the firm's equity securities.

If the firm has publicly traded stock, all the owners of that stock are the firm's owners. The workers could become capitalists by the simple expedient of purchasing the firm's common stock, or by having it purchased by pension funds and held in their pensions, in which apparently Marx believed.

There is no need to seize the means of production because there are now much easier ways to effectively own them. Instead of building aircraft, you can simply buy the publicly traded stocks of airline companies. Therefore, the alleged exclusive ownership of the means of production by the capitalists is not a feature of modern free-enterprise systems, although control issues remain.

If the firm is privately held, then the entrepreneurs own the equity, as well as all those who have purchased an equity stake. You can become an owner by starting your own company, and you can get funding through debt markets and venture capitalists (shark tank).

Profit Maximization

This excoriated goal focuses on profits, ignores costs, and assumes a one-period world of certainty. Given that, we can still look at its implications. Profit maximization requires cost minimization. To the lowest cost producer goes production. Competition provides incessant pressure towards producing efficiently, at the lowest cost. This benefits consumers and society by growing the pie and lowering prices.

The government, a monopolist, is hardly ever the lowest cost producer. There is little incentive for it to be so. Hence, it should provide the fewest goods to consumers, and extract the smallest taxes to do so. Why? Because there are almost always better producers and they compete, unlike the government monopoly that does not have to compete.

COMMUNISM

Communism is an ideology that arose in response to the alleged ills of capitalism, a system vehemently opposed by the partisans. Before we discuss it, there are several fallacies involved here. One is the pot-shot fallacy. It is a non-sequitur that critiquing an economic system immediately implies that the opponent has a better one. Another fallacy is the nirvana fallacy, that a system that does not measure up to nirvana is unacceptable. And the innuendo that those who promise nirvana must have an absolutely better system.

Then there is the fallacy related to alleged moral superiority. Opposition, even vehement opposition or selective moral outrage, does not imply the economic or any other form of superiority of the alternatives (if any) of those who use these tactics. It is a fatal error that those who complain the loudest and fight the hardest must be correct and their opponents dead wrong. Examples include Hitler, Stalin, Mao, Castro, Pol Pot, Maduro, and the list goes on.

None of these dictators had the slightest moral superiority (just the opposite) and yet they raved and ranted, and brainwashed the public with their rhetoric, while squandering their resources in the name of their ideologies. This was clearly known to the people who quickly lost confidence in the rhetoric after the honeymoon period but could do little about it once the rulers seized the *means of enforcement* (private guns, private wealth, the propaganda ministry, the military, the courts, the vote).

Communism is a utopian, collectivistic ideology bordering on being a religion with a large set of pre-requisites. To some partisans, opponents are not allowed to question it or its assumptions. The state implements it and it tolerates no nay saying. These prerequisites include philosophical concepts such as Georg Wilhelm Friedrich Hegel's dialectical materialism (a theory), the presumption of proof by historical forecasting as opposed to evidence, hypotheses on the nature of man and what and who creates their well-being, the fundamental transformation of humanity in conformity with an ideology and enforcement by the state, and a thorough understanding of capitalism at a stage when little empirical evidence about it was available. There are also assumptions including the alleged zero-sum game relationship between workers and capitalists. All of the above constitute joint hypotheses in tests of the alleged superiority of communism.

Fundamental differences between a free-enterprise system and communism are the roles of the individual and property rights. Under collectivism, the individual is secondary to the collective, an abstraction. The individual is eclipsed by the collective. Who represents the collective is a key question. The answer has always been the state and its army of government officials. The state is presumed to somehow represent the people, and it has the force to ensure its edicts.

The economy is also centrally planned, an interesting notion in the real world of uncertainty. You cannot plan what you cannot know, and there is much of that in the real world. For example, the demands and supplies of thousands of commodities cannot be known by any board of central planners. That kind of knowledge is inherently individualistic. Under capitalism, you do not have to know them in order for the system to work. It happens spontaneously.

There is no individual property under communism. The state owns it all. And yet the worker is sacrosanct. What safeguards are in place to protect the worker's private human capital and human rights? Statism has routinely violated those rights, which are apparently viewed as inimical to public ownership, a fact immediately evident from the historical record. Political freedom is related to economic freedom[13] and neither thrive under communism, a one-party system.

Placing the word "democratic" in front of the word "communism" produces a meaningless, fraudulent combination. That is why the partisans use the term "democratic socialism," a much easier rhetoric to manage. Unfortunately, socialism is a species of communism in that it requires public ownership of some industries.

The state endowed with the utopian goal of achieving the highest aspirations of humanity—as a collective—has the power of force to implement its government officials' interpretation. Human nature has to be first *fundamentally transformed* before ordinary citizens can participate in the utopian promise. If they do not accept the collective goal, they must be re-educated to buy the rhetoric in its entirety. If they cannot be re-educated, then they must be branded as *enemies of the people*, banned from the paradise, or otherwise disposed of.

The collective vision presumes that it is acting in the interests of the people (an abstraction). Individuals must learn that that is ultimately in their personal interest, otherwise why would they accept the implicit or explicit police state? Herein lies the difference between individualism and collectivism, between communism and free enterprise.

The assumption of the former is that the government can do better for individuals than individuals can do for themselves. Under a free enterprise system this is rejected. The role of the government is not to manage citizens. Rather, it is to create an infrastructure wherein individuals can make their *own* choices according to their own preferences, not a one-size fits all preference map for everyone. This will stimulate innovation, growth, and the consequent prosperity for all—the collective. Under communism, only the state can properly serve the collective (an abstraction).

Communism rejects the market for private claims and their exchange. How can there be such a market when there is no private ownership? With a market comes prices. Under communism, the people do not determine the prices of the numerous commodities they (the workers) produce and consume; the state does. Therefore, there is no democratic marketplace where individuals place their "votes" in determining and transacting at prices mutually acceptable—not enforced—to buyers and sellers.

Markets serve important economic functions as discussed. The fallacy is that the state can perform these functions, and in a better way. Both theory and the evidence contradict this claim. How does a planning board of government officials determine exactly what millions of individual citizens want or need? Markets equate demand and supply.

As an example, take agricultural foodstuffs. When prices are fixed, demand and supply imbalances naturally arise. When the demand for food is greater than the supply then people potentially starve. Communist production, wherever it has been tried, has suffered from state-induced starvation. Black markets are also characteristic of such regimes.

The elite central planning government officials have *privilege* and are presumably mandated to solve the fundamental problems of any economy; what and how to produce, and how to distribute the fruits of production. Without markets, their record is abysmal. Honest central planners have recognized the need for markets. Black markets are in utter contradiction to the state's goals, yet they arise from the failure of the central planners to meet the needs of the masses.

The communist utopian vision has never been attained in practice. Partisans simply ignore the reasons for its failure, lie that it has never been tried, re-write history, and repeat the Marxist rhetoric without change. When discussing private ownership one has to recognize that with ownership comes *control* over those assets. Thus, the notion of state capitalism is a fraud. This was the system of the German National Socialists party who lied by claiming there was private ownership. Yet the Nazis controlled everything. Nazism (labeled Fascism to allow the communists to distance themselves from it) shares many features of the communist regimes. Namely, utopianism which most have since recognized as dystopianism. What is common, among other things, are their failed ideologies, and economies based on state labor and state control, and their police states.

Richard Pipes's *Communism: A History* provides an interesting history.[14] Communism per se, with its history of failure, is not particularly popular these days. But what remains immensely popular is its rhetoric in the form of MCW, a combination of several fallacies as discussed. MCW is pervasive and it is powerful; its emotional appeal continues unabated, despite all the evidence. This tactic is used to this day by partisans; if evidence gets in the way of the rhetoric, simply ignore it or throw out red herrings hoping opponents will be blindsided.

SOCIALISM

Socialism is a variant of communism. It is not an entirely different system that has corrected the ills of the latter, as claimed by the rhetoric. It is another collectivist, utopian system built directly on MCW, and is distinguished by government ownership and/or control of selected industries and selected assets.

As such, socialism is subject to the same comments as communism. The difference is a matter of degree. We have already seen that price and wage controls tend to hurt the very people they are designed to help, and many others. Therefore, mandating prices is a fool's errand. The government is not able to make anything "affordable." For that, competition is needed. When a monopoly, private or government, is created it has control over prices and quality. It raises prices and lowers quality, and often in a discriminatory manner.

Further, if the government mandates a "fair" price for a commodity that is too low relative to the demand-supply market equilibrium, it will create excess demand (a shortage). Stubbornly refusing to raise the price will require non-price rationing. Waiting lines are common. No, they are not a good thing. They have obvious disastrous effects when it comes to single payer health care.

Promising something for free (paid for by others and/or in the future), is the ultimate rhetoric used by political operatives to get votes. Add selective moral outrage, victimology, hide the hypocrisy, and they think they have a winning combination—until the sham is exposed for what it is, empty rhetoric.

You cannot equitably (who decides?) divide the pie until you create the pie. Stealing the pie from others (for example, soak the rich schemes) will incentivize them not to further produce it. Both communism and socialism ignore these fundamentals. The costs include, for example, under-investment by private firms in curing deadly diseases like cancer.

Predatory government regulation by anti-corporate Marxist ideologues increases the production costs of legitimate producers, stifling their efforts. It also incentivizes black markets. That is one major reason drug prices are allegedly so high (note the absolutist rhetoric). It is cheaper to steal them and re-market. That is why some drug prices in Canada are relatively lower than of those who invent the drugs and pay the regulatory costs. This is a classic free-rider problem. Again, some politicians will use this rhetoric to get power.

Socialism suffers from the same problem as communism. The government keeps the masses in line by force, but who keeps the government and its army of unaccountable and unelected government officials in line? With government ownership and/or control comes monopoly and its well-known consequences such as the centralization of power and dictatorship.

"Democratic" Socialism

Consider the unlikely composite "democratic socialism." It is often used as rhetoric because political operatives who exploit it cannot explain it, and no one thinks to ask. As Benjamin Powell notes,

> But here's the problem. The word "democratic" is not magic fairy dust when put in front of "socialist." The socialist portion of democratic socialism still means the state—the government—has undue control over economic decision-making that will result in stagnation. . . . The reason is simple. Centrally planned socialist economic systems necessarily concentrate economic power in the hands of government officials and planners. Without such power they can't hope to "run things." Yet this same power limits citizens' ability to freely exercise their power when they become dissatisfied with the government. That's because the government can punish them financially if they choose to oppose those in power.
>
> Venezuela started off as a democratic socialist state when Hugo Chavez was freely elected in 1998. Then, with economic power centralized, his successor, Nicolas Maduro, tightened the screws in the predictable fashion of socialism. He took care of those who supported him, ignoring, jailing, harassing the rest, as the economy crumbled with falling oil prices. Now, the democratic portion of "democratic socialism" is no more in Venezuela—it is merely socialist.[15]

Just because people elect their leaders does not change the fact that under socialism such leaders have extra power to abuse. Look at how hard it is to get them out. Even if the people do succeed, that does not stop their abuses while in power, including voting themselves in for a lifetime and creating a one party system where voting is irrelevant. Further, the government can hijack the voting system itself and fraudulently win gerrymandered sham elections.

THE WELFARE STATE

The welfare state is often confused with socialism, particularly in the case of the Nordic countries, often used as examples to bolster up the partisans' case. You can have a welfare state and private ownership/free-enterprise as in the United States and in all the Nordic countries.

The problem here is (predatory) taxation to support the state in its unprovable welfare-increasing transfer system. Many citizens agree that the unfortunate should be aided by the state. The problem is to not incentivize free-riders to become unfortunates. That is to say, to not incentivize free riding.

How much welfare should a country have is the key issue. There are other ways to help those able to work, increasing production being one. Firms, not the government, engage in worthwhile production and job creation. Should the citizenry be forced to pay relatively high taxes to support government officials who tend to squander them on pursuing their political objectives? Should private citizens be forced to pay for government boondoggles like Solyndra and the unaccountable special prosecutor Robert Mueller's fiasco?

Welfare, such as free health insurance and social security benefits are debatable public goods, given the alternatives. A welfare state can turn socialist on the rhetoric (zero evidence) that only the government can do everything better and that it has the knowledge to do so at lower cost. A government monopolist does not have to pursue cost minimization to survive, as do entrepreneurs. Further, governments spend other peoples' money—while it lasts—a fact that produces numerous ill effects.

Contrary to the current redistributionist rhetoric, it is unable in principle to reallocate wealth from the capitalists to the workers.[16] The lesson here is feasibility and is so often ignored by rhetoric. Garett Jones notes, "Good economic policy doesn't try to do things that are impossible."[17] Nor should human beings be required to *do* the impossible such as prove themselves innocent, or to forcibly give up their freedoms to the collective.

Roger Scruton, in his *Fools, Frauds, and Firebrands* says,

> The contradictory nature of the socialist utopias is one explanation of the violence involved in the attempts to impose them; it takes infinite force to make people do what is impossible.[18]

Discussion Questions

(1) If it is impossible in principle to reallocate wealth from the capitalists to the workers, then what of all the income inequality rhetoric about how we should be doing precisely that? Would it appear to be moot in that it violates the requirement of feasibility?

(2) Does socialism, with its emphasis on moral superiority and reallocating the pie, beg the question of how to create the pie?

(3) Is item (2) why Marx declared that capitalism is a necessary stage that would have to precede socialism?

(4) How would socialism be able to operate in the absence of capitalism, in particular of market prices?

(5) Why have all real-world attempts to create socialist societies failed to deliver the promised utopia?

(6) Is the claim that real socialism has never been tried a red herring? Or a straw man? Evaluate it in light of the historical record.

(7) Is "fair" a relative or absolute term? How would you define it?

(8) Is socialism more fair than capitalism? In what sense? Why or why not?

(9) Define "sustainable." Is it a relative or absolute concept?

(10) Is socialism sustainable? In what sense?

(11) Is capitalism sustainable? In what sense?

NOTES

1. Witness the United States during the period 2016 to 2020. The Democrat party apparently rejected the rule that the winner of the majority of electoral votes is the duly elected President. Donald J Trump won the November 2016 Presidential election with 304 electoral votes. Hillary R. Clinton lost the election with 227 votes by the rules of election law, which she negates with rhetoric in the form of protestations, and disavowing any personal responsibility. Even though it was not a close election, the Democrat party and its media enablers immediately called for Donald J. Trump's "impeachment." (Winning an election is not an impeachable crime.) At the same time, the party and its echo chambers in the media hypocritically repeated the virtue signaling rhetoric that they were "defending our democracy," which presumably always and only has to be done when Democrats lose Presidential elections. Note the irrationality of the rhetoric and its counterfactual assertions. The United States is a constitutional republic.

2. Logically Fallacious, "Fallacy of Division," *Logically Fallacious*, n.d., https://www.logicallyfallacious.com/tools/lp/Bo/LogicalFallacies/89/Fallacy-of-Division (accessed January 6, 2020).

3. Alex Tabarrok, "Popularizing Arrow's Theorem II," *Marginal Revolution*, October 25, 2010, https://marginalrevolution.com/marginalrevolution/2010/10/popularizing-arrows-theorem-ii.html (accessed November 26, 2019).

4. Sean Ingham, "Pareto-Optimality," *Encyclopaedia Britannica, Social Sciences*, n.d., https://www.britannica.com/topic/Pareto-optimality (accessed November 26, 2019).

5. Michael Munger, "What Can and Cannot Be Planned," *American Institute for Economic Research*, August 3, 2018, https://www.aier.org/article/what-can-and-cannot-be-planned (accessed January 3, 2020).

6. Karl Marx and Friedrich Engels, "Manifesto of the Communist Party: II. Proletarians and Communists," n.d., *Avalon Project*, Yale Law School, Lillian Goldman Law Library, https://avalon.law.yale.edu/19th_century/manone.asp (accessed December 3, 2019).

7. See n4 of Murray N. Rothbard, "John Kenneth Galbraith and the Sin of Affluence," *Mises Institute*, September 13, 2008, https://mises.org/library/john-kenneth-galbraith-and-sin-affluence (accessed November 26, 2019).

8. Walter E. Williams, "Capitalism vs. Socialism," *Townhall*, May 30, 2018, https://townhall.com/columnists/walterewilliams/2018/05/30/capitalism-vs-socialism-n2484341 (accessed November 26, 2019); World Bank, "GDP per Capita, PPP (Constant 2011 International $)," 1990–2018, https://data.worldbank.org/indicator/NY.GDP.PCAP.PP.KD?most_recent_value_desc=true (accessed November 26, 2019).

9. Government funding ventures based on picking winners are usually fully partisan and agenda driven.

10. Garrett Hardin, "Tragedy of the Commons," *Library of Economics and Liberty*, n.d., https://www.econlib.org/library/Enc/TragedyoftheCommons.html (accessed November 26, 2019).

11. Steven E. Rhoads, "Marginalism," *Library of Economics and Liberty*, n.d., https://www.econlib.org/library/Enc/Marginalism.html (accessed November 25, 2019).

12. Henry Hazlitt, *Economics in One Lesson*, Fiftieth Anniversary ed. (Baltimore: Laissez Faire Books, 1996), 87–93.

13. Anders Ingemarson, "How 'Democratic Socialism' Wreaked Havoc on My Native Sweden," *Federalist*, September 5, 2018, https://thefederalist.com/2018/09/05/democratic-socialism-wreaked-havoc-native-sweden (accessed November 26, 2019).

14. Richard Pipes, *Communism: A History* (New York: Modern Library, 2001; repr. 2003).

15. Benjamin Powell, "'Democratic Socialist' Really Need to Learn More About Socialism," *Independent Institute*, November 15, 2018, https://www.independent.org/news/article.asp?id=10613 (accessed November 26, 2019).

16. Steve Landsburg, "A Quick Economics Lesson," *Bad Reasoning, Economics, and Policy*, January 27, 2010, http://www.thebigquestions.com/2010/01/27/a-quick-economics-lesson (accessed November 26, 2019).

17. Garett Jones, "Redistributing from Capitalists to Workers: An Impossibility Theorem," *Library of Economics and Liberty*, 2013, https://www.econlib.org/archives/2013/03/redistributing.html (accessed November 26, 2019).

18. Roger Scruton, *Fools, Frauds, and Firebrands: The Thinkers of the New Left* (London: Bloomsbury, 2015; repr. 2019), 6.

Bibliography

Abbot, J. W., et al. Preface in *Evidence-Based Climate Science (Second Edition)*, xiii–xiv. *Elsevier Science Direct*. September 23, 2016. https://www.sciencedirect.com/science/article/pii/B9780128045886050011 (accessed November 25, 2019).

Alinsky, Saul D. *Rules for Radicals: A Practical Primer for Realistic Radicals*. New York: Vintage, 1989.

Amadeo, Kimberly. "Capital Account, How It's Measured, with Examples." *Balance*. December 8, 2018. https://www.thebalance.com/what-is-the-capital-account-measurement-and-examples-3306266 (accessed November 25, 2019).

American Psychiatric Association. *The Principles of Medical Ethics: With Annotations Especially Applicable to Psychiatry*. Arlington, VA: American Psychiatric Association, 2013. https://www.psychiatry.org/File%20Library/Psychiatrists/Practice/Ethics/principles-medical-ethics.pdf (accessed November 24, 2019).

American Physical Society. "This Month in Physics History." *APS News* 15, no. 6 (2006). https://www.aps.org/publications/apsnews/200606/history.cfm (accessed November 23, 2019).

Arrow, Kenneth J. "What Has Economics to Say About Racial Discrimination?" *Journal of Economic Perspectives* 12, no. 2 (1998): 91–100.

Backman, Maurie. "How Bad Is Social Security's Fraud Problem? Nobody Knows." *Motley Fool*. May 21, 2017. https://www.fool.com/retirement/2017/05/21/how-bad-is-social-security-fraud-nobody-knows.aspx (accessed November 22, 2019).

Bailey, Ronald. "Global Warming Hiatus Is Real." *Reason*. February 24, 2016. https://reason.com/2016/02/24/global-warming-hiatus-is-real (accessed November 25, 2019).

Barr, Bob. "Show Me the Man and I'll show You the Crime." *Townhall*. June 28, 2017. https://townhall.com/columnists/bobbarr/2017/06/28/draft-n2347508 (accessed November 19, 2019).

Barr, William. "Mueller Report: AG William Barr's Full Press Conference." *USA TODAY*. YouTube video. 21.23 min. Streamed live on April 18, 2019. https://www.youtube.com/watch?v=FeFGk6JbkJo (accessed November 20, 2019).

Becker, Gary S. *The Economics of Discrimination.* 2nd ed. London and Chicago: University of Chicago Press, 1971.

Becker, Gary S., and Guity Nashat Becker. *The Economics of Life: From Baseball to Affirmative Action to Immigration, How Real-World Issues Affect Our Everyday Life.* New York: McGraw-Hill, 1997.

Bell, David A. "Why Sanders Should Stop Talkin' 'Bout a Revolution." *Politico.* February 29, 2016. https://www.politico.com/magazine/story/2016/02/bernie-sanders-revolution-donald-trump-2016-213684 (accessed November 25, 2019).

Bergh, Andreas. "Embracing Capitalism: The Real Success of Sweden's Universal Welfare State." *ElgarBlog from Edward Elgar Publishing* (blog). September 9, 2014. https://elgar.blog/2014/09/09/embracing-capitalism-the-real-success-of-swedens-universal-welfare-state (accessed December 5, 2019).

Bessel, Richard. *Nazism and War.* New York: Modern Library Chronicles, 2004.

Bird, Alexander. "Thomas Kuhn." *Stanford Encyclopedia of Philosophy.* Winter 2018. Edited by Edward N. Zalta. https://plato.stanford.edu/entries/thomas-kuhn (accessed November 23, 2019).

Blinder, Alan S. "Free Trade." *Library of Economics and Liberty.* N.d. https://www.econlib.org/library/Enc/FreeTrade.html (accessed November 25, 2019).

Boaz, David. "Solyndra: A Case Study in Green Energy, Cronyism, and the Failure of Central Planning." *CATO Institute.* August 27, 2015. https://www.cato.org/blog/solyndra-case-study-green-energy-cronyism-failure-central-planning (accessed November 19, 2019).

Bodeen, Christopher. "China Accuses US of Prejudice Over Human Rights Issues." *Washington Times.* March 14, 2019. https://www.washingtontimes.com/news/2019/mar/14/china-accuses-us-of-prejudice-over-human-rights-is (accessed December 17, 2019).

Book, Robert. "Yes, It Was the 'Affordable' Care Act That Increased Premiums." *Forbes.* March 22, 2017. https://www.forbes.com/sites/theapothecary/2017/03/22/yes-it-was-the-affordable-care-act-that-increased-premiums/#796c4b0211d2 (accessed November 25, 2019).

Boorman, Georgi. "How the Theory of White Privilege Leads to Socialism." *Federalist.* June 26, 2018. https://thefederalist.com/2018/06/26/theory-white-privilege-leads-socialism (accessed December 2, 2019).

Boskin, Michael J. *A Closer Look at the Left's Agenda: Scientific, Economic, and Numerical Illiteracy on the Campaign Trail.* Stanford, CA: Hoover Institution, Stanford University, 2019. Available online at http://hoover.org/sites/default/files/research/docs/a-closer-look-at-the-lefts-agenda-scientific-economic-and-numerical-illiteracy-on-the-campaign-trail.pdf (accessed November 25, 2019).

Bourne, Ryan. "Do Minimum Wage Increases Raise Crime Rates?" *CATO Institute* (blog). March 18, 2019. https://www.cato.org/blog/do-minimum-wage-increases-raise-crime-rates (accessed December 4, 2019).

Brennan Center for Justice. New York University School of Law. "Debunking the Voter Fraud Myth." March 12, 2017. https://www.brennancenter.org/sites/default/files/analysis/Briefing_Memo_Debunking_Voter_Fraud_Myth.pdf (accessed November 29, 2019).

Brennan, John O. Interview on *MSNBC*, March 25, 2019, video interview, posted by Wojciech Pawelczyk, March 29, 2019, 9:08 a.m., *Twitter*, https://twitter.com/PolishPatriotTM/status/1110211940104704001/video/1 (accessed November 22, 2019).

———. (@JohnBrennan). Posted March 17, 2018, 5:00 a.m. to @realDonaldTrump. *Twitter*. https://twitter.com/johnbrennan/status/974978856997224448?lang=en (accessed November 22, 2019).

Brinklow, Adam. "California High-Speed Rail Cost May Approach $100 Billion." *Curbed San Francisco*. March 12, 2018. https://sf.curbed.com/2018/3/12/17110190/high-speed-rail-cost-money-bullet-train (accessed January 3, 2020).

Burke, Michael. "Ocasio-Cortez: 'Capitalism Is Irredeemable.'" *Hill*. March 10, 2019. https://thehill.com/homenews/house/433394-ocasio-cortez-capitalism-is-irredeemable (accessed November 24, 2019).

Camarota, Steven A., and Karen Zeigler. "The Impact of Legal and Illegal Immigration on the Apportionment of Seats in the U.S. House of Representatives in 2020." *Center for Immigration Studies*. December 19, 2019. https://cis.org/Report/Impact-Legal-and-Illegal-Immigration-Apportionment-Seats-US-House-Representatives-2020 (accessed December 25, 2019).

Caplan, Bryan. " Utopian Experimental Socialism." *Library of Economics and Liberty*. 2012. https://www.econlib.org/archives/2012/10/utopian_experim.html (accessed November 25, 2019).

Caracas Chronicles Team. "ENCOVI 2017: A Staggering Hunger Crisis, in Cold, Hard Numbers." *Caracas Chronicles*. February 21, 2018. https://www.caracaschronicles.com/2018/02/21/encovi-2017 (accessed December 7, 2019).

Carter, Robert M. "Why Scientists Disagree About Global Warming." *Heartland Institute*. November 30, 2015. https://www.hcartland.org/news-opinion/news/why-scientists-disagree-about-global-warming (accessed November 25, 2019).

Cesario, Joseph, and David Johnson. "Our Database of Police Officers in Fatal Shootings Reveals Who Shot Citizens." *Foundation for Economic Education*. July 23, 2019. https://fee.org/articles/our-research-of-police-shootings-reveals-who-is-the-likeliest-to-be-shot-by-police (accessed November 19, 2019).

CFACT editors. "Seeing the CO2 Greening of Plant Earth." *CFACT*. March 8, 2018. https://www.cfact.org/2018/03/08/seeing-the-co2-greening-of-planet-earth (accessed November 25, 2019).

Chalfin, Aaron, and Justin McCrary. "Criminal Deterrence: A Review of the Literature." *Journal of Economic Literature* 55, no. 1 (2017): 5–48. https://doi.org/10.1257/jel.20141147; https://eml.berkeley.edu/~jmccrary/chalfin_mccrary2017.pdf (accessed January 27, 2020).

Coalition Against Insurance Fraud. "Healthcare: Recoveries & Improper Payments." *Insurance Fraud*. March 2019. https://insurancefraud.org/fraud-stats/ (accessed November 22, 2019).

Collins English Dictionary. HarperCollins. 2019. https://www.collinsdictionary.com/.

Cooper, Anderson. "Alexandria Ocasio-Cortez: The Rookie Congresswoman Challenging the Democratic Establishment." *CBS News*. *60 Minutes*. January 6, 2019.

https://www.cbsnews.com/news/alexandria-ocasio-cortez-the-rookie-congress woman-challenging-the-democratic-establishment-60-minutes-interview-full -transcript-2019-01-06/?ftag=CNM-00-10aab7d&linkId=62017632 (accessed January 28, 2020).

Crime Prevention Research Center. "Comparing Murder Rates and Gun Ownership Across Countries." *CPRC* (Original Research). March 31, 2014. https://crime research.org/2014/03/comparing-murder-rates-across-countries (accessed November 23, 2019).

———. "Do States with Stricter Gun Control Laws Have Fewer Gun Deaths? No. Do They Have Fewer Homicides and Suicides? Definitely Not." *CPRC* (Original Research). March 27, 2018. https://crimeresearch.org/2018/03/states-stricter-gun -control-laws-fewer-gun-deaths-no-fewer-homicides-suicides-definitely-no (accessed December 28, 2019).

———. "Responding To John Donohue's Responses to Our Evaluation of His New Study." *CPRC* (Original Research). July 12, 2017. https://crimeresearch.org/ 2017/07/responding-john-donohues-responses-evaluation-new-study (accessed November 23, 2019).

C-SPAN. "Statement from Special Counsel Robert Mueller." YouTube video. 10:30 min. Posted by C-SPAN. May 29, 2019. https://www.youtube.com/ watch?v=3ah7mneJ32A (accessed November 26, 2019).

Curry, Judith. "Spinning the Climate Model—Observation Comparison [Part I]." *Climate Etc.* February 22, 2013. https://judithcurry.com/2013/02/22/spinning-the -climate-model-observation-comparison (accessed January 22, 2020);

———. "Spinning the Climate Model—Observation Comparison: Part II." *Climate Etc*. October 2, 2013. https://judithcurry.com/2013/10/02/spinning-the-climate -model-observation-comparison-part-ii (accessed January 22, 2020).

———. "Spinning the Climate Model—Observation Comparison: Part III." *Climate Etc*. October 13, 2013. https://judithcurry.com/2013/10/13/spinning-the-climate -model-observations-comparison-part-iii (accessed January 22, 2020).

Curtis, Claire, Ishmael Russell, and Lucas Russell. "Increasing Carbon Dioxide Levels Affect Plant Growth." YouTube video. 10:10 min. Posted by G Morwong. October 29, 2015. https://www.youtube.com/watch?v=0NFu4QBIXRw (accessed November 25, 2019).

Data USA. "Police Officers: Race and Ethnicity." N.d. https://datausa.io/profile/ soc/333050 (accessed January 7, 2019).

Depken II, Craig A. *Microeconomics DeMystified*. Emeryville, CA: McGraw-Hill, 2006.

Dershowitz, Alan M. "The Mueller Waiting Game." *Gatestone Institute, International Policy Council*. April 4, 2019. https://www.gatestoneinstitute.org/14005/ mueller-report-waiting (accessed November 19, 2019).

Dictionary.com. 2019. https://www.dictionary.com/.

Ditch, David. "California's High-Speed Rail Failure Shows the Insanity of Green New Deal." *Daily Signal*. February 12, 2019. https://www.dailysignal.com/2019/02/12/ californias-high-speed-rail-failure-shows-the-insanity-of-green-new-deal (accessed January 3, 2020).

Donohue, John J., Abhay Aneja, and Kyle D. Weber. "Right-to-Carry Laws and Violent Crime: A Comprehensive Assessment Using Panel Data and a State-Level Synthetic Control Analysis." *National Bureau of Economics Research*. NBER Working Paper No. 23510. June 2017. Revised November 2018. https://www.nber.org/papers/w23510 (accessed November 23, 2019).

Durden, Tyler. "All the World's Carbon Emissions In One Chart." *ZeroHedge*. June 7, 2019. https://www.zerohedge.com/news/2019-06-06/all-worlds-carbon-emissions-one-chart (accessed November 25, 2019).

Easterbrook, D. J. "Greenhouse Gases." In *Evidence-Based Climate Science (Second Edition)*. *Elsevier Science Direct*. September 23, 2016, 163–73. https://www.sciencedirect.com/science/article/pii/B9780128045886000094 (accessed November 25, 2019).

———."The Medieval Warm Period (900 A.D. to 1300 A.D.)." In *Evidence-Based Climate Science (Second Edition)*. *Elsevier Science Direct*. September 23, 2016, 137–60. https://www.sciencedirect.com/topics/earth-and-planetary-sciences/medieval-warm-period (accessed January 14, 2020).

———. "Pacific Decadal Oscillation." In *Evidence-Based Climate Science (Second Edition)*. *Elsevier Science Direct*. September 23, 2016, 395–411. https://www.sciencedirect.com/topics/earth-and-planetary-sciences/pacific-decadal-oscillation (accessed November 25, 2019).

———. "Water Vapor." In *Evidence-Based Climate Science (Second Edition)*. *Elsevier Science Direct*. September 23, 2016, 163–73. https://www.sciencedirect.com/topics/earth-and-planetary-sciences/water-vapor (accessed November 25, 2019).

Eastman, John C. "The General Warrant and the Politics of Personal Destruction." *American Greatness*. June 20, 2017. https://amgreatness.com/2017/06/20/general-warrant-politics-personal-destruction (accessed November 30, 2019).

Ebeling, Richard M. "Socialism, Like Dracula, Rises Again from the Grave." *American Institute for Economic Research*. July 16, 2018. https://www.aier.org/article/socialism-like-dracula-rises-again-from-the-grave (accessed December 18, 2019).

eHealth. "Health Insurance Price Index Report: 2018 Open Enrollment Period." *eHealth*. September 2018. http://news.ehealthinsurance.com/_ir/68/20188/eHealth%20Health%20Insurance%20Index%20Report%20for%20the%202018%20OEP.pdf (accessed November 25, 2019).

Erikson, Robert, and Christopher Wlezien. "How To Read the Polls—And Keep Your Sanity—In Two Easy Steps." *Washington Post*. June 8, 2016. https://www.washingtonpost.com/news/monkey-cage/wp/2016/06/08/how-to-read-the-election-polls-and-keep-your-sanity-in-two-easy-steps (accessed November 26, 2019).

Evans, David M. W. "I Was on the Global Warming Gravy Train." *Mises Institute*. May 28, 2007. https://mises.org/library/i-was-global-warming-gravy-train (accessed November 25, 2019).

Executive Office for Immigration Review (EOIR). "Asylum Rates." April 16, 2018. https://www.justice.gov/eoir/file/1061586/download (accessed December 3, 2019).

Ferrara, Peter. "The Disgraceful Episode of Lysenkoism Brings Us Global Warming Theory." *Forbes*. April 28, 2013. https://www.forbes.com/sites/peterferrara/

2013/04/28/the-disgraceful-episode-of-lysenkoism-brings-us-global-warming-theory/#1d3664207ac8 (accessed November 25, 2019).

Feynman, Richard P. *The Pleasure of Finding Things Out: The Best Short Works of Richard P. Feynman*. Edited by Jeffrey Robbins. New York: Basic Books, 1999. Reprint. 2005.

Figueres, Christiana. "UN Climate Change Warns That the World Economy Is Transformed Intentionally." *World Press* (blog). May 2, 2015. https://blogsl2n.wordpress.com/2015/02/05/the-top-un-climate-change-official-warns-that-first-time-the-world-economy-is-transformed-intentionally-christiana-figueres (accessed November 23, 2019).

Fox News. "Venezuelans Regret Gun Ban: 'A Declaration of War Against an Unarmed Population.'" *Education News*. December 14, 2018. https://www.educationviews.org/venezuelans-regret-gun-ban-a-declaration-of-war-against-an-unarmed-population (accessed January 2, 2020).

Franklin, Charles H. "The 'Margin of Error' for Differences in Polls." Posted by *ABC News* October 27, 2002; revised February 9, 2007. https://abcnews.go.com/images/PollingUnit/MOEFranklin.pdf (accessed November 26, 2019).

Frazis, Harley. "Employed Workers Leaving the Labor Force: An Analysis of Recent Trends." *Monthly Labor Review*. U.S. Bureau of Labor Statistics. May 2017. https://doi.org/10.21916/mlr.2017.16 (accessed January 10, 2020).

Fredericks, Bob. "Michael Bloomberg Says He Won't Run for President in 2020 but Could Beat Trump." *New York Post*. March 5, 2019. https://nypost.com/2019/03/05/michael-bloomberg-says-he-wont-run-for-president-in-2020-but-could-beat-trump (accessed November 23, 2019).

Friedmann, Sarah. "What Is a Certificate of Ascertainment? It Provides a Link between the Popular Vote & the Electors' Votes." *Bustle*. November 3, 2016. https://www.bustle.com/articles/191177-what-is-a-certificate-of-ascertainment-it-provides-a-link-between-the-popular-vote-the (accessed November 3, 2019).

Fyfe, John C., Gerald A. Meehl, Matthew H. England, Michael E. Mann, Benjamin D. Santer, Gregory M. Flato, Ed Hawkins, Nathan P. Gillett, Shang-Ping Xie, Yu Kosaka, and Neil C. Swar. "Making Sense of the Early-2000s Warming Slowdown." *Nature Climate Change* 6 (2016): 224–28. https://doi.org/10.1038/nclimate2938 (accessed January 21, 2020).

Gallup. "Presidential Job Approval Center." *Gallup*. N.d. https://news.gallup.com/interactives/185273/presidential-job-approval-center.aspx (accessed November 3, 2019).

Gibbs, John. "Voter Fraud Is Real. Here's the Proof." *Federalist*. October 13, 2016. https://thefederalist.com/2016/10/13/voter-fraud-real-heres-proof (accessed November 29, 2019).

GoodTherapy. "Psychobabble." *GoodTherapy* (blog). 2016. https://www.goodtherapy.org/blog/psychpedia/psychobabble (last updated January 29, 2016).

Goodwill Community Foundation. "What Is an Echo Chamber?" *Digital Media Literacy*. 1998–2019. https://edu.gcfglobal.org/en/digital-media-literacy/what-is-an-echo-chamber/1 (accessed November 19, 2019).

Goodwin, Michael. "Goodwin: Why are Democrats Acting Like They Have Something to Hide?" *New York Post*. October 26, 2019. https://nypost.com/2019/10/26/goodwin-why-are-democrats-acting-like-they-have-something-to-hide (accessed November 23, 2019).

Gould David, and Roy J. Ruffin. "Trade Deficits: Causes and Consequences." *Economic and Financial Policy Review* (January 1996): 10–20. https://www.researchgate.net/publication/5029945_Trade_Deficits_Causes_and_Consequences (accessed November 25, 2019).

Gratzer, David. "The Ugly Truth About Canadian Health Care." *City Journal*. Summer 2007. https://www.city-journal.org/html/ugly-truth-about-canadian-health-care-13032.html (accessed November 25, 2019).

Greenfield, Daniel. "The Environmental Apocalypse: The Movement to Destroy Human Civilization as We Know It." *Frontpage*. July 13, 2013. https://www.frontpagemag.com/fpm/198937/environmental-apocalypse-daniel-greenfield (accessed November 25, 2019).

Halbrook, Stephen P. *Gun Control in the Third Reich*. Oakland, CA: Independent Institute, 2013.

Happer, William. "C02 Is Not a Pollutant: Debunking a Global-Warming Myth." *Public Discourse*. December 1, 2009. https://www.thepublicdiscourse.com/2009/12/1037 (accessed November 26, 2019).

Hardin, Garrett. "Tragedy of the Commons." *Library of Economics and Liberty*. N.d. https://www.econlib.org/library/Enc/TragedyoftheCommons.html (accessed November 26, 2019).

Harinam, Vincent, and Rob Henderson. "Why White Privilege Is Wrong—Part 1." *Quillette*. August 22, 2019. https://quillette.com/2019/08/22/why-white-privilege-is-wrong-part-1 (accessed December 30, 2019).

Harris, Tim. "Mueller Makes First Statement: 'The Report Is My Testimony,' I Hope This Is the Only Time I Speak." *RealClear Politics*. May 29, 2019. https://www.realclearpolitics.com/video/2019/05/29/watch_live_special_counsel_robert_mueller_to_make_statement.html (accessed November 26, 2019).

Hawley, George. "The Demography of the Alt-Right." *Institute for Family Studies (IFS)*. August 9, 2018. https://ifstudies.org/blog/the-demography-of-the-alt-right (accessed December 29, 2019).

Hayek, F [Friedrich]. A. *Law, Legislation and Liberty*. Volume 2. *The Mirage of Social Justice*. Chicago: University of Chicago Press, 1976.

———. *The Road to Serfdom: The Definitive Edition* (Text and Documents). Edited by Bruce Caldwell. Chicago: University of Chicago Press, 2007.

Hazlitt, Henry. *Economics in One Lesson*. Fiftieth Anniversary ed. Baltimore: Laissez Faire Books, 1996.

Heilbroner, Robert. "The World After Communism." *Dissent* (Fall 1990): 429–30. Reprint. Rev. ed. "Socialism." *Library of Economics and Liberty*. N.d. https://www.econlib.org/library/Enc/Socialism.html (accessed November 25, 2019).

Hemingway, Mollie, and Carrie Severino. *Justice on Trial: The Kavanaugh Confirmation and the Future of the Supreme Court*. Washington, DC: Regnery Publishing, 2019.

Henderson, David R. "Demand." *Library of Economics and Liberty.* N.d. https://www.econlib.org/library/Enc/Demand.html (accessed November 25, 2019).

———. "Rent Seeking." *Library of Economics and Liberty.* N.d. https://www.econlib.org/library/Enc/RentSeeking.html (accessed November 19, 2019).

Heritage Foundation. "Election Fraud Cases [by state]." 2019. https://www.heritage.org/voterfraud/search (accessed November 22, 2019).

Heshmat, Shahram. "What Is Confirmation Bias?" *Psychology Today* (online; blog). April 23, 2015. https://www.psychologytoday.com/us/blog/science-choice/201504/what-is-confirmation-bias (accessed November 23, 2019).

Higgs, Robert. *Against Leviathan: Government Power and a Free Society.* Oakland, CA: Independent Institute, 2005.

———. "Fear: The Foundation of Every Government's Power." *Independent Institute.* May 17, 2005. https://www.independent.org/publications/article.asp?id=1510 (accessed November 25, 2019).

Hitler, Adolf. "'Why We Are Anti-Semites'—Text of Adolf Hitler's 1920 Speech at the Hofbräugaus." *Carolyn Yeager.* January 29, 2013. https://carolynyeager.net/why-we-are-antisemites-text-adolf-hitlers-1920-speech-hofbr%C3%A4uhaus (accessed January 26, 2020).

Holtz-Eakin, Douglas, Dan Bosch, Ben Gitis, Dan Goldbeck, and Philip Rossetti. "The Green New Deal: Scope, Scale, and Implications." *American Action Forum (AAF).* February 25, 2019. https://www.americanactionforum.org/research/the-green-new-deal-scope-scale-and-implications (accessed December 18, 2019).

Huang, Yi, and Maziar Bani Shahabadi. "Why Logarithmic? A Note on the Dependence of Radiative Forcing on Gas Concentration." *Journal of Geophysical Research: Atmospheres* 119, no. 24 (December 28, 2014): 13683–89. https://doi.org/10.1002/2014JD022466 (accessed January 14, 2020).

Humlum, Ole, Kjell Stordahl, and Jan-Erik Solheim. "The Phase Relation between Atmospheric Carbon Dioxide and Global Temperature." *Global and Planetary Change.* 2013. https://doi.org/10.1016/j.gloplacha.2012.08.008 (accessed January 22, 2020).

Ingemarson, Anders. "How 'Democratic Socialism' Wreaked Havoc on My Native Sweden." *Federalist.* September 5, 2018. https://thefederalist.com/2018/09/05/democratic-socialism-wreaked-havoc-native-sweden (accessed November 26, 2019).

Ingham, Sean. "Pareto-Optimality." *Encyclopaedia Britannica, Social Sciences.* N.d. https://www.britannica.com/topic/Pareto-optimality (accessed November 26, 2019).

Intergovernmental Panel on Climate Change (IPCC). "Climate Change 2001: The Physical Science Basis." *Contribution of Working Group I (WGI) to the Third Assessment Report (AR3) of the Intergovernmental Panel on Climate Change (IPCC).* 2001. https://archive.ipcc.ch/ipccreports/tar/wg1/505.htm (accessed December 17, 2019).

———. "Climate Change 2007: The Physical Science Basis." *Contribution of Working Group I (WGI) to the Fourth Assessment Report (AR4) of the Intergovernmental Panel on Climate Change (IPCC).* 2007. https://www.ipcc.ch/site/assets/uploads/2018/05/ar4_wg1_full_report-1.pdf (accessed December 17, 2019).

———. "Climate Change 2013: The Physical Science Basis." *Contribution of Working Group I (WGI) to the Fifth Assessment Report (AR5) of the Intergovernmental Panel on Climate Change (IPCC)*. 2013. http://www.climatechange2013.org/report/full-report (accessed December 17, 2019).

———. "Principles Governing IPCC Work." 2013. https://archive.ipcc.ch/pdf/ipcc-principles/ipcc-principles.pdf (accessed December 17, 2019).

"Is Social Justice, Just?" *Independent Review: A Journal of Political Economy* 24, no. 1 (2019).

Johnson, David J., Trevor Tress, Nicole Burkel, Carley Taylor, and Joseph Cesario. "Officer Characteristics and Racial Disparities in Fatal Officer-Involved Shootings." Edited by Kenneth W. Wachter. *PNAS* 116, no. 32 (2019): 15877–82. https://www.pnas.org/content/116/32/15877 (accessed November 19, 2019).

Johnston, Louis D. "Why Falling Unemployment Doesn't Always Mean Rising Employment." *MinnPost*. December 7, 2011. https://www.minnpost.com/macro-micro-minnesota/2011/12/why-falling-unemployment-doesnt-always-mean-rising-employment (accessed November 23, 2019).

Johnston, Matthew. "How Labor Force Participation Rate Affects U.S. Unemployment." *Investopedia*. June 25, 2019. https://www.investopedia.com/articles/investing/103015/how-labor-force-participation-rate-affects-us-unemployment.asp (accessed November 23, 2019).

Jones, Garett. "Redistributing from Capitalists to Workers: An Impossibility Theorem." *Library of Economics and Liberty*. 2013. https://www.econlib.org/archives/2013/03/redistributing.html (accessed November 26, 2019).

Karlsson, Stefan. "The Sweden Myth." *Mises Institute*. August 7, 2016. https://mises.org/library/sweden-myth?sms_ss=facebook&at_xt=4d91345528ba2b1c%2C0 (accessed November 23, 2019).

Karpman, Stephen B. *A Game Free Life: The New Transactional Analysis of Intimacy, Openness, and Happiness*. San Francisco: Drama Triangle Publications, 2014.

Kauppinen, J. [Jyrki], and P. [Pekka] Malmi. "No Experimental Evidence for the Significant Anthropogenic Climate Change." *arXiv* (Cornell University Open Access). July 13, 2019. https://arxiv.org/pdf/1907.00165.pdf (accessed November 25, 2019).

Keefer, Philip, and Stephen Knack. "Boondoggles, Rent-Seeking, and Political Checks and Balances: Public Investment under Unaccountable Governments." *Review of Economics and Statistics* 89, no. 3 (2007): 566–72. Available online at http://pscourses.ucsd.edu/ps200b/Keefer%20Knack%20Boondoggles,%20Rent-Seeking,%20and%20Political%20Checks%20and%20Balances.pdf (accessed November 19, 2019).

Kiely, Eugene. "Obama's Economic Sleight of Hand." *FackCheck.org*. June 15, 2012. https://www.factcheck.org/2012/06/obamas-economic-sleight-of-hand (accessed November 23, 2019).

Klein, Philip. "AOC's Chief of Staff Comments Just Killed the Green New Deal." July 12, 2019. *Washington Examiner*. https://www.washingtonexaminer.com/opinion/aocs-chief-of-staff-just-killed-the-green-new-deal (accessed November 25, 2019).

Klimek, Peter, Yuri Yegorov, Rudolf Hanel, and Stefan Thurner. "Statistical Detection of Systematic Election Irregularities." *Proceedings National Academy Science USA* (*PNAS*) 109, no. 41 (October 9, 2012): 16469–73. https://dx.doi.org/10.1073%2Fpnas.1210722109 (accessed November 22, 2019).

Kline, Audrey D. "Gun Control in Nazi Germany." *Mises Daily Articles. Mises Institute*. May 9, 2014. https://mises.org/library/gun-control-nazi-germany (accessed January 2, 2020).

Kling, Arnold. "Ricardo's Difficult Idea Eludes Wonks." *Econlog at Econlib*. January 13, 2004. https://www.econlib.org/archives/2004/01/ricardos_diffic.html (accessed November 25, 2019).

Knutson, Thomas R., Rong Zhang, and Larry W. Horowitz. "Prospects for a Prolonged Slowdown in Global Warming in the Early 21st century." *Nature Communications* 7, no. 13676 (2016): 1–12. https://doi.org/10.1038/ncomms13676 (accessed January 18, 2020).

Koerth, Maggie. "How Much Is the Government Spending On Climate Change? We Don't Know, and Neither Do They." *FiveThirtyEight*. February 8, 2019. https://fivethirtyeight.com/features/how-much-is-the-government-spending-on-climate-change-we-dont-know-and-neither-do-they (accessed January 26, 2020).

Landsburg, Steve. "A Quick Economics Lesson." *Bad Reasoning, Economics, and Policy*. January 27, 2010. http://www.thebigquestions.com/2010/01/27/a-quick-economics-lesson (accessed November 26, 2019).

Lang, Kevin, and Jee-Yeon K. Lehmann. "Racial Discrimination in the Labor Market: Theory and Empirics." *Journal of Economic Literature* 50, no. 4 (2012): 959–1006.

Larsen, Emily. "Fact Check: Are 80% of Asylum Court Cases Not Approved?" *Daily Signal*. July 5, 2018. https://www.dailysignal.com/2018/07/05/fact-check-are-80-of-asylum-court-cases-not-approved (accessed December 3, 2019).

Learn Liberty. "Shaming Someone Doesn't Change Their Mind: People Are Prone to Believe What They Want to Believe." YouTube video. 1:57 min. February 1, 2017. https://www.youtube.com/watch?v=4qU7KVTAMIU (accessed November 23, 2019).

L & E Global. "Anti-Discrimination Laws in USA." March 24, 2017. *L & E Global*. https://knowledge.leglobal.org/anti-discrimination-laws-in-usa (accessed November 20, 2019).

Lemieux, Pierre. "Are Imports a Drag on the Economy?" *Regulation* (Fall 2015): 6–8. https://www.cato.org/sites/cato.org/files/serials/files/regulation/2015/9/regulation-v38n3-6_0.pdf (accessed November 25, 2019).

———. "Free Trade Isn't Killing Jobs." *Foundation for Economic Education* (*FEE*). October 16, 2017. https://fee.org/articles/free-trade-isnt-killing-jobs (accessed November 25, 2019).

———. "The Poverty of Protectionism and the Impact of Tariffs." *Library of Economics and Liberty*. N.d. https://www.econlib.org/the-poverty-of-protectionism-and-the-impact-of-tariffs (accessed November 25, 2019).

Leonard, Thomas C. *Illiberal Reformers: Race, Eugenics, and American Economics in the Progressive Era*. Princeton, NJ: Princeton University Press, 2016. Reprint. 2017.

Lexico. 2019. http://www.lexico.com.

Library of Economics and Liberty. "Adam Smith (1723-1790)." *Library of Economics and Liberty*. N.d. https://www.econlib.org/library/Enc/bios/Smith.html (accessed November 22, 2019).

Lind, Bill. "The Origins of Political Correctness." *Accuracy in Academia*. February 5, 2000. https://www.academia.org/the-origins-of-political-correctness (accessed December 25, 2019).

Logically Fallacious. "Affirming the Consequent." *Logically Fallacious*. N.d. https://www.logicallyfallacious.com/tools/lp/Bo/LogicalFallacies/14/Affirming-the-Consequent (accessed November 23, 2019).

———. "Appeal to Authority." *Logically Fallacious*. N.d. https://www.logicallyfallacious.com/tools/lp/Bo/LogicalFallacies/21/Appeal-to-Authority (accessed January 6, 2020).

———. "Causal Reductionism." *Logically Fallacious*. N.d. https://www.logicallyfallacious.com/tools/lp/Bo/LogicalFallacies/64/Causal-Reductionism (accessed January 6, 2020).

———. "Cherry Picking." *Logically Fallacious*. N.d. https://www.logicallyfallacious.com/logicalfallacies/Cherry-Picking (accessed November 23, 2019).

———. "Fallacy of Division." *Logically Fallacious*. N.d. https://www.logicallyfallacious.com/tools/lp/Bo/LogicalFallacies/89/Fallacy-of-Division (accessed January 6, 2020).

———. "Nirvana Fallacy." *Logically Fallacious*. N.d. https://www.logicallyfallacious.com/logicalfallacies/Nirvana-Fallacy (accessed November 25, 2019).

———. "Political Correctness Fallacy." *Logically Fallacious*. N.d. https://www.logicallyfallacious.com/tools/lp/Bo/LogicalFallacies/141/Political-Correctness-Fallacy (accessed November 23, 2019).

———. "Proving Non-Existence." *Logically Fallacious*. N.d. https://www.logicallyfallacious.com/tools/lp/Bo/LogicalFallacies/145/Proving-Non-Existence (accessed November 25, 2019)

———. "Subjectivist Fallacy." *Logically Fallacious*. N.d. https://www.logicallyfallacious.com/tools/lp/Bo/LogicalFallacies/171/Subjectivist-Fallacy (accessed November 23, 2019).

Lomborg, Bjørn. "How Green Policies Hurt the Poor." *Spectator*. April 5, 2014. https://www.spectator.co.uk/2014/04/let-them-eat-carbon-credits (accessed December 18. 2019).

Lott Jr., John R. "Weak Evidence for New Gun Control Laws." *Townhall*. July 23, 2018. https://townhall.com/columnists/johnrlottjr/2018/07/23/weak-evidence-for-new-gun-control-laws-n2502786 (accessed December 19, 2019).

MacDonald, Steve. "The Unemployment Rate vs. the Labor Force Participation Rate in 90-Seconds." *Granite Grok* (blog). September 2, 2016. https://granitegrok.com/blog/2016/09/unemployment-rate-vs-labor-force-participation-rate-90-seconds (accessed November 23, 2019).

Mangu-Ward, Katherine. "Tariffs Are Self-Imposed Sanctions." *Reason*. June 2018. https://reason.com/2018/05/01/tariffs-are-self-imposed-sanct (accessed January 3, 2020).

Marjanovic, Boris. "Don't Be Fooled by Stock Market Noise." *Seeking Alpha*. April 16, 2015. https://seekingalpha.com/article/3074086-dont-be-fooled-by-stock-market-noise (accessed November 26, 2019).

Martín, Karina. "Maduro Drops All Pretense, Vows to Become a Dictator to Ensure 'Economic Peace' in Venezuela." *Panam Post*. September 10, 2017. https://panampost.com/karina-martin/2017/09/10/maduro-dictator-ensure-economic-peace-in-venezuela (accessed December 7,2019).

Marx, Karl, and Friedrich Engels. "Manifesto of the Communist Party: I. Bourgeois and Proletarians." N.d. *Avalon Project*. Yale Law School. Lillian Goldman Law Library. https://avalon.law.yale.edu/19th_century/manone.asp (accessed December 3, 2019).

Maue, Ryan. "You Ought to Have a Look: Time for a New 'Hiatus' in Warming, or Time for an Accelerated Warming Trend?" *Cato Institute* (blog). May 25, 2017. https://www.cato.org/blog/you-ought-have-look-time-new-hiatus-warming-or-time-accelerated-warming-trend (accessed November 25, 2019).

Mcardle, Mairead. "Conservative Group Hits AOC with Ethics Complaint." *National Review*. March 7, 2019. https://www.nationalreview.com/news/conservative-group-hits-aoc-with-ethics-complaint (accessed January 28,2020).

McBride, Jessica. "Popular Vote 2016: How California Drove Hillary Clinton's Lead." *Heavy*. November 18, 2016. https://heavy.com/news/2016/11/popular-vote-results-2016-clinton-trump-2012-2008-vs-electoral-college-california-uncounted-ballots-new-york-update-totals-final (accessed November 3, 2019).

McCann, Daryl. "Alt-Right vs Alt-Left." *Quadrant Online*. March 22, 2017. https://quadrant.org.au/magazine/2017/03/alt-right-v-alt-left (accessed December 29, 2019).

McCarthy, Andrew C. "Is 'Guilty Until Proven Innocent' the New Standard?" *National Review*. April 26, 2018. https://www.nationalreview.com/2018/04/trump-russia-investigation-guilty-until-proven-innocent-new-standard (accessed November 30, 2019).

McConnell, Michael, and Steve Thompson. "What Is a Revolution?" *Alpha History*. June 20, 2018. https://alphahistory.com/vcehistory/what-is-a-revolution (accessed November 25, 2019).

McIntyre, Stephen, and Ross McKitrick. "Hockey Sticks, Principal Components, and Spurious Significance." *Geophysical Research Letters* 32. L03710. February 12, 2005. http://www.climateaudit.info/pdf/mcintyre.mckitrick.2005.grl.pdf (accessed November 25, 2019).

McQuillan, Lawrence J., and Graham H. Walker. "Housing, Human Dignity and 'State of Emergency.'" *Independent Institute*. October 25, 2019. http://www.independent.org/news/article.asp?id=12962 (accessed November 25, 2019).

Michaels, Patrick J. "The 'BEST' Global Warming Science Goes Lukewarm." *Cato Institute*. August 2, 2012. https://www.cato.org/publications/commentary/best-global-warming-science-goes-lukewarm (accessed January 11, 2020).

Mises, Ludwig von. *The Anti-Capitalistic Mentality*. Princeton, NJ: D. Van Nostrand, 1956. Reprint. Auburn, AL: Ludwig Von Mises Institute, 2008. Available online at https://mises.org/library/anti-capitalistic-mentality (accessed November 25, 2019).

Mitchell, Dan. "In One Chart, Everything You Need to Know about Big Government, the Welfare State, and Sweden's Economy." *International Liberty*. October 24, 2016. https://danieljmitchell.wordpress.com/2016/10/24/in-one-chart-everything-you-need-to-know-about-big-government-the-welfare-state-and-swedens-economy (accessed December 5, 2019).

———. "The Rise and Fall (and Rise) of Sweden." *International Liberty*. November 3, 2016. https://danieljmitchell.wordpress.com/2016/11/03/the-rise-and-fall-and-rise-of-sweden (accessed December 5, 2019).

Moore, Dylan. "How Gun Ownership Protects Citizens from an Abusive Government." *Federalist*. April 4, 2018. https://thefederalist.com/2018/04/04/guns-help-americans-protect-abusive-government (accessed January 1, 2020).

Morin, Rich, Kim Parker, Renee Stepler, and Andrew Mercer. "Behind the Badge." *Pew Research Center, Social & Demographic Trends*. January 11, 2017. https://www.pewsocialtrends.org/2017/01/11/behind-the-badge (accessed November 19, 2019).

Morningstar. "Course 407: Psychology and Investing, Selective Memory." 2015. http://news.morningstar.com/classroom2/course.asp?docId=145104&page=3 (accessed November 23, 2019).

Morrow, Brendan. "How Many Popular Votes Did Clinton & Trump Win in Each State?" *Heavy*. December 19, 2016. https://heavy.com/news/2016/11/how-many-popular-votes-did-hillary-clinton-donald-trump-win-2016-election-state-by-state (accessed November 3, 2019).

Mullen, Tom. "You Deserve a Tax Break and Your Boss Does Too." *Foundation for Economic Education*. November 16, 2017. https://fee.org/articles/you-deserve-a-tax-break-and-your-boss-does-too (accessed November 21, 2019).

Muller, Richard. "Global Warming Bombshell: A Prime Piece of Evidence Linking Human Activity to Climate Change Turns Out to be an Artifact of Poor Mathematics." *MIT Technology Review*. October 15, 2004. https://www.technologyreview.com/s/403256/global-warming-bombshell (accessed November 25, 2019).

Mundi Index. "CO2 Emissions (Metric Tons per Capita)—Country Ranking." *MundiIndex*. 2014. https://www.indexmundi.com/facts/indicators/EN.ATM.CO2E.PC/rankings (accessed November 24, 2019).

Munger, Michael. "What Can and Cannot Be Planned." *American Institute for Economic Research*. August 3, 2018. https://www.aier.org/article/what-can-and-cannot-be-planned (accessed January 3, 2020).

Murphy, Robert P. "Using IPCC to Defeat UN Climate Agenda." *Institute for Energy Research (IER)*. September 23, 2014. https://www.instituteforenergyresearch.org/climate-change/using-ipcc-defeat-un-climate-agenda (accessed November 25, 2019).

Murray, Chris. "Why Brett Kavanaugh Should Sue Christine Blasey Ford for Defamation." *Federalist*. October 17, 2018. https://thefederalist.com/2018/10/17/brett-kavanaugh-sue-christine-blasey-ford-defamation (accessed November 21, 2019).

Musumeci, Natalie. "Ocasio-Cortez Finds Amazon's HQ2 in NYC 'Extremely Concerning.'" *New York Post*. November 13, 2018. https://nypost.com/2018/11/13/

ocasio-cortez-finds-amazons-hq2-in-nyc-extremely-concerning (accessed November 24, 2019).

New York Post editors. "Mueller's Conclusions Expose Disgrace of Obama's Spy Chiefs." *New York Post*. March 26, 2019. https://nypost.com/2019/03/26/muellers-conclusions-expose-disgrace-of-obamas-spy-chiefs (accessed November 22, 2019).

Nilsson, Jeff. "The Long Tradition of the Smear Campaign." *Saturday Evening Post* (Weekly Newsletter). August 25, 2012. https://www.saturdayeveningpost.com/2012/08/tradition-dirty-politics (accessed November 23, 2019).

Nova, Joanne. "The 800 Year Lag in CO2 After Temperature—Graphed." *JoNova*. N.d. http://joannenova.com.au/global-warming-2/ice-core-graph (accessed January 14, 2020).

———. "Shock: Global Temperatures Driven by US Postal Charges." *JoNova*. N.d. http://joannenova.com.au/2009/05/shock-global-temperatures-driven-by-us-postal-charges (accessed January 14, 2020).

Ortiz-Ospina, Esteban, and Max Roser. "Financing Healthcare." *OurWorldInData.org*. 2019. https://ourworldindata.org/financing-healthcare (accessed November 25, 2019).

Orwell, George. "Appendix: The Principles of Newspeak." *Nineteen Eight-Four: A Novel*. London: Secker and Warburg, 1949. Reprint. New York: Penguin Books, 1990. http://orwell.ru/library/novels/1984/english/en_app (accessed November 22, 2019).

O'Sullivan, John. "Breaking: Fatal Courtroom Acts Ruins Michael "Hockey Stick" Mann." *Principia Scientifica*. July 4, 2017. https://principia-scientific.org/breaking-fatal-courtroom-act-ruins-michael-hockey-stick-mann (accessed November 25, 2019).

Pavlich, Katie. "New and Rare Durham Statement Shows IG Report Doesn't Come Close to Telling the Whole Story." *Townhall*. December 09, 2019. https://townhall.com/tipsheet/katiepavlich/2019/12/09/durham-we-disagree-with-the-igs-findings-on-how-the-investigation-into-trump-officials-started-n2557706 (accessed December 10, 2019).

Perry, Mark J. "18 Spectacularly Wrong Predictions Made Around the Time of First Earth Day in 1970, Expect More This Year." *AEIdeas* (blog). April 20, 2017. https://www.aei.org/carpe-diem/18-spectacularly-wrong-predictions-made-around-the-time-of-first-earth-day-in-1970-expect-more-this-year (accessed November 25, 2019).

Pierce, Tony. "As Unemployment Falls to a Two-Year Low, Obama Says There's Still Work To Do." *Los Angeles Times*. April 1, 2011. https://latimesblogs.latimes.com/washington/2011/04/obama-unemployment.html (accessed November 23, 2019).

Pipes, Richard. *Communism: A History*. New York: Modern Library, 2001. Reprint. 2003.

Pipes, Sally C. *The False Promise of Single-Payer Health Care*. New York: Encounter Broadside, 2018.

Pomerleau, Kyle. "How Scandinavian Countries Pay for Their Government Spending." *Tax Foundation*. June 10, 2015. https://taxfoundation.org/how-scandinavian-countries-pay-their-government-spending (accessed December 5, 2019).

Poor, Jeff. "Krugman Warns Not to Celebrate Last Week's Unemployment Data: 'It's Still Terrible.'" *Daily Caller*. April 3, 2011. https://dailycaller.com/2011/04/03/krugman-warns-not-to-celebrate-last-weeks-unemployment-data-its-still-terrible (accessed November 23, 2019).

Popper, Karl. *The Logic of Scientific Discovery*. Abingdon-on-Thames: Routledge, 1959.

———. *The Poverty of Historicism*. Abingdon-on-Thames: Routledge, 2002.

Powell, Benjamin. "'Democratic Socialists' Really Need to Learn More About Socialism." *Washington Examiner*. November 14, 2018. https://www.washingtonexaminer.com/opinion/op-eds/democratic-socialists-really-need-to-learn-more-about-socialism (accessed November 26, 2019). Reprint. *Independent Institute*. November 15, 2018. https://www.independent.org/news/article.asp?id=10613 (accessed November 26, 2019).

Powell, Jim. *FDR's Follies: How Roosevelt and His New Deal Prolonged the Great Depression*. New York: Three Rivers Press, 2003.

Prager, Dennis. "The Fallacy of 'White Privilege.'" *National Review*. February 16, 2016. https://www.nationalreview.com/2016/02/white-privilege-myth-reality (accessed December 31, 2019).

Price, Gary, and Tim Norbeck. "A Look Back at How the President Was Able to Sign Obamacare Into Law Four Years Ago." *Forbes*. March 26, 2014. https://www.forbes.com/sites/physiciansfoundation/2014/03/26/a-look-back-at-how-the-president-was-able-to-sign-obamacare-into-law-four-years-ago/#71ebfca526b7 (accessed November 25, 2019).

Psychology iResearch. "Recency Effect." *IresearchNet*. N.d. https://psychology.iresearchnet.com/social-psychology/decision-making/recency-effect (accessed November 23, 2019).

Rhoads, Steven E. "Marginalism." *Library of Economics and Liberty*. N.d. https://www.econlib.org/library/Enc/Marginalism.html (accessed November 25, 2019).

Richardson, Craig. "The 'Green New Deal' Is a Prescription for Poverty." *Washington Examiner*. January 28, 2019. https://www.washingtonexaminer.com/opinion/op-eds/the-green-new-deal-is-a-prescription-for-poverty (accessed December 18, 2019).

Roberts, Russell. "Incentives Matter." *Library of Economics and Liberty*. June 6, 2006. https://www.econlib.org/library/Columns/y2006/Robertsincentives.html (accessed November 25, 2019).

Roper, James E., and David M. Zin, eds. "Revealed Preference Theory." *Encyclopaedia Britannica, Economics*. December 30, 2013. https://www.britannica.com/topic/revealed-preference-theory (lasted updated May 24, 2016; accessed November 19, 2019).

Rossiter, Caleb. "The Scientific Consensus on Global Warming Does Not Support the Green New Deal." *Federalist*. March 7, 2019. https://thefederalist

.com/2019/03/07/scientific-consensus-global-warming-not-support-green-new-deal (accessed November 25, 2019).

Rothbard, Murray N. "John Kenneth Galbraith and the Sin of Affluence." *Mises Institute*. September 13, 2008. https://mises.org/library/john-kenneth-galbraith-and-sin-affluence (accessed November 26, 2019).

Saavedra, Ryan. "Pelosi Scraps Presumption of Innocence: Trump Needs to Prove He Is Innocent." *Daily Wire*. November 17, 2019. https://www.dailywire.com/news/pelosi-scraps-presumption-of-innocence-trump-needs-to-prove-he-is-innocent (accessed November 30, 2019).

Sanandaji, Nima. *Debunking Utopia: Exposing the Myth of Nordic Socialism*. Washington, DC: WND Books, 2016.

———. "The Nordic Democratic-Socialist Myth." *National Review*. July 26, 2016. https://www.nationalreview.com/2016/07/nordic-democratic-socialist-model-exposing-lefts-myth (accessed December 5, 2019).

Saunders, Joe. "Christine Blasey Ford's Attorney Admits Protecting Abortion Was Part of Her Motivation." *Western Journal*. September 4, 2019. https://www.westernjournal.com/christine-blasey-fords-attorney-admits-protecting-abortion-part-motivation (accessed January 26, 2020).

Schön, Lennart. "Sweden—Economic Growth and Structural Change, 1800-2000." *EH-Net. Economic History Association*. N.d. https://eh.net/encyclopedia/sweden-economic-growth-and-structural-change-1800-2000 (accessed December 5, 2019).

Schuettinger, Robert L., and Eamonn F. Butler. *Forty Centuries of Wage and Price Controls: How Not to Fight Inflation*. Washington, DC: Heritage Foundation, 1979.

Scruton, Roger. *Fools, Frauds, and Firebrands: The Thinkers of the New Left*. London: Bloomsbury, 2015. Reprint. 2019.

Shackford, Scott. "California's Bullet Train Project Doesn't Deserve Your Moist-Eyed Love Letters." *Reason*. February 14, 2019. https://reason.com/2019/02/14/californias-bullet-train-project-doesnt (accessed January 3, 2020).

Sheffield, Rachel, and Robert Rector. "The War on Poverty After 50 Years." *Heritage Foundation*. September 15, 2014. https://www.heritage.org/poverty-and-inequality/report/the-war-poverty-after-50-years (accessed January 8, 2020).

Shmueli, Galit. "To Explain or to Predict?" *Statistical Science* 25, no. 3 (2010): 289–310. https://www.stat.berkeley.edu/~aldous/157/Papers/shmueli.pdf (accessed January 21, 2020).

Shughart II, William F. "Public Choice." *Library of Economics and Liberty*. N.d. https://www.econlib.org/library/Enc/PublicChoice.html (accessed November 21, 2019).

Smiley, Gene. *Rethinking the Great Depression: A New View of Its Causes and Consequences*. Chicago: I. R. Dee, 2002.

Smith, Adam. *An Inquiry into the Nature and Causes of the Wealth of Nations* (1776). Edited by Edwin Cannan. London: Methuen, 1904.

Smith, Keri. "Yes, the Alt-Left Exists and It's Terrifying." *Foundation for Economic Education* (*FEE*). September 6, 2017. https://fee.org/articles/yes-the-alt-left-exists-and-its-terrifying (accessed December 29,2019).

Sowell, Thomas. *Basic Economics: A Common Sense Guide to the Economy*. 4th ed. New York: Basic Books, 2011.

———. "Discrimination, Economics, and Culture." In *Beyond the Color Line: New Perspectives on Race and Ethnicity in America*, edited by Abigail Thernstrom and Stephan Thernstrom, 167-80. Stanford, CA: Hoover Institution Press, 2002. Available online at https://www.hoover.org/sites/default/files/uploads/documents/0817998721_167.pdf (accessed November 19, 2019).

———. *Economic Facts and Fallacies*. 2nd ed. New York: Basic Books, 2011.

———. "Lessons from the Past." *Townhall*. January 28, 2019. https://townhall.com/columnists/thomassowell/2019/01/28/lessons-from-the-past-n2540365 (accessed January 26, 2020).

———. *Marxism: Philosophy and Economics*. London: George Unwin, 1985.

Spakovsky, Hans A. von. "The Electoral College: A Safeguard for Stable Elections." October 2, 2017. https://www.heritage.org/election-integrity/commentary/the-electoral-college-safeguard-stable-elections (accessed November 3, 2019).

Statista Research Department. "People Shot to Death by U.S. Police, by Race 2017-2019." Last edited October 30, 2019. https://www.statista.com/statistics/585152/people-shot-to-death-by-us-police-by-race (accessed November 19, 2019).

Stein, Herbert. "Balance of Payments." *Library of Economics and Liberty*. N.d. https://www.econlib.org/library/Enc/BalanceofPayments.html (accessed November 25, 2019).

Stossel, John. "Governments Don't Create Prosperity: The Truth About Economic Growth." *Reason*. September 29, 2011. https://reason.com/2011/09/29/governments-dont-create-prospe (accessed November 26, 2019).

Sullum, Jacob. "Do Strict Firearm Laws Give States Lower Gun Death Rates?" *Reason*. September 2, 2015. https://reason.com/2015/09/02/do-strict-firearm-laws-give-states-lower (accessed December 28, 2019).

Syrios, Andrew. "Fact Checking Paul Krugman's Claim To Be 'Right About Everything.'" *Mises Wire*. June 10, 2015. https://mises.org/library/fact-checking-paul-krugmans-claim-be-right-about-everything (accessed December 30, 2019).

Tabarrok, Alex. "Popularizing Arrow's Theorem II." *Marginal Revolution*. October 25, 2010. https://marginalrevolution.com/marginalrevolution/2010/10/popularizing-arrows-theorem-ii.html (accessed November 26, 2019).

Tegel, Simeon. "Why Do Many on the Global Left Still Support Venezuela's Maduro?" *NBC News*. October 26, 2017. https://www.nbcnews.com/storyline/venezuela-crisis/latin-american-leftists-defend-nicol-s-maduro-s-regime-n803866 (accessed December 7, 2019).

Texas State University. Department of Philosophy. "Begging the Question." *Texas State*. N.d. https://www.txstate.edu/philosophy/resources/fallacy-definitions/Begging-the-Question.html (accessed November 24, 2019).

Tobin, Jonathan S. "Doubling Down on Global-Warming Alarmism." *National Review*. October 11, 2018. https://www.nationalreview.com/2018/10/global-warming-ipcc-doubles-down (accessed November 25, 2019).

Toobin, Jeffrey. Post to *Twitter*. April 18, 2019. 7:34 a.m. https://twitter.com/JeffreyToobin/status/1118885464914714624 (accessed November 20, 2019).

Tracinski, Robert. "ClimateGate: The Fix Is In" *Real Clear Politics*. November 24, 2009. https://www.realclearpolitics.com/articles/2009/11/24/the_fix_is_in_99280.html (accessed January 22, 2020).

———. "Global Warming: The Theory that Predicts Nothing and Explains Everything." *Federalist*. June 8, 2015. https://thefederalist.com/2015/06/08/global-warming-the-theory-that-predicts-nothing-and-explains-everything (accessed November 25, 2019).

Tuttle, Ian. "The 97 Percent Solution." *National Review*. October 8, 2015. https://www.nationalreview.com/2015/10/climate-change-no-its-not-97-percent-consensus-ian-tuttle (accessed November 25, 2019).

University of Chicago Press. Interview with John R. Lott Jr. 1998. https://www.press.uchicago.edu/Misc/Chicago/493636.html (accessed November 23, 2019).

U.S. Bureau of Labor Statistics. "Calculating Approximate Standard Errors and Confidence Intervals for Current Populations Survey Estimates." November 2018. https://www.bls.gov/cps/calculating-standard-errors-and-confidence-intervals.pdf (accessed November 26, 2019).

———. "Career Outlook: Blacks in the Labor Force." February 2018. https://www.bls.gov/careeroutlook/2018/article/blacks-in-the-labor-force.htm (accessed November 20, 2019).

———. FRED. Federal Reserve Bank of St. Louis. https://fred.stlouisfed.org (accessed November 4, 2019).

———. FRED. Federal Reserve Bank of St. Louis. "All Employees, Total Nonfarm." November 1, 2019. https://fred.stlouisfed.org/series/PAYEMS (accessed November 21, 2019).

———. FRED. Federal Reserve Bank of St. Louis. "Federal Net Outlays as Percent of Gross Domestic Product." 2019. https://fred.stlouisfed.org/series/FYONGDA188S (accessed November 25, 2018).

———. Glossary. "Unemployed Persons (Current Population Survey)." 2019. https://www.bls.gov/bls/glossary.htm#U (accessed November 22, 2019).

———. "Graphics for Economic News Release, Civilian Labor Force Participation Rate." 1999-2019. https://www.bls.gov/charts/employment-situation/civilian-labor-force-participation-rate.htm (last updated October 2019).

———. "Graphics for Economic News Release, Civilian Unemployment Rate." 1999–2019. https://www.bls.gov/charts/employment-situation/civilian-unemployment-rate.htm (last updated October 2019).

———. "Graphics for Economic News Release, HOUSEHOLD DATA, Table A-15. Alternative Measure of Labor Underutilization." 2018–2019. https://www.bls.gov/news.release/empsit.t15.htm (last updated October 2019).

———. Handbook of Methods. "Error Measurement." 2019. https://www.bls.gov/opub/hom/topic/error-measurements.htm (accessed November 21, 2019).

———. "HOUSEHOLD DATA ANNUAL AVERAGES, 3. Employment Status of the Civilian Noninstitutional Population by Age, Sex, and Race." 2016. https://www.bls.gov/cps/aa2016/cpsaat03.htm (last modified date: January 18, 2019).

———. "HOUSEHOLD DATA ANNUAL AVERAGES, 3. Employment Status of the Civilian Noninstitutional Population by Age, Sex, and Race." 2017. https://www.bls.gov/cps/aa2017/cpsaat03.htm (last modified date: January 16, 2019);

———. "HOUSEHOLD DATA ANNUAL AVERAGES, 3. Employment Status of the Civilian Noninstitutional Population by Age, Sex, and Race." 2018. https://www.bls.gov/cps/aa2018/cpsaat03.htm (last modified date: January 18, 2019).

———. "HOUSEHOLD DATA ANNUAL AVERAGES, 5. Employment Status of the Civilian Noninstitutional Population by Age, Sex, and Race." 2016–2017. https://www.bls.gov/cps/aa2017/cpsaat05.htm (last modified date: January 16, 2019).

———. "HOUSEHOLD DATA NOT SEASONALLY ADJUSTED QUARTERLY AVERAGES, E-16. Unemployment Rates by Age, Sex, Race, and Hispanic or Latino Ethnicity." 2018–2019 Q3. https://www.bls.gov/web/empsit/cpsee_e16.htm (last modified date: October 4, 2019).

———. "Labor Force Characteristics by Race and Ethnicity." 2017. https://www.bls.gov/opub/reports/race-and-ethnicity/2017/home.htm (last modified date: August 2018).

———. "Labor Force Statistics from the Current Population Survey, How the Government Measures Unemployment." 2015. https://www.bls.gov/cps/cps_htgm.htm (last updated October 8, 2015).

U.S. Census Bureau. "About Race." January 23, 2018. https://www.census.gov/topics/population/race/about.html (accessed November 19, 2019).

———. "Quick Facts." July 1, 2018. https://www.census.gov/quickfacts/fact/table/US/PST045217 (accessed November 19, 2019).

———. Thom File. Social, Economic and Housing Statistics Division. "Voting in America: A Look at the 2016 Presidential Election." May 10, 2017. *Census Blogs.* https://census.gov/newsroom/blogs/random-samplings/2017/05/voting_in_america.html (accessed November 22, 2019).

U.S. Citizenship and Immigration Services. "Victims of Criminal Activity: U Nonimmigrant Status." 2019. https://www.uscis.gov/humanitarian/victims-human-trafficking-other-crimes/victims-criminal-activity-u-nonimmigrant-status/victims-criminal-activity-u-nonimmigrant-status (last updated June 12, 2019).

U.S. Department of Justice. Federal Bureau of Investigation. "2018 Crime in the United States, Murder Offenders by Age, Sex, Race, and Ethnicity." 2018. https://ucr.fbi.gov/crime-in-the-u.s/2018/crime-in-the-u.s.-2018/tables/expanded-homicide-data-table-3.xls (accessed November 19, 2019).

———. Federal Bureau of Investigation. "2018 Crime in the United States, Race, Sex, and Ethnicity of Victim by Race, Sex, and Ethnicity of Offender." 2018. https://ucr.fbi.gov/crime-in-the-u.s/2018/crime-in-the-u.s.-2018/tables/expanded-homicide-data-table-6.xls (accessed November 19, 2019).

———. Office of the Inspector General. "Review of Four FISA Applications and Other Aspects of the FBI's Crossfire Hurricane Investigation." [Redacted]. Compiled by Michael E. Horowitz. December 9, 2019. https://www.justice.gov/storage/120919-examination.pdf (accessed December 10, 2019).

———. Office of Justice Programs. Bureau of Justice Statistics. "Source and Use of Firearms Involved in Crimes: Survey of Prison Inmates, 2016." Compiled by Mariel Alper and Lauren Glaze. Special Report. January 2019. https://www.bjs.gov/content/pub/pdf/suficspi16.pdf (accessed January 3, 2020).

———. Special Counsel Robert S. Mueller III. "Report on the Investigation Into Russian Interference in the 2016 Presidential Election." [redacted]. Volume 1. March 2019. https://www.justice.gov/storage/report_volume1.pdf (accessed November 20, 2019).

———. Special Counsel Robert S. Mueller III. "Report on the Investigation Into Russian Interference in the 2016 Presidential Election." [redacted]. Volume 2. March 2019. https://www.justice.gov/storage/report_volume2.pdf (accessed November 20, 2019).

U.S. Environmental Protection Agency (EPA). "Greenhouse Gas Inventory Data Explorer." N.d. https://cfpub.epa.gov/ghgdata/inventoryexplorer (accessed January 24, 2020).

U.S. Senate. Committee on the Judiciary. Memo by Rachel Mitchell. "Memorandum: Analysis of Dr. Christine Blasey Ford's Allegations." September 30, 2018. https://static.politico.com/28/7f/80157df74b96bb352b10f8b7aa66/09-30-18-mitchell-memo-ford-allegations.pdf (accessed December 7, 2019).

Vigen, Tyler. *Spurious Correlations*. New York: Hachette Books, 2015. http://tylervigen.com/spurious-correlations (accessed January 13, 2020).

Vincent, Isabel, and Melissa Klein. "Gas-Guzzling Car Rides Expose AOC's Hypocrisy Amid Green New Deal Pledge." *New York Post*. March 2, 2019. https://nypost.com/2019/03/02/gas-guzzling-car-rides-expose-aocs-hypocrisy-amid-green-new-deal-pledge (accessed December 18, 2019).

Volokh, Eugene. "Zero Correlation between State Homicide Rate and State Gun Laws." *Reason*. Volokh Conspiracy. October 6, 2015. 12:32 p.m. https://reason.com/2015/10/06/zero-correlation-between-state (accessed December 30, 2019).

Washington Examiner editors. "Gun Control Is a Fantasy. Start a Realistic Conversation About Preventing School Massacres." *Washington Examiner*. February 21, 2018. https://www.washingtonexaminer.com/gun-control-is-a-fantasy-start-a-realistic-conversation-about-preventing-school-massacres (accessed November 25, 2019).

Washington Post. "Fatal Force: 994." 2015. *Washington Post*. https://www.washingtonpost.com/graphics/national/police-shootings (last accessed November 19, 2019). Website also provides data links for years 2015–2019.

Williams, Walter E. "Capitalism vs. Socialism." *Townhall*. May 30, 2018. https://townhall.com/columnists/walterewilliams/2018/05/30/capitalism-vs-socialism-n2484341 (accessed November 26, 2019).

———. *Race and Economics: How Much Can Be Blamed on Discrimination?* Stanford, CA: Hoover Institution Press, 2011.

Williamson, Kevin D. "Capitalism Is Clean(er)." *National Review*. September 25, 2014. https://www.nationalreview.com/2014/09/capitalism-cleaner-kevin-d-williamson (accessed November 25, 2019).

Wilson, Peter. "Venezuela's Season of Starvation." *Foreign Policy Group* (*FP*), June 19, 2016. https://foreignpolicy.com/2016/06/19/venezuela-maduro-food-shortages-price-controls-political-unrest (accessed November 22, 2019).

WISQARS. "Compare Causes / States for Fatal Injury Data Visualization Tool." *Centers for Disease Control and Prevention.* N.d. https://www.cdc.gov/injury/wisqars/fatal.html (accessed December 29, 2019).

Wistrich, Robert S. *Hitler and the Holocaust.* New York: Modern Library Chronicles, 2003.

World Bank. "GDP per Capita, PPP (Constant 2011 International $)." 1990–2018. https://data.worldbank.org/indicator/NY.GDP.PCAP.PP.KD?most_recent_value_desc=true (accessed November 26, 2019).

World Data Info. "Greenhouse Gases Emissions by Country." *WorldData.* c. 2012. https://www.worlddata.info/greenhouse-gas-by-country.php (accessed November 24, 2019).

Young, Cathy. "The Pecking Disorder: Social Justice Warriors Gone Wild." *Observer.* June 11, 2015. https://observer.com/2015/06/the-pecking-disorder-social-justice-warriors-gone-wild (accessed January 23, 2020).

Zeiler, David. "Warning: Hidden Obamacare Taxes Will Cost You More Than You Think." *Money Morning.* August 5, 2012. https://moneymorning.com/2012/08/05/warning-hidden-obamacare-taxes-will-cost-you-more-than-you-think (accessed November 25, 2019).

Zhang, Jerry, Darrell Carpenter, and Myung Ko. "Online Astroturfing: A Theoretical Perspective." AMCIS 2013 Proceedings, *bepress.* http://works.bepress.com/xiao_zhang/2 (accessed November 23, 2019).

Zwolinski, Matt, and Alan Wertheimer. "Exploitation." In *The Stanford Encyclopedia of Philosophy* (Summer 2017 edition), edited by Edward N. Zalta. https://plato.stanford.edu/archives/sum2017/entries/exploitation (accessed November 23, 2019).

Zycher, Benjamin. "Earth Day 2019: The Sixth Mass Extinction and the Imperative of Apocalypse." *AEIdeas.* April 22, 2019. https://www.aei.org/articles/earth-day-2019-the-sixth-mass-extinction-and-the-imperative-of-apocalypse (accessed November 25, 2019).

Index

ACC hypothesis. *See* Anthropogenic Climate Change hypothesis
accountability issues/considerations: expert fallacy and, 68–69, 117–18; with political partisans, 4, 35, 38, 70, 79, 88n17, 117–18, 120–21, 130n76; with psychobabble, 139–40; valid investigations and, 130n76
ad hominem attacks, 4, 5n4, 30, 121, 134
affordability claims, 166–67
African American population: CNIP data on, 41–42, *42*; crime statistics for, 23–24, 25, 26n4, 27n18; educational attainment rates for, *58*, 58–59; employment to population ratio, 47, *48*, 49, *49*, 99, *101*, 103; gang/internecine killings, 25; labor market discrepancies, evidence-based approach to, 44–57; labor market discrepancies, rhetoric-based data on, 35–36, 42–44, 52, *54*, *55*, *56*, 57; police discrimination against, evidence-based analysis of, 19–26; police discrimination against, rhetoric-based argument for, 17–19; "twice the rate" rhetoric for unemployment of, 52, *54*, *55*, *56*; U3 unemployment rate, 50, *51*, 52, *53–54*, 61n16; unemployment discrepancies from 2016 to 2019 between whites and, 50, *50*, *51*, 52

Against Leviathan (Higgs), 77
aggregates as individuals fallacy: "American people" assumption and, 73–75; definition of, 29, 73; in dictatorship collective will rhetoric, 76, 198; discriminatory states and, 78–79; fallacy of composition relation to, 195; fallacy of division relation to, 108, 194; moral authority and threats with, 163–64; presidential election (2016) example and, 74–76; public good rhetoric and, 163–64, 194–96; religious ideology claims and, 79; with statistics, 76–77
Alinsky, Saul D., 5n4
alt-left identity, 133
alt-right identity, 67–68, 133
Amazon, 152, 159
Anthropogenic Climate Change (ACC) hypothesis, 112–15
Antifa movement, 133, 163
applied statistics. *See* statistical concepts/methods
Arrow, Kenneth J., 15n6, 57, 195
Arrow's Impossibility Theorem, 15n6, 195

Asian population, 18, 24, 58, *58*
asylum seekers and process, 84, 90n38, 170–72

Barr, William, 35
Becker, Gary S., 57, 72
begging the question: climate change debates and, 116; definition of, 30, 138; "gun control" phrase and, 190n4; Marxist ideology and, 132, 138–39; rhetoric-based approach use of, 13, 14, 27n13, 43; smear campaigns and, 95
Beria, Lavrentiy, 13, 14, 185
bias, confirmation: avoidance of, 65; common sense claims relation to, 98; correlation-confused-as-causation fallacy with, 93; in data acquisition and analysis, 41, 91–97, 189; definition of, 91; echo chambers role in, 9, 92; moral authority claims relation to, 96–97; Mueller report and, 186; in police discrimination case study, 18; poll data and, 189; presidential election (2016) turnout and, 75; rhetoric-based approach use of, 3, 9, 10, 14, 18, 35, 91–97; in science, 66; smear campaigns use of, 93–95
Bloomberg, Michael, 118, 129n66
Boaz, David, 14–15
Booker, Cory, 93
boondoggles, government: climate change rhetoric and, 115–16, 128n58, 159, 190n3; correlation-confused-as-causation fallacy and, 105; discrimination rhetoric goals and, 59; with hypotheses testing without valid evidence, 121; income and wealth transfer through, 14; Mueller investigation and, 35, 206; policymaking by rhetorical-approach and, 14–15, 66, 153; subsidization and taxation example of, 14–15, 35, 206

Boorman, Georgi, 44
border wall, 80–81, 135
Brennan, John O., 69–70, 88n17
Butler, Eamonn F., 66

capitalism: climate change debates from detractors of, 115–16, 128n58; competition and serving populace needs under, 77; correlation-confused-as-causation fallacy in debates about, 104; defining, 197–98; free exchange criteria for, 175, 197–99, 200–201; Marxist begging the question about, 138–39; Nordic countries adoption of, 105, 206; profits and, understanding, 200–201; property rights role in, 197–98; state, fallacy, 204; uncertainty and, 202; victimology fallacy lacking with, 200; zero sum game debunked in, 199
carbon emissions. *See* climate change debates
causation: causal reductionism fallacy and, 17, 103, 112, 141–42, 172; characteristics of, 109–10; climate change computer models and issues in, 110, 112–13, 126n47, 158; logical conditions for, 109–12; temporal sequence role in, 110, 112. *See also* correlation-confused-as-causation fallacy
centrally planned systems (non-market systems): communism, 78, 154, 201–4; dictatorship threat with, 97, 196, 198, 205; moral authority tactic in, 96–97, 201; price and wage control issues under, 199, 203, 204–5; socialism, 71–73, 96, 104, 115–16, 132–33, 145, 204–6; socialism, democratic, 145, 202, 205–6; uncertainty in free-market compared with, 202; unfree/coerced exchange in, 198, 199–200
change, incremental, 162–64

cherry-picked data: in climate change arguments, 104, 158, 161; fallacy of composition relation to, 97; gun control debates and, 107; history re-written with, 145; in partisans performance claims, 97–98; in police discrimination debates, 19, 21–22; polls and, 189, 190; in rhetoric-based approach, 9–10, 14, 19, 21–22, 35, 91, 97–98, 104, 158, 161; in welfare state debates, 105
China, 131, 155, 156, 173
civilian non-institutionalized population (CNIP), 41–42, *42*, 44–45, 47
climate change debates, 176n12; ACC hypothesis and, 112–15; anti-capitalist agenda in, 115–16, 128n58; begging the question in, 116; cherry-picked data in, 104, 158, 161; computer models and causation issues in, 110, 112–13, 126n47, 158; correlation-confused-as-causation fallacy in, 104, 109–16, 157–58; "deniers" of majority science in, attacks on, 87n2, 114–15, 157–58, 162; dichotomous thinking fallacy in, 87n4; economic assumptions in, 160–61; fallacies, summary of, 157; fallacy of composition example in, 113; falsifiability lack in hypotheses in, 114–15, 157, 158, 161–62; fear mongering use in, 155, 158, 161; government boondoggles and, 115–16, 128n58, 159, 190n3; hypocrisy behind, 156–57, 177n21; IPCC data and claims in, 109–14, 126n45, 158–59, 161; Marxist ideology in, 115, 116, 128n58; natural climate variations and, 111–12, 155, 158, 160; nonlinear correlation and, 110–11; opportunity costs/ cost-benefit analysis in, 159–61, 177n21; shaming rhetoric with, 87n2; single variable assumptions in, 160; socialism ideology relation to, 115–16; temporal sequence condition in, 110, 112. *See also* green energy/ green new deal
Clinton, Hillary R., 74–76, 207n1
CNIP. *See* civilian non-institutionalized population
collectivism: definition and examples of, 76, 195, 198, 201–2, 204–5; individualism compared with, 193–97, 202, 203; public good fallacies in, 163–64, 194–96
common sense claims, 98–103, 107
communism: democratic, meaningless rhetoric of, 202; dialectical materialism theory in, 201–2; fallacies involved with, 201; individual and property rights under, 78, 202, 203–4; socialism relation to, 204; success of, historical perspective, 203–4; utopian/nirvana fallacy in, 154, 201, 202
Communism (Pipes), 204
comparative advantage, 37–38, 167, 171
comparisons and analogies, false, 30, 98, 136–38, 142–43
composition, fallacy of: aggregates as individuals relation to, 195; cherry picking relation to, 97; in climate change debates, 113; collective will as example of, 76; definition, 29, 68; expert fallacy and, 68–69, 117; in immigration debates and policy, 68, 171; in labor market discrimination rhetoric, 52; in Marxism, 132; Nazis and, 144; with polls, 70–71; on socialism, 71–73; in social justice rhetoric, 196–97; victimology and, 143–45
confirmation bias. *See* bias, confirmation
conspiracy theories, 25, 28n22, 116, 123n9
correlation: linear, 109–12, 157; nonlinear, 110–11, 126

correlation-confused-as-causation fallacy: in anti-capitalism/pro-socialism debates, 104; in climate change debates, 104, 109–16, 157–58; confirmation bias relation to, 93; definition of, 29, 103; government boondoggles and, 105; in gun rights/control debates, 105–8; in Nordic welfare states debates, 104–5

cost-benefit analysis, 197; in climate change debates, 159–61, 177n21; in comparing projects, 155; gun rights/control and, 169–70; health insurance, government compared with private, 165–69; immigration policy, 170–72; incremental, 162–64; trade/trade policy, 172–75. *See also* marginalism; opportunity costs

crime rates: African American, 23–24, 25, 26n4, 27n18; cross-sectional across countries data issues for, 120; illegal immigration and, 68, 83–87, 171–72; by race and ethnicity, 20, 22–24, 26n4; sanctuary cities, 171–72; white, 23. *See also* homicide statistics

criminal guilt/innocence: Beria's dictum on proving, 13, 14, 185; confidence, appeal to, 185; costs incurred in investigations of, 186, 206; evidence absence in determining, 13–14, 35; exoneration and, 34–35; hypothesis testing example with, 12–13; Kavanaugh, rhetoric-based approach to, 93–95; negative hypothesis proof/disproof in, 11–14, 34–35, 59–60, 91, 115, 184–86; non sequitur fallacy with, 138; Trump Campaign, rhetoric-based approach to, 34–35; uncertainty and, recognizing, 184–86

data: collection and availability of valid, 119–20; common sense claims with analysis of, 98–103; confirmation bias role in analysis of, 41, 91–97, 189; dichotomous thinking fallacy in analysis of, 43–44, 49, 99; gun control, collection and analysis of, 105–8, 120; labor market discrepancies, acquisition and analysis of, 41–60, 98–103; noise and filtering issues, 120, 184, 188–89; noise confused with signal, 184; police discrimination, 19–20, 22, 25, 27n13; randomization issues in, 9, 22, 27n13; rhetoric-based compared with evidence-based selection of, 9–10; sampling, correct method of, 119; sampling error considerations with, 45, 52, 62n20, 73, 184; source, identifying and focusing on, 41. *See also* cherry-picked data; employment/unemployment data; evidence; polls; statistics

decision-making: fallacies impact on, 3, 29, 93; hallmarks of government, 14–15; opportunity costs role in, 35, 151–52, 153, 154–55, 165, 195; public compared with private sector approach to, 34–35; relative compared with absolute thinking in, 153–55. *See also* cost-benefit analysis

Democrats, influenced by Marxist hypotheses, 62n19

dialectical materialism, 201–2

dichotomous thinking fallacy: alt-right opposed to neo-Marxism and, 67–68; in climate change debates, 87n4; defining, 29, 65; gun control debates and, 105–6; with immigration policy debates, 135, 171; in labor market data analysis, 43–44, 49, 99; in Marxism, 4, 44, 67–68, 132, 199–200; nirvana fallacy relation to, 154; partisan use of, 27n19, 67–68; with price and wage controls, 66–67

dictators/totalitarian regimes, 92–93; centrally planned systems and threat of, 97, 196, 198, 205; collective will rhetoric of, 76, 198; "ends justifying the means" trope of, 132; gun confiscation consequences and, 106; moral authority use by, 134, 141, 201; nirvana fallacy and, 146; rhetoric mastery of, 61n3

discrimination: aggregates as individuals fallacy and, 78–79; comparative advantage theory and, 37–38, 171; defining, 21; hypocrisy with claims of, 144; mind-reading as evidence of, 18, 24; necessary and sufficient conditions of, differences between, 36–38, 57; proportionality/non-proportionality considerations with, 20, 22–24, 27n19, 35–37, 42–43, 47, 50, 52, 57; racism and, 5n4, 27n18, 44, 67–68; rhetoric, goals of, 59; shaming tactics with rhetoric around, 59, 121; Sowell on assumptions of, 24; statistics as evidence of, problems with, 19; theoretical and empirical studies on, 57–60. *See also* labor market discrepancies/discrimination; police discrimination

drug smuggling, 80–81, 85

economic concepts: Pareto inefficient, 195; of profits, 200–201; of stocks compared with flows, 29, 81–87; behind trade/trade policy, 172–75, 182n70. *See also* cost-benefit analysis; marginalism; opportunity costs

Economic Facts and Fallacies (Sowell), 172

The Economics of Discrimination (Becker), 57

economic systems, ideological underpinnings for: collectivism, definition and examples of, 76, 195, 198, 201–2, 204–5; collectivism, public good fallacies in, 163–64, 194–96; criteria for defining and comparing, 193; individualism, government role in, 203; individualism compared with collectivism, 193–97, 202, 203; property rights and, 78, 116, 197–98, 202, 203–4; state as instrument of coercion and, 198

educational attainment, *58*, 58–59
educational system, 153
electoral system, 74–75
elitist fallacy, 142, 157
employment/unemployment data, 61n13; CNIP, 41–42, *42*, 44–45, 47; LPR and, 43–45, *46*, 47, *47*, 49–50, 99, *100*, 103; to population ratio, 47, *48*, 49, *49*, 99, *101*, 103; sampling error considerations with, 45, 52, 62n20; "twice the rate" rhetoric for discrepancies in, 52, *54*, 55, *56*; 2016 to 2019 discrepancies by race in, 50, *50*, *51*, 52; U3, 50, *51*, 52, *53–54*, 61n16, 99, *102*, 103; U3 and U6, compared, 52, *53*, 61n16; welfare states and, 104–5

Engels, Friedrich, 61n3, 90n37, 105, 198

evidence: cherry-picked data used as, 9–10, 14, 19, 21–22, 35, 91, 97–98, 104, 158, 161; citizen responsibility to demand, 70, 130n78; in criminal guilt/innocence, absence of, 13–14, 35; empirical, sourcing and sharing of, 15n2; about gun-related deaths, 108; hypotheses testing and gathering of, 9, 15nn2–3, 120–21; justice system dependence on, 185; on media sources, discerning rhetoric from, 21, 130n78; mind-reading taken as, 18, 24, 33, 117; monitoring and verifying claims of, 121–22, 123n20, 130n77; in Mueller report, 184–86; rhetoric use of tactics over, 95, 97; rhetoric volume and intensity relation to available, 181n61; scientific method acceptance of,

119–20; true from false, knowing and collecting, 119–22

evidence-based approach: to alternative viewpoints, 3; data selection in rhetoric-based contrasted with, 9–10; empirical evidence used in, 9, 15n2; goals/purpose in addressing, 2–3; to labor market discrimination claims, 44–57; in media sources, discerning rhetoric from, 21; to police discrimination claims, 19–26; policy understanding and making under, 3–4, 9; rhetoric-based compared with, topics overview, 2–4. *See also specific topics*

exchange: free/voluntary, 175, 197–99, 200–201; trade deficit and balance in, 173–75; unfree/coerced, 198, 199–200, 205

exoneration, 34–35

expert fallacy, 68–70, 117–18

fallacies: ad hominem attack, 4, 5n4, 30, 121, 134; begging the question, 13, 14, 27n13, 30, 43, 95, 116, 132, 138–39, 190n4; with comparisons and analogies, 30, 98, 136–38, 142–43; of confusing rates with stocks, 29, 81–87; of correlation-confused-as-causation, 29, 103–16, 157–58; decision-making impacted by, 3, 29, 93; of division, 108, 194; of doing something over nothing, 1–2; elitist, 142, 157; expert, 68–70, 117–18; knowing-more-than-we-know-or-can-know, 19, 29, 71, 80–81, 132, 171, 186; list of common, 29–30; mind-reading, 18, 24, 33, 90n39, 117, 138; of necessary and sufficient conditions differences, failure to understand, 29, 30–38, 57, 139; nirvana, 95, 146, 153–54, 162, 170, 201, 202; non sequitur, 30, 67, 78, 80, 116, 138; police discrimination case study, 17–19; pot shot, 30,

145–46; psychobabble, 30, 33, 117, 139–40; recognizing, in research process, 4n1; straw man argument, 30, 108, 135–36; of two wrongs make a right, 29, 131; unique cause/causal reductionism, 17, 103, 112, 141–42, 172. *See also* aggregates as individuals fallacy; composition, fallacy of; dichotomous thinking fallacy; moral authority fallacy; personal attack-based fallacies; victimology fallacy

FBI, 23, 25

Figueres, Christiana, 115, 116, 128n58

flows. *See* rates and stocks confusion fallacy

Fools, Frauds, and Firebrands (Scruton), 206

Ford, Christine Blasey, 94–95

Foreign Intelligence Surveillance Act, 130n76

Forty Centuries of Wage and Price Controls (Schuettinger and Butler), 66

freedoms: government health care and loss of, 166–67, 168; labor market choice, 38; utopian schemes and loss of, 154. *See also* property rights

free-market system. *See* capitalism

A Game Free Life (Karpman), 144

global warming. *See* climate change debates

GND. *See* green energy/green new deal

Goldwater, Barry, 139

government officials. *See* policy/policymaking; political partisans

green energy/green new deal (GND), 14–15; assumptions and fallacies behind, 157, 160–62; benefit-cost/opportunity costs analysis lacking with, 159–60, 177n21; historical perspective, 158; opportunity cost applied to, 159; premise of, 158

guilt. *See* criminal guilt/innocence

Index   239

gun rights/control: begging the question in rhetoric behind, 190n4; black market gun acquisition and, 169–70; common sense claims in debates on, 98, 107; correlation-confused-as-causation fallacy in debates on, 105–8; cross-sectional across countries data issues on, 108, 120; data collection and analysis, 105–8, 120; dichotomous thinking fallacy and, 105–6; homicide statistics and, 105–8, 129n73, 169; marginalism and cost-benefit analysis with, 169–70; moral authority tactic in debates on, 107; suicide statistics role in data on, 107–8; totalitarian states and, 106

Halbrook, Stephen P., 106
Harris, Kamala, 93
Hayek, Friedrich A., 134
health insurance, 153; cross-sectional across countries data issues in debates on, 166; freedoms with government compared to private, 166–67, 168; marginalism and cost-benefit analysis of, 165–69; negative impacts from government, 167–68; opportunity costs consideration with, 165–66; socialist price controls and, 204
Hegel, Georg Wilhelm Friedrich, 201–2
Hemingway, Mollie, 93
Heshmat, Shahram, 91
Higgs, Robert, 77
Hispanic population, 20, 58, *58*
Hitler, Adolf, 61n3, 141, 142, 145
homicide statistics: African American, 23–24, 25, 27n18; gun-related, 105–8, 129n73, 169; illegal immigration and, fallacies around, 85–86; by race, 23–24; white, 23–24
Horowitz, Michael E., 130n76
housing market, 153, 167
human rights violations, 131

hypocrisy. *See* Tu Quoque fallacy
hypotheses: climate change (ACC), testing of, 112–15; conspiracy theories and testing of, 28n22; evidence for testing, gathering valid, 9, 15nn2–3, 120–21; facts difference from, understanding, 4n1, 119; falsifiable, fabrication of, 66; falsifiable requirement for well-formulated, 3, 10–13, 28n22, 65–66, 95, 114–15, 157, 158, 161–62; mathematical negative, proving, 15n6; negative, proof/disproof of, 4n1, 11–14, 34–35, 59–60, 91, 114–15, 184–86; null, definition and testing of, 3, 10–12, 187–88; testing, 2–3, 9, 10–13, 15nn2–3, 19, 28n22, 65–66, 112–15, 120–21, 187–89; testing, criminal guilt/innocence example of, 12–13, 59–60; testing, statistics in, 19, 187–88; for testing, choosing, 9, 15nn2–3, 120–21; testing obstacles in policy/policymaking, 12

identity politics, 68, 95, 96, 133, 137–38, 142–43
Illiberal Reformers (Leonard), 154
immigration debates and policy, 146n6; asylum seekers and process and, 84, 90n38; crime rate considerations and fallacies in, 68, 83–87, 171–72; dichotomous thinking fallacy with, 135, 171; fallacy of composition in, 68, 171; knowing-more-than-we-know-or-can-know fallacy with, 171; marginalism and cost-benefit analysis with, 170–72; sanctuary cities and, 84, 86–87, 90n39, 170–72; straw man arguments in, 135–36; unique cause fallacy in, 172
imperialism terminology, 136–37
income and wealth transfer systems: government boondoggles and, 14; re-distribution, 76–77, 105, 159–60,

206; soak the rich schemes and, 24, 153, 205; welfare state as, 206
income equality, 76–77
income mobility, 77
individualism, collectivism compared with, 193–97, 202, 203
innocence. *See* criminal guilt/innocence
Inquiry into the Nature and Causes of the Wealth of Nations (Smith), 69
Intergovernmental Panel on Climate Change (IPCC), 109–14, 126n45, 158–59, 161

Justice on Trial (Hemingway and Severino), 93

kangaroo courts, 60, 94, 95, 138, 143, 144
Karpman, Stephen B., 144
Kavanaugh, Brett, 93–95
Krugman, Paul, 117

Labor Force Participation Rate (LPR), 43–45, *46*, 47, *47*, 49–50, 99, *100*, 103
labor market: comparative advantage considerations in, 37–38; educational attainment by race and ethnicity relation to, *58*, 58–59; expert fallacy and specialization role in, 69; freedom of choice in, 38. *See also* employment/unemployment data
labor market discrepancies/discrimination: business cycle consideration in, 50; common sense claims with data on, 98–103; data acquisition and analysis for, 41–60, 98–103; data supporting decreasing, 42–43, 45, 49–50, 61n15; dichotomous thinking fallacy in, 65; employment to population ratio considerations in, 47, *48*, 49, *49*, 99, *101*, 103; evidence-based approach to, 44–57; fallacy of composition in rhetoric around, 52, 69; logical conditions in debates on, 35–38, 57; LPR data and analysis of, 43–45, *46*, 47, *47*, 49–50, 99, *100*, 103; Marxism worker exploitation rhetoric on, 44, 62n19, 77–78; rhetoric-based approach to, 35–36, 41–44, 52, *54*, *55*, *56*, 57

Lang, Kevin, 57–58
Lehmann, Jee-Yeon K., 57–58
Leonard, Thomas C., 154
logical conditions: for causation, 109–12; happiness and obstruction of justice example of fallacy in, 33–35; Marxist example of error in, 138–39; Nazi-nationalist example of fallacy in, 31–32; necessary, examples of, 32, 109–10, 111; necessary and sufficient, failure to understand distinction between, 29, 30–38, 57, 139; sufficient, examples of, 32, 34, 110
Lott, John R., 120
LPR. *See* Labor Force Participation Rate

Mann, Michael, 115, 157
marginalism, 159; defining, 164; gun rights/control debates and, 169–70; health insurance debates and, 165–69; in immigration debates and policy, 170–72; minimum wage debates and, 164; in trade/trade policy, 172–75; zero sum game contrasted with win-win of, 199
market systems. *See* capitalism
Marxism: begging the question fallacy and, 132, 138–39; classical, 44; class polarization/warfare rhetoric of, 4, 61n3, 62n19, 67–68, 77–78, 90n37, 95, 132–33, 143–44, 195, 197, 198–200, 204; climate change debates relation to, 115, 116, 128n58; cultural, 68, 92–93, 96; Deus ex machina and, 78; dichotomy fallacy in, 4, 44, 67–68, 132, 199–200;

"ends justifying the means" trope of, 132; fallacy of composition in, 132; identity politics of, 95, 96, 133; knowing-more-than-we-know-or-can-know fallacy in, 132; labor market discrimination rhetoric and, 44, 62n19, 77–78; logical condition error example with, 138–39; moral authority claims of, 61n3, 62n19, 96, 97; neo, 44, 67–68, 147n14, 153; on property rights, 78, 198; racial and ethnic polarization framework in, 44, 147n14; on societal growth and prosperity, 105; tragedy of the commons with, 198; victimology fallacies in, 61n3, 62n19, 95, 144, 198; working class term in, 90n37; zero sum game and class warfare rhetoric of, 62n19, 77, 143–44, 199, 202. *See also* communism
mathematical theorems, 15n6
McIntosh, Peggy, 141, 147n14
McQuillan, Lawrence J., 167
media sources: discerning evidence from rhetoric on, 21, 130n78; echo chamber role of, 4, 92, 116, 130n78, 138, 172, 207n1; expert fallacy and, 69, 117–18; internet astroturfing and, 93
mercantilism, 173, 174
mind-reading fallacy, 18, 24, 33, 90n39, 117, 138
minimum wage debates, 67, 81–83, 153, 164
moral authority fallacy: aggregates as individuals fallacy relation to, 163–64; in centrally planned systems, 96–97, 201; confirmation bias relation to, 96–97; definition of, 30, 140–41; dictators use of, 134, 141, 201; false comparisons and, 142–43; Marxist use of, 61n3, 62n19, 96, 97; minimum wage and fallacy of, 67, 81, 82–83, 153; as partisan tactic, 39n2, 91, 107, 153, 175n2, 175n4;

as personal attack-based fallacy, 134, 140–43; revolutionaries and, 162; socialist rhetoric and, 96; social justice rhetoric and, 197; spurious reasons for, 141–42; theatrical moves role in, 142; white privilege concept and, 141–42
Mueller, Robert S., 35, 184–86, 191n8, 206

national (income) accounting identity, 172–73, 174, 182n70
Nazi Germany: aggregates as individuals fallacy and, 78–79; state capitalism fallacy of, 204
Nazis: confirmation bias use in propaganda tactics of, 92; fallacy of composition and, 144; false comparisons to, 136, 143; logical condition fallacy example with nationalists relation to, 31–32; rhetoric used by, 61n3, 92; shaming tactic in use of term, 5n4, 121. *See also* Hitler, Adolf
necessary conditions. *See* logical conditions
New York, 152
nirvana fallacy, 95, 146, 153–54, 162, 170, 201, 202
non sequitur fallacy, 30, 67, 78, 80, 116, 138
Nordic countries: capitalism embraced by, 105, 206; correlation-confused-as-causation in debates on welfare state of, 104–5; fallacy of composition about socialism of, 71–73; welfare state and free-enterprise in, 206

Obama, Barack, 69, 98, 166, 183
Ocasio-Cortez, Alexandria, 96, 116, 145, 152, 156–57, 159, 177n21
online resources, 4, 4n1
opportunity costs: climate change policies and debate and, 159–61,

177n21; in decision-making, role of, 35, 151–52, 153, 154–55, 165, 195; definition of, 154; examples, 155–57; government health insurance and, 165–66; minimum wage laws and, 82–83; taxation and, 152

partisans. *See* political partisans

personal attack-based fallacies: ad hominem, 4, 5n4, 30, 121, 134; false comparisons and analogies as, 136–38; on majority science deniers, 66, 87n2, 114–15, 157–58, 162; moral authority claims as, 134, 140–43; pot shot, 30, 145–46; psychobabble, 30, 33, 117, 139–40; straw man argument, 30, 108, 135–36; Tu Quoque (hypocrisy), 29, 131–34, 144, 146n1; victimology as, 30, 143–45, 147n18. *See also* shaming tactics; smear campaigns

Pipes, Richard, 204

police discrimination, 26n4; cherry-picked data on, 19, 21–22; confirmation bias in claims of, 18; evidence-based analysis of, 19–26; fatal shootings data and, 19–20, 25; race of officer importance in arguments about, 21–22; randomization issues in data around, 22, 27n13; rhetoric-based approach and fallacies with, 17–19; statistics, challenges with, 21–22, 27n13

policy/policymaking: ad hominem attacks focus on person over, 134; citizen empowerment over, 26, 28n23; correlation-confused-as-causation fallacy in, 104–5; cost-benefit analysis in, 152, 155, 160, 164–72, 197; evidence-based path to, 3–4, 9; fallacy of doing something over nothing in, 1–2; government boondoggles and, 14–15, 66, 153; hypotheses testing obstacles in, 12; research sources, 4n1; rhetoric-based support of, impacts, 1–4, 9, 14–15, 38n1, 66, 153; stocks and rates/flows confusion fallacy in, 81–87; trade, 172–75, 182n70; valid investigations into, 130n76; victimology fallacy used in, 39n3, 80–87. *See also* decision making; immigration debates and policy

political partisans: accountability issues/considerations with, 4, 35, 38, 70, 79, 88n17, 117–18, 120–21, 130n76; cherry-picked data for performance claims of, 97–98; correlation-confused-as-causation fallacy in stock market relation to, 104; dichotomous thinking fallacy tactic of, 27n19, 67–68; economic principles ignorance of, 151; evidence claims by, monitoring and verifying, 121–22, 123n20, 130n77; expert fallacy use by and for, 68–70, 117–18; history re-writing tactic of, 32, 122, 145, 203–4; identity politics and, 68, 95, 96, 133, 137–38, 142–43; Marxist class warfare rhetoric adopted by, 204; moral authority claims tactics of, 39n2, 91, 107, 153, 175n2, 175n4; power abuses historically by, 134; SIGs influence on, 1, 9, 94, 137, 175n4, 194–96; smear campaigns rhetoric/tactics with, 69–70, 93–95; victimology tactic of, 39n3, 80–87, 143

polls: approval, 187, 189; cherry-picked data and, 189, 190; confirmation bias role in, 189; fallacy of composition with, 70–71; horserace, 187, 189–90; knowing-more-than-we-know-or-can-know fallacy with, 19; noise in, data, 188–89; predictive, problems with, 71, 189–90; sampling errors with, 73; statistical concepts behind, 187–89; statistical errors with, 71, 73, 186–89; voter preference, 186, 189–90

pollution, 155–57
Popper, Karl, 65–66
post hoc ergo propter hoc. *See* correlation-confused-as-causation fallacy
Powell, Benjamin, 205
Powell, Jim, 158
presidential election (1964), 139
presidential election (2016): aggregates like individuals fallacy and, 74–76; Bloomberg self-speculations about, 118, 129n66; Democratic party rejection of results of, 207n1; horserace polls, 190; popular and electoral votes in, 74–76, 207n1; Russian collusion in, rhetoric/debates on, 34–35, 70, 121, 123n9
presidential election (2020), 93
price and wage controls: under centrally planned systems, 199, 203, 204–5; dichotomy fallacies about, 66–67; minimum wage debates and, 67, 81–83, 153, 164
profits, understanding, 200–201
property rights: in capitalism, 197–98; communism rejection of, 78, 202, 203–4; environmental protection and, 116; Marx on, 78, 198; tragedy of the commons and, 198
psychobabble, 30, 33, 117, 139–40
public good, 163–64, 194–96

race and ethnicity: categories, 17, 26n3; CNIP by, 41–42, *42*; crime rates by, 20, 22–24, 26n4; educational attainment by, *58*, 58–59; labor market data acquisition and analysis by, 41–60; Marxist framework on polarization by, 44, 147n14; of police officer importance in discrimination debates, 21–22. *See also* African Americans
"Racial Discrimination in the Labor Market" (Lang and Lehmann), 57–58
racism. *See* discrimination
rates and stocks confusion fallacy: definitions, 29, 81; illegal immigration and crime rates case study and, 83–87; minimum wage case study and, 81–83
Republicans, influenced by Marxist hypotheses, 62n19
research sources and goals, 2–3, 4n1
revealed preference theory, 10
revolution/revolutionaries, 162–63, 194
rhetoric-based approach: begging the question (conclusion assumption) in, 13, 14, 27n13, 30, 43, 95, 116, 132, 138–39, 190n4; to border wall and drug smuggling debate, 80–81; challengers of, ad hominem attacks on, 5n4; cherry-picked data role in, 9–10, 14, 19, 21–22, 35, 91, 97–98, 104, 158, 161; confirmation bias role in, 3, 9, 10, 14, 18, 35, 91–97; data selection in evidence-based contrasted with, 9–10; echo chambers of media role in, 4, 92, 116, 130n78, 138, 172, 207n1; evidence availability relation to emphasis on, 181n61; evidence-based compared with, topics overview, 2–4; "fact" claims in, 9; goals in addressing, 2–3, 4n1; green energy case example of, 14–15; to labor market discrepancies, 35–36, 41–44, 52, *54*, *55*, *56*, 57; in media sources, discerning evidence from, 21; to minimum wage laws, 81–83; polarization agenda under, 4; policy understanding and making under, 1–4, 9, 14–15, 38n1, 66, 153; resistance to emotional appeal of, 1; revealed preference theory and, 10; in smear campaigns, 69–70, 93–95. *See also specific topics*
ridicule. *See* personal attack-based fallacies; shaming tactics; smear campaigns
The Road to Serfdom (Hayek), 134
Roosevelt, Franklin D., 158, 160

sanctuary cities, 84, 86–87, 90n39, 170–72
Schuettinger, Robert L., 66
science: confirmation bias in, 66; "deniers" of majority, attacks on, 66, 87n2, 114–15, 157–58, 162; "deniers" of majority, historical perspective, 65–66, 87n2, 158; fallacies in, 66, 87n2; shaming tactics in rhetoric-based approach to, 66, 87n2. *See also* climate change debates
scientific method: alternative viewpoints addressed with, 3; evidence accepted through, 119–20; falsifiable hypotheses criteria for, 3, 10–12, 65–66, 95, 157, 158, 161–62
Scruton, Roger, 206
Severino, Carrie, 93
shaming tactics: with climate change debates, 87n2; with discrimination rhetoric, 59, 121; majority science, 66, 87n2; "Nazi" term used as, 5n4, 121; power-grab process with, 129n67
SIGs. *See* special interest groups
smear campaigns: anti-Trump, 69–70; Kavanaugh, 93–95
Smith, Adam, 69
Smith, Keri, 133
social good, 163–64, 194–96
socialism: class warfare rhetoric and, 132–33; climate change debates relation to, 115–16; communism relation to, 204; correlation-confused-as-causation fallacy in arguments for, 104; definition of, 204; democratic, rhetoric of, 145, 202, 205–6; fallacy of composition about Nordic welfare state and, 71–73; in Hitler ideology, 145; moral authority rhetoric of, 96; power abuses and, 205–6; price and wage control issues with, 204–5; as utopian system, 154, 204; welfare state relation to, 71–73, 206
social justice rhetoric: fallacy of composition in, 196–97; of Hitler, 145; moral authority fallacy and, 197; terminology, 137–38
social media. *See* media sources
social utility, 195
social welfare, 163–64, 194–96
Solyndra, 14–15, 198, 206
Sowell, Thomas, 24, 172
special interest groups (SIGs), 1, 9, 94, 137, 175n4, 194–96
Stalin, Joseph, 13, 94, 95, 141, 198, 201
statistical concepts/methods, 15n3; applied, 19; confidence intervals, 184, 187–89; correlation, linear, 109–12, 157; correlation, nonlinear, 110–11, 126; polls, 187–89; sampling statistic in, 188; statistical significance in, 108, 188
statistics: absolute compared with relative, 19–20, 22–23; aggregates as individuals fallacy with, 76–77; crime rates and, issues around, 22–23, 85; homicide, African American, 23–24, 25, 27n18; police discrimination, challenges with, 21–22, 27n13; polls and errors of, 71, 73, 186–89; predictive, problems with, 71, 110; proportionality/non-proportionality considerations with, 20, 22–24, 27n19, 35–37, 42–43, 47, 50, 52, 57; race categories used for, 17, 26n3; uncertainty in using, 19. *See also* employment/unemployment data; homicide statistics
stock market, 184
stocks. *See* rates and stocks confusion fallacy
straw man argument, 30, 108, 135–36
sufficient conditions. *See* logical conditions
suicide rates, 107–8

taxation: of Amazon in New York, benefit-cost analysis of, 152; GND and, 159; government boondoggles and, 14–15, 35, 206; government health care and, 165–66; as income and wealth re-distributionist system, 105, 159, 206; opportunity costs and, 152; without representation, historical perspective of, 166, 180n50; stealth/hidden, 166; welfare state and, 206

terrorists, 133, 171

theocracies, 194

Toobin, Jeffrey, 33

totalitarian regimes. *See* dictators/ totalitarian regimes

trade/trade policy, 172–75, 182n70

Trump, Donald: Democrats rejection of 2016 election win by, 207n1; expert fallacy example around campaign of, 69–70; popular and electoral votes (2016) for, 74–76, 207n1; Russian collusion with, rhetoric/debates on, 34–35, 70, 121, 123n9; smear campaigns rhetoric/tactics against, 69–70

Tu Quoque (hypocrisy) fallacy: climate change debates and, 156–57, 177n21; defining, 29, 131; examples of, 131–34, 144, 146n1, 156–57, 177n21; in Trump 2016 win debate, 207n1

uncertainty: in centrally planned compared to free-market systems, 202; Mueller report case study on recognizing, 184–86; noise compared with signal and, 184; statistics and nature of, 19; utopian schemes conflict with reality of, 183

unemployment. *See* employment/ unemployment data; labor market

unique cause (causal reductionism) fallacy, 17, 103, 112, 141–42, 172

utopian arguments: capitalism contrasted with, 197; in communism, 154, 201, 202; nirvana fallacy in, 95, 146, 153–54, 162, 170, 201, 202; uncertain/changing realities conflict with, 183

Venezuela, 67, 92, 205

victimology fallacy, 30; capitalism avoidance of, 200; fallacy of composition relation to, 143–45; lionizing of "victimhood" in, 144–45, 147n18; Marxism use of, 61n3, 62n19, 95, 144, 198; as partisan tactic, 39n3, 80–87, 143

voter fraud, 10–11, 74, 76, 80

voter preferences, 74–76, 188–90

Walker, Graham H., 167

welfare dependency, 63n26, 105

welfare state, 71–73, 104–5, 206

"What Has Economics to Say about Racial Discrimination?" (Arrow), 57

white population, homicide statistics for, 23–24

white privilege: fallacy of composition and attacks on, 143–44; moral authority claims in attacks on, 141–42; neo-Marxist concept of, 147n14

white supremacy, 44, 67–68. *See also* Nazis

zero sum game, 62n19, 77, 143–44, 199, 202

About the Author

David H. Goldenberg holds a doctorate in financial economics as well as masters degrees in pure and applied mathematics, and is a financial economist with many years as a professor at Rensselaer Polytechnic University, Temple University, University of Maryland, and internationally. He is now an independent researcher. His background includes training in logic, philosophy, data-analysis and applied statistics, economics, risk analysis and decision-making under uncertainty, and he has taught behavioral finance. In addition, his careful study of fallacies and how they operate, rhetoric, and history provides context for this book. He notes that all of the great economists were interested in public policy and informing the public in non-technical terms. His publications include: *Derivatives Markets* (2016); and "Risk Neutral Valuation: Convenience Or Consensus?" *Social Science Research Network* (*SSRN*) (2015): 1–39.